CUSTOMER WHAT?

The honest and practical guide to
customer experience

IAN GOLDING

Visit the author's website at ijgolding.com

ISBN 978-1-5272-2216-8

To Naomi, Ciara, Caitie and Jack.

Dedication

This book is the culmination of 24 years of working-life experiences. It is dedicated to, and my gift to, everyone who, like me, aspires to do what is right – for the customer, for the employee, and for the shareholder. Whether you work directly on the front line or sit around an expensive mahogany table as a member of the most senior group of executives, my admiration for everyone who fights to do the right thing for customers is overwhelming.

I also dedicate this book and everything I do to my wonderful family – my wife Naomi and my three children, Ciara, Caitie, and Jack. (And my two dogs, Rosie and Poppy, and my tortoise, Chester.) Their love, support, belief, and tremendous patience have enabled me to have the experiences that allow me to support and guide others. While they often lose me to my work, they know that everything I do is ultimately for all of us.

I must also dedicate this book to the 100 amazing people who believed in me enough to support my Kickstarter campaign to get this book published – you have enabled my dream to become a reality.

I am also hugely grateful to Bruce Temkin, Jeanne Bliss, Diane Magers, Lesley Lykins, and everyone who has played a part in creating, establishing, and building the customer experience profession. Without their drive, dedication, and courage, I and many other professionals around the world would not have our work recognised as something of substance – something that requires a tremendous amount of knowledge, capability, and competency.

Finally, I want to recognise the efforts of my friend and colleague Beth Richardson. Beth and I have known each other for several years, but it is only recently that we have officially started to work together. It would not have been possible for me to produce this work without Beth – her commitment, focus, skill, and passion are immeasurable – she is not only an amazing wordsmith but an amazing customer experience professional – and I am delighted that together we will continue to change the world, one customer journey at a time.

Contents

Preface
The why and how of this book 01

Foreword
Christina Dolding, Head of Customer Experience and Innovation at Old Mutual Wealth
Steve West, Customer Management and Brand Protection Specialist 03

Introduction
Life as a customer experience professional
The secret diary of a customer experience professional (aged 41¾) 04

PART 1. THE FUNDAMENTALS
Establishing a firm footing – an introduction to the fundamentals 12

Chapter 1 – Readiness
Understanding how ready your organisation is for a customer experience strategy 17
The Customer Experience Readiness Scale 18
Customer experience commitment – the story of JC Penney 28

Chapter 2 – Belief = authority (outward) and skills (inward)
Building your authority 31
Assessing your own readiness 34
The CEO who waits on tables 36

Chapter 3 – Strategy
Customer experience strategy - the missing link 39
Creating a strategy statement 42
Authenticity, the key to unlocking the greatest customer experiences 46

PART 2. CULTURE: CONNECTING PEOPLE TO THE STRATEGY
Employees, customers, and leadership – in that order! 52

Chapter 4 – Employees
The importance of employee experience 57
Customer-centric role profiles – creating a direct connection to customers 58
The curious case of the business that lived up to its name 59

Chapter 5 – Customers
Walking in customers' shoes – something we do, not something we say 62
Getting comfortable with getting close 64
Clear and direct communication – how O2 turned employees into fans 65

Chapter 6 – Leaders
Helping your leaders trust their people 68
Choose one thing, and say "Yes!" 70
The British Airways pilot who got out of his seat 71
Bringing it all together 72

PART 3. MAKING IT HAPPEN IN PRACTICE
The tools of the trade – knowing how (and when) to apply them **76**

Chapter 7 – Doing / the journey map
The six functions of your journey map **80**
Map-building step by step **81**
Cost out, experience in – a tale of two banks **97**

Chapter 8 – Doing / measurement
Establishing the facts **102**
How to align measurement to your journey **105**
Feedback as a touchpoint – a lesson in how not to do it **111**

Chapter 9 – Doing / priorities
Constructing your roadmap **115**
The vital five – completing your strategy statement **116**
Random to intentional. Right skills, right priorities **119**

Chapter 10 – Doing / design
Start with the customer goal, and work from there **122**
Designing for value **129**
Correctly framing the challenge **131**
Personas **133**
Collaborating with customers **137**
One customer, three hotel experiences **139**

PART 4. SUSTAINING
From starting the movement to safeguarding momentum **148**

Chapter 11 – Governance and reward
Establishing accountability **152**
Top down and bottom up **153**
A supporting framework **155**
True accountability needs freedom and safety **156**
18 hours – how a loaf of bread helped improve customer experience **157**

Chapter 12 – Writing your story
What if? Seven common challenges **161**
Square pegs in round holes **163**

Thank you
Customer experience heroes **167**

Closing thoughts
Diane Magers, CEO of the Customer Experience Professionals Association (CXPA) **171**
Beth Richardson, CCXP **172**

Endnotes **173**

Index **186**

Preface

The why and how of this book

"What exactly do you do then?" I get asked this question a lot.

I always describe myself as a customer experience professional. I help organisations put customers and employees at the forefront of their business. This book is the story of my 24 years in the profession, and I have distilled my learning into these pages.

Part practice handbook, part novel, part therapy, this is a practical guide to creating and sustaining the focus on customers, despite everything that may block your way.

I haven't edited out the failures and flops – they are an important part of the story I want to tell. And let me say right up front that one of the critical learning points is that every organisation is different. I'm afraid there is no one-size-fits-all approach. What drives value for customers and shareholders in one business may not work for another.

A large part of my message is that you need to understand not only the customers of a business but the business itself. If you find yourself wanting to dive into the later chapters of this book before you have read Part 1, don't! Even if you think the things that need to be done are blindingly obvious, and must be done by next week, take a deep breath, slow down, and ensure that you are going at the right pace for your business.

The raw materials – people, culture, business model, resources, and commitment – should always shape your approach.

This book will help you understand where you are now, and find the right way to move forward.

> "YOU NEED TO UNDERSTAND NOT ONLY THE CUSTOMERS OF A BUSINESS BUT THE BUSINESS ITSELF.

How it works

This book is written in four parts.

1. The fundamentals – essentials for success; take them for granted and they will cause you to fail.
2. Culture – connecting people to the strategy, and creating the right conditions for action.
3. Making it happen – tools and tactics for delivering the strategy.
4. Sustaining – continuously advocating for change.

Each of these four parts contains an overview of what needs doing; a set of practical activities and approaches to help you do it; and a story or two to illuminate your path.

There is a good reason why I have organised the book in this way. You cannot set about changing customer experience until you have established the right supporting culture. And you cannot do that unless your senior leadership team has an unshakeable belief that this strategy is right for the organisation. You must work your way through each part in turn.

How you go about driving this change is every bit as important as what you do, and in what order. I will introduce you to five guiding principles, or mantras, which have served me very well over the years.

Before you start reading, I would like to leave you with a quote from one of the most humble and inspirational leaders I have ever met. She is so humble that she doesn't want anyone to know that these words are hers, but they are words that perfectly sum up the nature of the journey this book will take you on – happy reading!

"I always knew that customer experience was important – but I did not realise it was a science – and behind that science is a heart."

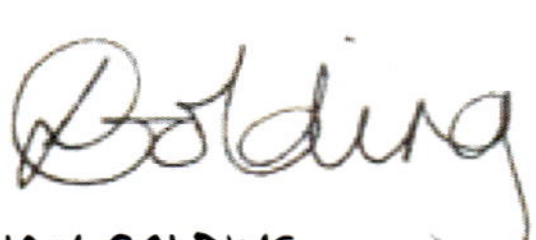

IAN GOLDING

> “I ALWAYS KNEW THAT CUSTOMER EXPERIENCE WAS IMPORTANT - BUT I DID NOT REALISE IT WAS A SCIENCE - AND BEHIND THAT SCIENCE IS A HEART.

Foreword

Christina Dolding, Head of Customer Experience and Innovation at Old Mutual Wealth

It was 16th June 2015 and I was on yet another company two-day off-site which, I have to confess, I was not particularly looking forward to. Apparently, one of the trainers was this so-called customer experience specialist. Really?! I had seen some slides in advance of the session and I could not see how this was going to engage people for two days.

Well how wrong can one person be? Ian has a unique and wonderful way of bringing the story of customer experience to life. Those two days were both inspirational and transformational, and I watched a fairly motley crew of people go on this magical journey together. When we came out of that session, we knew our work life would never be the same again... and it wasn't. How often does that happen? In my experience, this was a first and a never-to-be-forgotten moment.

This book is gold dust. It contains absolutely everything you need to know – and things you didn't even know you needed to know. It is a joy to read and takes you on a seamless journey to achieve consistent, scalable, and repeatable customer experiences.

Ian uses accessible language and provides you with clear and easy strategies you can deploy to make a change. Unquestionably, you will immediately think of practical ways of implementing new thinking in your business.

There are real-life stories which will bring joy to your heart as you explore some incredible, and often simple, ways companies have got this right... and learn how things can go very badly wrong. It never ceases to amaze me how many people fail to recognise that customer experience is simply the art of being lovely: creating positive emotions at every point in the journey.

Most importantly, this stuff is not expensive. You don't need a huge resource base, project managers, and a large budget. Nearly everything in this book can be done within your business using what you have to hand. You just need to be prepared to roll your sleeves up, settle in for a fun ride, and know your destination will not only be wonderful for your customers but will be for you too.

Ian is the 'David Attenborough of customer experience'. He is undoubtedly a national treasure with global influence and appeal. Ian's thinking and approach transcends business sector, geography, and your own personal experiences. Read this book and be transported into a world of possibility. Revel in the opportunity and make lasting change in your organisation. Be brave, be bold, and be different. You won't regret it.

CHRISTINA

Steve West, Customer Management and Brand Protection Specialist

On a cold, rainy November evening in 2010 I telephoned my wife from a service station and revealed, "I've finally met a guy that really understands what customer experience means!"

Ian Golding had been speaking at one of the many CX industry events I'd attended that year and it was immediately obvious that there was something very different about him. He appeared to be a humble man giving an honest appraisal of how he had fought tooth and nail to get the company he worked for to invest in 'customer experience', what he and his colleagues had learned from this, and how his efforts had paid off for his employer and himself. And he had the whole audience hanging on his every word.

Ian is not afraid to say things that you may not want to hear. But he says them because he truly believes they will make a positive difference to the way your customers engage with you. And most importantly, Ian understands that there is always a commercial element to customer experience. He doesn't say fluffy things that won't make or save your business money.

Ian's writing is informative, entertaining, and often hilarious. This book includes fantastic advice and guidance and great examples of CX, so sit back and enjoy the ride!

STEVE

Introduction

Life as a customer experience professional

I have observed, and been part of, a tidal wave of focus on customer experience. It has always existed (although few realised it), and customers have always been willing to give feedback. But businesses have only recently started to recognise that doing the right thing by their customers, and actively managing the experience, might make sense.

A few years back, my family and I were honoured to take part in a BBC1 'living history' programme called *Turn Back Time: The Family.*[1] It was an experience like no other, and we were transported back in time to the turn of the 20th century to experience life as our ancestors lived it and understand how life for the family unit has changed over time[2].

Our experience started in 1904. Life in pre-war Britain felt much simpler than it is today. Although shopping by mail order had been invented, most shopping happened in person, in a physical shop, with real things in it! The overwhelming majority of people didn't own a car, so most customers would shop locally with independent traders in the high street (remember them?). Payment was also pretty simple – cash or cheque, with no plastic in sight.

As a father in 1904, I learned how important etiquette was. Manners and politeness were evident in all interactions – at home, at work, and as a customer. Shops were very orderly places, staffed by smartly dressed shopkeepers standing behind tall counters. They knew most of their customers by name, and would pick, and wrap, products by hand while chatting to customers – products they had chosen, or even made, especially for their customers. Most of the time the shopkeepers did not even have to ask what their customers wanted to buy – they knew already. There was not a great deal of variety in terms of the products on offer, but the shopkeeper knew each customer's preferences, their family's preferences, and their budget, and customers trusted them to help find just the right thing, just as they would trust their children's head teacher or the family doctor.

Fast-forward 100 or so years. Today, customers do not just have two purchase channels to choose from. We have ten that I can think of – physical stores; the telephone; the web; mobile; live chat; SMS; mail order; TV; social; AI-assisted. I am sure I have forgotten one or two! Local availability is not a consideration either - we can buy anything and everything we want, in any way we want, from anywhere in the world. We can, in theory, live our lives without ever talking to anyone or setting foot outside our front door.

It is not at all uncommon to conduct an entire transaction without a human being involved, and even if one is, they are often just reading back a pre-written script. In shops, it is unlikely that anyone will know you personally. Trust isn't the currency it used to be – it's likely you are so well informed by technology that the people working in the shop won't need to help you make your purchase. In fact, if you need help you are likely to turn to Google – you trust the wisdom of the crowd to tell you what others think about an item before you commit to buying it.

So, when was the best time to be a customer? The personal, simple experience of 1904 or the global, convenience-led experience of today?

I am not advocating that we literally turn back time – far from it. It is impossible to deny the remarkable ease and convenience afforded today's consumer by the amazing connected world we are part of. However, the experience is less fulfilling somehow. It does not always feel good being a customer of the global corporations that distribute the products and services we buy. We create and share stories of organisations that fail to connect emotionally with us. Not only do they not know our names, but very few seem to understand us. Ironically, we're looking for something we've lost: trust. And feeling known and understood and valued, a little like we used to feel in the good old days of 1904.

Is the customer always right?

Many will argue that today's experience looks the way it does because consumers have demanded it, and will

> IN THE RUSH TO CHASE CONVENIENCE, EFFICIENCY, AND LOWER COSTS, MANY BUSINESSES HAVE UNKNOWINGLY AND GRADUALLY BROKEN THE BOND OF TRUST THAT EXISTED BETWEEN THEM AND THEIR CUSTOMERS.

continue to demand more and more. Is that really true, though? The power consumers have today has definitely changed the relationship between business and customer.

In the rush to chase convenience, efficiency, and lower costs, many businesses have unknowingly and gradually broken the bond of trust that existed between them and their customers.

But some businesses have adapted to the change better than others. These are the customer experience leaders. They offer all the benefits of today's experience – choice, convenience, and speedy access at affordable prices – but they have done it without ever losing trust. They have consistently made it their mission to extend the personal, empathetic, emotional flavour of the shopping experience of 1914 to our modern day, connected experience.

Today, business leaders who have taken customers for granted in the past are reconsidering their strategy. Even Ryanair CEO, Michael O'Leary – infamous for his very public disdain for customers – claims to have had an epiphany,[3] saying, "If I had known being nicer to our customers was going to work so well I would have done it years ago."[4]

A whole consulting industry has grown up around creating wonderful-looking customer journey maps. New roles are emerging with 'customer experience' in their job titles. Ten years ago, the CCO (or chief customer officer) did not exist. Today, increasing numbers of CCOs are appearing on the scene, alongside customer experience directors; heads of customer experience; customer experience transformists; customer experience futurologists; and VPs of customer success.

Now, more than ever, should be a wonderful time to be a customer

So why do I continue to be on the receiving end of inconsistent, uninspiring, and often substandard customer experiences? Why do I encounter more people who have no idea what customer experience is, than those who do?

Because organisational understanding of customer experience as a discipline is still in its fledgling state. Differentiating on customer experience requires you to embed customers in the psyche of your organisation and every individual who works within it. It is a long-term business strategy, not a quick fix. It requires strategic thinking, scientific measurement, and emotional intelligence. It is an organisation-wide collaborative effort, needing committed leadership and hardcore change management.

This is why groups like the Customer Experience Professionals Association (CXPA),[5] founded by Bruce Temkin and Jeanne Bliss, are so vital to the development of our industry. And why a new professional qualification has been created to recognise our complex and ever-evolving skill set.

At times, being a customer experience professional can be lonely and frustrating. Putting the needs of customers and employees at the forefront of everyone's thinking requires a bucketload of inspiration, dedication, and perspiration. I have seen and heard it all, and believe me I have developed a very thick skin!

No matter what role you play in your organisation (regardless of whether you have customer experience in your job title or not!) you can drive this change. Never give up. Remind yourself every day that our businesses exist to serve customers, and without them we would not exist.

story

THE SECRET DIARY OF A CUSTOMER EXPERIENCE PROFESSIONAL (AGED 41¾)

The secret diary of a customer experience professional (aged 41¾)

The exploits of one customer experience professional as he went about his business during a working week back in 2014. Whether it makes you laugh, cry, or feel pity for me, I genuinely hope that my diary provides a useful perspective on the challenges of our profession.

Monday 29th September 2014

As has become normal recently, I am up at 4:30 am to embark on a long journey from the north-west of England down to the south. Wiping the sleep from my eyes, I load my car up with a suitcase, laptop bag, and enough sticky notes and sweets to sink a battleship. This week will see me delivering two workshops for two different companies and I need plenty of supplies!

By the time I arrive at a McDonald's close to my location, I start to feel ready for the week ahead. Sipping my Americano, I go about dealing with my first task of the day, of most days to be honest, dealing with my emails. Getting them out of the way before the working day really begins is essential. I need my mind fully focused on the major task for this particular Monday morning - the delivery of a current state customer journey mapping workshop for a relatively new client.

Having already spent time immersing myself with said client, I am not expecting the day to be an easy one. A challenge for any customer experience professional is assessing the readiness of a business to transform, to become more customer centric. This particular business has fantastic people, yet their desire to accept change is less overt. The workshop proves to be as challenging as anticipated. Ultimately, we achieve what is necessary, but it is not easy. Sometimes it can be so frustrating working with people who on the face of it appear to be resistant to change, even if on the inside they are not.

I believe that a good customer experience professional will determine the pace that an organisation can work at as it embarks on or continues on a customer experience transformation. We must be patient and sensitive in understanding the issues, behaviours, and mindsets of the people we work with. I must admit that I struggled with this today, something I openly admitted to the participants of the workshop. Although I said the right thing, I said it in an inappropriate way. It is so easy to do! I must apologise to the person I spoke to as soon as possible.

Back in my car driving further south, I am tired and reflective. It never ceases to amaze me just how different every business I interact with seems to be from another - this is why I love doing what I do. I learned a lot today, and continue to do so on a weekly basis.

Tuesday 30th September 2014

I spend the night at my parents' flat in North London. I am immensely grateful for their kind hospitality and generosity. In the early days as an independent practitioner, keeping costs low for me and my clients is important. Today is an exciting one. I am visiting a potential new client. Business development is a vital component for any consultant (I hate that word, although that is what I technically am) and I must admit I do not particularly like doing it.

This is a business that has been introduced to me by a long-term friend of mine. I am very confident that the company will want to work with me, especially with his endorsement. Arriving early (as I always do), I find a lovely café in West London and catch up on my emails over a coffee and a pain au chocolat.

I have just come out of the meeting. It did not go quite as I expected. In fact, it went far worse than I could have imagined! I learned a long time ago that not everyone is going to like me, my style, or my view on the world. The meeting this morning saw me present to two people who did not appear to connect with anything I said or did. I keep going over everything in my head. Did I say something to upset them?

Meetings like this are so frustrating. I put so much time, energy, and passion into my work. Yet to come across people who do not appear to recognise it at all is very demotivating. I am sure that the expectation set prior to the meeting was the major contributor to the problem. I must work harder on ensuring that everyone I meet going forward is clear about expectation to avoid meetings like this.

Walking back to the tube station I feel so deflated. After the challenges of yesterday, it has been a tough week already... and it is only Tuesday lunchtime! I cheer myself up by going back to the café and writing my weekly blog post: a review of the 2014 Customer Experience Awards. Reminiscing about the fabulous event goes some way to restoring my faith and mood.

Blog written, I telephone the person who I had a disagreement with in the workshop yesterday. I apologise for what I perceived to be my insensitivity. He was very grateful for my humility. We both understand each other's perspectives better after the call; it was a very useful call to have made.

Back in the car on the way south, I do not have long to dwell on anything. On Wednesday and Thursday I move on to another client and the delivery of a two-day customer experience workshop - happy days!

Wednesday 1st October 2014

Up at 4:30 am for my morning run. I love running, but do not have much time to fit it in... unless I get up at silly o'clock! It does make me feel good, though. Today is the start of a new month and it could not be starting better. A few years ago, I became a full-time Six Sigma trainer for GE. I never realised how much I would enjoy training other people. And that is still the case today. I am excited about spending two days imparting knowledge to another of my clients. Surely the week can only get better from here?

I arrive at the clients' offices at 7:30 am. The sun is shining and everything seems good. As the delegates, with smiles on their faces, start to arrive, I become even more optimistic about the day ahead. I was right to be. I am blown away by the energy, enthusiasm, passion, and drive of the 18 people in the room. The mood could not have been more different from Monday.

Again, it is astounding how different my two clients this week have been - different industries with completely different people. Both have very different challenges. The common denominator is that through their people they can both make a difference; they can transform for the good of customers and colleagues. I have no doubt they both will.

The day has come to an end. I feel radically different from yesterday. My faith in myself has been restored. I shall sleep well tonight.

Thursday 2nd October 2014

I did not think I could improve on yesterday. I was wrong. The delegates arrived early for the workshop today - early! I am inspired by their desire to want to know more. I so hope this company succeeds in its mission to become more customer centric. I will do everything in my power to help it do so.

There is not much more to write about today because it continued as it started. At the end of the day, the delegates presented their learnings to me. It sent a shiver down my spine (a good one, that is).

The last two days validate to me why my job is so important. To be able to help people influence their own organisations to change is a wonderful thing. The questions and requests that followed the workshop bowled me over.

The only slightly sad thing about the two days was the absence of any senior leader. They had said that they were committed to attending, but work emergencies ruled them out at the last minute.

Sometimes I do not believe it when senior leaders abandon their commitment to attend a workshop. In this case I do believe them. It is such a shame, though. I wish they could have witnessed the passion of their people. Hopefully the feedback they deliver will do the trick.

I arrive home in Chester at 11:30 pm. It was a very long day, but so rewarding. I feel energised rather than exhausted. My happy head hits the pillow for a very good night's sleep.

Friday 3rd October 2014

Where has the week gone? Another week? Seeing my beautiful wife and children is a real bonus. I can no longer take it for granted that I will see them more than one day a week these days. I drop them off at school before returning home to catch up on everything I have been unable to do for the last couple of days.

Emails and invoices take up most of my morning; it is a productive few hours. Feedback keeps coming in from the workshop on Monday and the two-day training workshop. It is all good news.

Despite Monday being a challenge, our client is very happy with progress. They know how hard change will be, yet they are delighted that we are making the right progress. They do not see my behaviour as insensitive - they see it as necessary.

The delegates from the two-day training workshop keep emailing. Some of them are telling me about the customer-centric things they have done since the course ended yesterday!!! I wish I could share some of their immediate stories with you, but now is not the time. Safe to say that they are acting successfully on the things they have learned - the best outcome to the week I could ever have anticipated.

I have another call with a different client, not one I have worked with this week. Their challenges are different yet again. On Monday, I am to present to their executive committee. We expect the presentation to be challenging; nothing new there! Some of my client's colleagues do not think there is much to do on the customer experience front - we do not agree. I have just finished the presentation and am happy that I have a good story to tell to help influence them. I am hopeful that my start to next week will be a good one.

It is time to turn off the laptop for another week. The weekend is for my family, not for work. What a week it has been. The typical rollercoaster ride of a customer experience professional - the ups and downs are constant and continuous. I would not have it any other way.

PART 1.
THE FUN-DAMENTALS

A customer is the most important visitor on our premises. He is not dependent on us. We are dependent on him. He is not an interruption in our work. He is the purpose of it. He is not an outsider in our business. He is part of it. We are not doing him a favour by serving him. He is doing us a favour by giving us an opportunity to do so.

MAHATMA GANDHI

theory

What is it? Definitions

Customer experience – the sum of all interactions a customer has with a supplier of goods and/or services for the duration of their relationship with that supplier. This can include awareness, discovery, attraction, interaction, purchase, use, cultivation, and advocacy. The quality of the experience as a whole will determine whether it is a one-off or a continuous relationship.

User experience – generally refers to customer interactions through digital platforms – web, mobile, and apps. It is a subset of the customer experience.

Customer service – the assistance and advice provided by the supplier. It involves providing help to the customer so that they can answer a question or get information, or make a change. Also known as service experience, this is also a subset of the customer experience.

Customer journey – the steps customers take to complete their goals at each stage of the relationship – finding information, weighing up options, and deciding whether to trust you, right through to using a product or service and deciding whether to use it again.

Touchpoints – points of interaction with the supplier. These can be direct, through sales and servicing interactions, product designs, and propositions. Or indirect, through what they see and hear in the media, or by word-of-mouth from current, former, and 'nearly' customers, friends, and family.

Customer experience management – the practice of delivering successful interactions across the entire journey to drive the commercial goals of the supplier organisation.

Customer centricity – putting customers' interests first in everything you do. Very often this involves decisions which look unprofitable in the short term, but ultimately lead to increased customer satisfaction and loyalty, which will in turn increase profitability.

> TO BE EFFECTIVE WE MUST BE EXPERT AT GUIDING OUR IDEAS AND PLANS AT A PACE THE ORGANISATIONS WE ARE WORKING WITHIN, OR FOR, CAN COPE WITH.

Establishing a firm footing - an introduction to the fundamentals

Given that you have taken the time to pick up and open this book, it's likely you are reading these words from a similar perspective to mine. You have an interest in, or even a passion for, the subject of customer experience.

But I learned a long time ago that just because it's obvious to you and me, does not mean it will be obvious to someone else. For every one of us who has the luxury of working in an organisation that wants to listen, another ten of us will be faced with the prospect of having our ideas met with cynicism, or outright rejection.

During my working life, I have often felt I am the only person who understands that the organisation needs to do something different to genuinely put its customers first. I have had days when I could see light at the end of the tunnel, only for it to be extinguished before I could get anywhere near it. I have been accused of being emotionally immature; naive; ignorant; arrogant; even insignificant!

Occasionally, I have even wondered if I am deluding myself.

It can be very tempting for the overenthusiastic customer experience professional to rush in like an excited puppy. We run the risk of moving too fast. We get carried away with the plethora of potential opportunities laid out in front of us.

Enthusiasm and passion are vital, and should never be suppressed, but to be effective we must be expert at guiding our ideas and plans at a pace the organisations we are working within, or for, can cope with.

Driving a customer experience programme can take a significant amount of time – especially in a business that has never been customer centric before. When I say significant time, I am measuring this in years, not months. Treading carefully, and slowly bringing people at all levels of the organisation along, is what will get us there. Going too quickly may set us back.

Before we start the doing, we must establish a firm footing for customer experience. There are three fundamentals we need to attend to. Address them early, do this thoroughly, and do it with an open mind. The critical thing here is to be honest. If we can see things for how they really are, rather than how we would like them to be, it will set us up for success.

Those fundamentals are as follows:

→ Assessing how ready our organisation is to become customer focused **(readiness)**

→ Helping key influencers to 'get it' in the context of business objectives **(belief)**

→ Developing a link between customer experience and business objectives **(strategy)**

In the first part of this book we will explore each one in turn.

CHAPTER 1 - READINESS

Change is hard at first, messy in the middle, and gorgeous at the end.

ROBIN SHARMA

theory

Understanding how ready your organisation is for a customer experience strategy

If you find yourself wanting to dive into the later chapters of this book before you have read Part 1, don't! Even if you think the things that need to be done are blindingly obvious, and must be done by next week, take a deep breath, slow down, and ensure that you are going at the right pace for your business. You need to take others on this journey with you. I have seen countless customer experience programmes fail because the basic foundations were not in place.

The first thing you need to do is understand how ready your organisation is for a customer experience strategy. The more ready your organisation is (or the people are within it), the easier it will be to embed an all-encompassing customer experience programme that will be sustained. The less ready, the more difficult it will be.

So, the first practical exercise in this book is a readiness assessment, to help you determine which approach to take, at what pace, and who can best help you.

> **"ENSURE THAT YOU ARE GOING AT THE RIGHT PACE FOR YOUR BUSINESS. YOU NEED TO TAKE OTHERS ON THIS JOURNEY WITH YOU.**

The Customer Experience Readiness Scale

practice

The scale shown in Figure 1-1 is used like a chart to plot your business readiness: **D** is the lowest state of readiness; **A** is the highest. Your overall goal is to help your business move from left to right, to achieve an **A** rating in each level. But your aim in completing this exercise is to create a clear-eyed assessment of where the business is now. It's important to be objective and honest with yourself.

Figure 1-1 The Customer Experience Readiness Scale

The customer experience readiness scale

1 **Acknowledge.** The role of and benefit of customer experience management in the business.	Benefits not acknowledged at any level of the organisation. ❑	Benefits acknowledged at lower levels of the organisation only. ❑	Benefits partially acknowledged at leadership level. ❑	Benefits acknowledged at all levels of the organisation. ❑
2 **Diagnose.** Recognise strengths and weaknesses of current state and underlying drivers.	No recognition at any level of the organisation. ❑	Partial recognition at lower levels only. ❑	Partial recognition at leadership level only. ❑	Complete recognition at all levels. ❑
3 **Improve.** Commit to a series of appropriate actions to embed strengths and address weaknesses.	No commitment to act at any level of the organisation. ❑	No formal action – employees make tactical decisions at function level. ❑	Partial agreement and investment in addressing specific 'burning' issues. ❑	Priorities identified and investment and resource allocated. ❑
4 **Embed.** Commit to a roadmap with ongoing investment to embed capability and continuously meet changing customer needs.	No specific focus on continuous improvement at any level of the organisation. ❑	Need for continuous improvement recognised but not actioned. ❑	Investment in some areas, but with finite scope, budget, and timescale. ❑	Customer experience continuous improvement programme embedded. ❑
NOTES				

Download a blank template at ijgolding.com[6]

Make a list of every function of your business. Areas like sales, service, and marketing are obvious. They design and deliver the customer journey and their actions can be linked directly to customers. But the functions which are less 'on show' – finance, facilities, HR, risk, IT, distribution, and internal communication – need to be part of your assessment. They influence the environment, culture, and context in which decisions about customers are made, and as such their views and readiness are an essential part of your analysis. Do not leave anybody out.

Round one: Identify the key stakeholders and decision makers in each function and interview them.

Ask them to respond to the following six questions:

1. What role do customers play in this business?
2. What benefit will managing customer experience deliver to this business?
3. How good is the customer experience today?
4. When making decisions, to what extent does this business consciously consider whether the decision will positively or negatively affect customer experience?
5. What actions are being taken to fix, maintain, or improve the experience?
6. Describe three things that are either enabling or preventing a focus on customer experience.

> **"THE FUNCTIONS WHICH ARE LESS 'ON SHOW' - FINANCE, FACILITIES, HR, RISK, IT, DISTRIBUTION, AND INTERNAL COMMUNICATION - NEED TO BE PART OF YOUR ASSESSMENT. THEY INFLUENCE THE ENVIRONMENT, CULTURE, AND CONTEXT IN WHICH DECISIONS ABOUT CUSTOMERS ARE MADE.**

If possible, include the executive committee – the most senior executives in your business who are accountable for executing the business strategy. This would include the chief executive officer (CEO), chief financial officer (CFO), chief operating officer (COO), and so on. But a word of caution – your senior executive team may be less in touch with customers than they like to admit. Your questions may prove challenging for them to answer, and might even trigger a defensive response. Regardless of the reaction, this is a conversation you need to have. But be ready to pause a little longer on the benefits, or offer examples of any positive organisational behaviours you have witnessed.

Round two: Identify two or more line managers in each function and interview them. Ask them the same questions. For larger functions speak to more people – enough to give you a balanced view of sentiment.

Round three: Repeat the exercise with colleagues at a lower level in the organisation. Again, not just those with customer facing roles, but colleagues from all functions.

Wherever you report to in the organisation, remember to include your own leadership line. Do not take for granted that they are ready for change just because they hired you. They don't yet know what's involved!

Do not try to influence people at this stage. You are interviewing people to understand their perceptions and point of view; listen, clarify, and make notes.

When you have your responses, use them to plot your stakeholders on the chart in Figure 1-1. Plot them on each of the four horizontals: acknowledge; diagnose; improve; embed.

Why? It's not unusual to find a business with an ambitious improvement plan where the customer experience team is constantly firefighting competing priorities, barriers to collaboration, and budget challenges. This can happen when the acknowledge stage has never been fully developed – people either do not know what customer experience is, or cannot articulate specific benefits in the context of the business. They will sense it as something we care about and do because it's the right thing. And they might quote research from Forrester[7] or KPMG Nunwood[8] to support their viewpoint, but in the face of a head-on challenge from a chief finance officer or an urgent change mandated by the regulator, they will be severely challenged to prove the benefit of maintaining focus on customer experience. The plan will not have resilience.

If you find functions or stakeholders are polarised in their views, create separate versions of the Readiness Scale for different functions, or levels of seniority, together with a summary version depicting your business readiness as a whole.

NOTES

Interpreting results – the levels explained:

Level 1. Acknowledge the role of and benefit of customer experience management in the business.

Level 1 is about recognising a need or opportunity. Some organisations will not recognise that customer experience is a strategic discipline, or will believe they are exempt.

1D. If your organisation is here, it is possible to introduce a customer experience strategy, but it will be challenging. You will need to operate tactically at first, doing whatever it takes to help the business understand what customer experience is and how the business can benefit from it. There are many underlying factors that could be driving this view, and they are usually linked to culture. Being in 1D does not mean you can give up. Far from it! It means this business (and its customers) need you more than most!

1C and 1B. There is evidence that people in your business believe there is a link between customer experience and business performance. Finding the link, building evidence, and communicating it will be your next step.

1A. The business has fully woken up to the possibilities. You still need to build the evidence, but the business is ready for the conversation.

Level 2. Diagnose. Recognise strengths and weaknesses of current-state and underlying drivers.

> **“POSITIVE REINFORCEMENT IS AN AMAZINGLY POWERFUL WAY TO ENGAGE PEOPLE AND TO BUILD BELIEF AND ENERGY IN AN ORGANISATION.**

Level 2 is about facts and the underlying characteristics of the business which brought them about. This phase of readiness requires your business to both recognise the current state of customer experience and understand the causes.

2D, 2C, and 2B. The facts about your customer experience are either poorly understood or have not been communicated. Concentrate on remedying this and helping people understand which characteristics of your business – capability, culture, or focus – are propelling you forward or holding you back. Alongside the negative aspects of the experience or missed opportunities, remember to talk passionately about what the business does well. By finding the positive attributes of your customer experience, you are focusing the business on what customers value and highlighting potential competitive advantage. Not only can you ensure the business continues to deliver that value, but positive reinforcement is an amazingly powerful way to engage people and to build belief and energy in an organisation.

2A. You are probably hearing "Yes, I agree, and something needs to be done". That's good. But do not underestimate how common it is for people to become defensive when faced with an honest assessment of causation. This can be difficult for business leaders to hear.

Level 3. Improve. Commit to a series of appropriate actions to embed strengths and address weaknesses.

Level 3 is about committing to action. It is only when you have identified priorities and committed the resource that you know your business is ready and your customer experience efforts are on the right track. Don't underestimate the change management effort and skill required – the same cross-functional collaboration required to be successful in Level 2 is required on a sustained basis.

3D and 3C. By now, you will be building a picture of what is happening in your business. If you are at D or C in the preceding levels, it's unlikely you will be any higher than a 3C. If you find yourself here, you need to refocus on Levels 1 and 2 to convince your decision makers to prioritise customer experience.

3B and 3A. You are in a very strong position but don't be complacent. I have often been in the situation where I have successfully got to 3A only for the key decision makers to change their minds when they see what they are being asked to commit to.

Level 4. Embed. Commit to a roadmap with ongoing investment to embed capability and continuously meet changing customer needs.

Level 4 is about investing for sustainability. The ideal state is securing commitment to a long-term focus on customer experience which sees your organisation embedding continuous customer experience improvement in its very fabric.

4D, 4C, and 4B. If you are driving action at Level 3A, you are ready to start work on embedding. Focus your efforts on reinforcing belief. Customer experience is not a project or an initiative, it is a long-term business strategy requiring sustained commitment. If you are not yet driving action in Level 3 you need to focus there first. You are not ready to move to Level 4 yet.

4A. This is the pinnacle. This is Amazon, First Direct, and Lush territory, where meeting and exceeding customer needs is a way of life. It means that the mechanisms are in place to ensure that whatever needs to be done to improve the customer experience will be forever. The question is this – are you here because you have worked through the levels and embedded thinking throughout your organisation? Or are you here purely because you have a visionary on the executive committee who is driving the strategy through? Do not become dependent on borrowed authority from a single person. Plan for stability and sustainability in the event of a change of leadership.

NOTES

The big picture

The objective is to create a sustainable, always-improving customer experience by aiming to reach column A in every level. If your results are straightforward, and you can see you are mostly landing in one column or a close neighbour on all levels, read on and work through the chapters.

If you are seeing something less straightforward, you are not going mad. I have worked with organisations which exhibit every possible permutation of scores on that chart. Figure 1-2 provides some examples.

Remember that each organisation is different, and this means that their ability to change is different. The phrase 'customers are at the heart of everything we do' is one of the most prevalent clichés in business. Not every organisation is ready to become customer centric – even if they say they are, or think they are. Plotting your organisation and key stakeholders on the scale is an iterative process. You might move up, down, left, or right, depending on what is happening in your business or market environment.

This is a tool to help you as a customer experience professional. It is your choice whether or not to share your detailed findings with anyone in your business. Over time you will become practised at understanding where your key stakeholders sit in terms of their support for your efforts. You will know who the advocates are, and be even more aware of your detractors.

"NOT EVERY ORGANISATION IS READY TO BECOME CUSTOMER CENTRIC - EVEN IF THEY SAY THEY ARE, OR THINK THEY ARE.

Figure 1-2 Change readiness results

Strong belief in doing the right thing and building capability, but more needs to be done to establish the facts about the journey and focus on priorities. The business is focused on investing for the long term to achieve an ambitious customer experience vision, but may have overlooked short- and medium-term benefits, which can be realised alongside the transformational change.

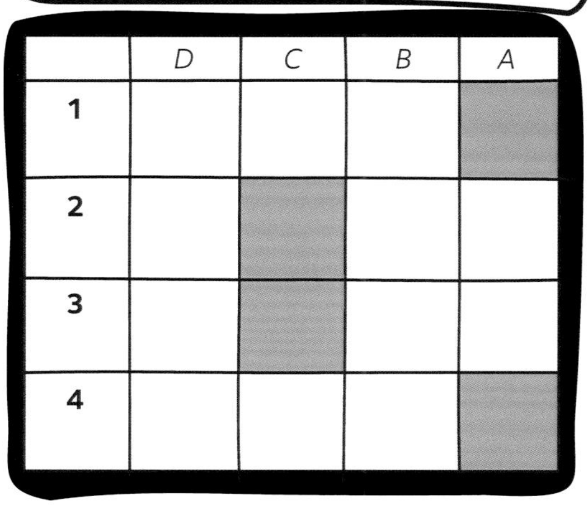

Customer experience improvements are being driven from the inside out by a desire to drive short-term growth, or perhaps control costs or reduce risk. This is a common situation. There are likely to be silos with conflicting objectives. Work on finding areas of overlap between the silos and helping the business connect with its customers.

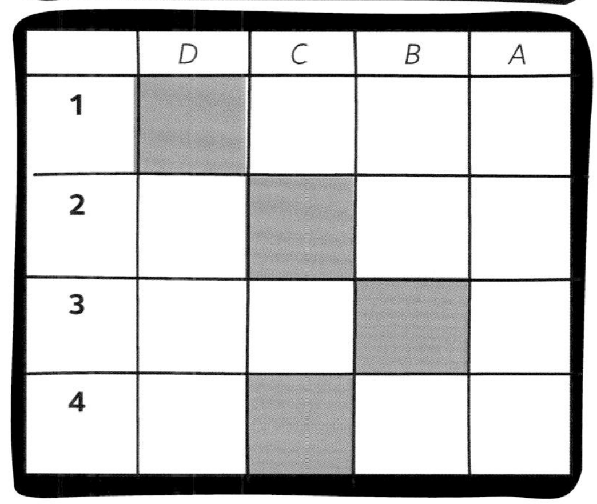

It's likely some journey analysis has been completed, as this organisation has clarity on strengths and weaknesses. There is change activity happening in pockets, but there is little commitment to driving change collectively – the strategic case has not been made. Create a stronger case for investment by uniting initiatives.

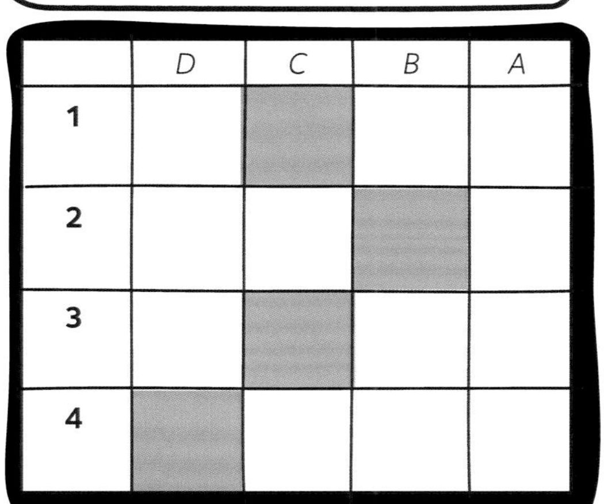

Strong belief and appreciation of the benefits, and broad understanding of the current state of customer experience. But the business is falling short on following through, with functions left to deliver their own actions and no roadmap for longer-term change. What's needed here is a unifying leadership presence and a single change roadmap.

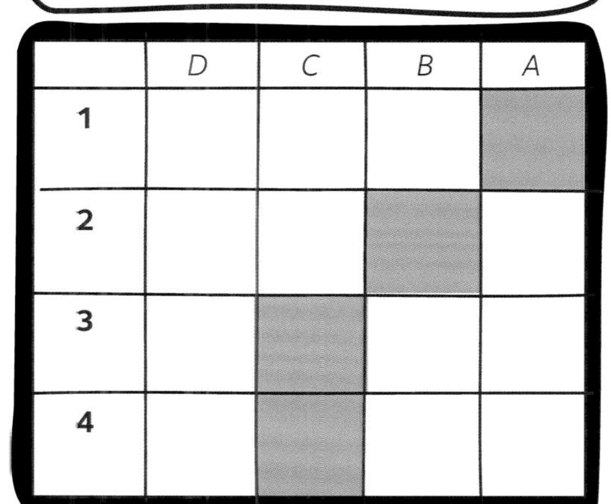

Organisations get in their own way

Getting to the higher reaches of the Readiness Scale requires a sustained focus over time, and I spend a lot of time talking to my clients about commitment.

The number of organisations and leaders who cite customer experience as central to their business strategy steadily increases year on year. If I was given £1 for every time I have heard a member of the executive committee say this, I would be modestly rich by now.

Most of the time I don't believe it. In fact, I can tell from my experiences as a customer that it isn't true.

Together with my friend and colleague Jerry Angrave,[9] I asked my peers working in organisations across the globe whether *they* believe it.[10] I put two questions to them. You will recognise them from the readiness assessment:

Q1. When making decisions, does your business consciously consider whether the decision will positively or negatively affect customer experience?

Q2. What are the main enablers, or barriers, to a focus on customer experience?

Figure 1-3 Does your business consciously consider how decisions will affect customer experience?

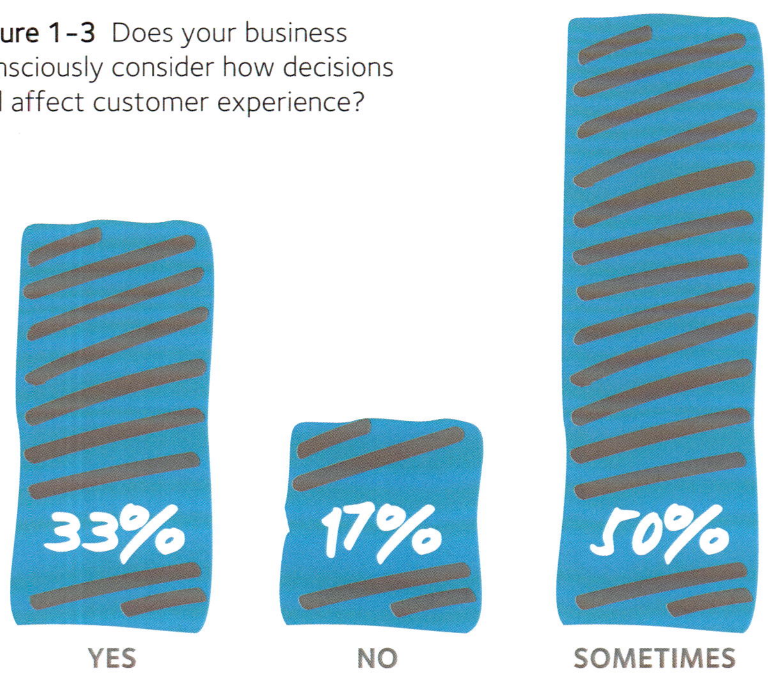

The answers:

NOTES

Q1 – decisions. Only a third of respondents said "Yes". Despite all the good rhetoric, two-thirds of businesses are making decisions without considering the effect on customer experience. Half said their organisations consider the impact "Sometimes", and **17%** of respondents said a concrete "No". The fact that **67%** of organisations are not acting in line with the rhetoric should not surprise anyone. I expected the percentage to be higher – customer experience strategy is not an easy path to tread.

Q2 – enablers and barriers. The key enablers are as follows:

- Seeking to understand customers, rather than looking inward – 22%
- Enabling people to do the right things without fear of challenge – 12%
- Dedicated resource to champion the customer experience cause – 10%
- Leadership commitment – 8%

Major barriers are as follows:

- Short-term focus: revenue; sales; restructures; cost-cutting at all costs; wrong metrics in performance management - 29%
- Organisational silos: differing agendas, lack of incentive to collaborate - 15%
- Leadership - specifically an inability to translate customer experience into commercial benefits - 11%

Does every transformation need a transformational leader?

As Jerry put it, the overriding sentiment is that organisations get in their own way. In fact, the view held by many of the people we spoke to is that for customer experience to get on the agenda, you need one of two things: a transformational leader or a burning platform.

Truly transformational leaders will do what is right for the long-term health of their business, irrespective of the financial state that business is in. From Jack Welch to Jeff Bezos to Richard Branson, all of them started from the same point, with the belief that doing the right things for their customers and their people would deliver commercial results as well as loyal customers. Transformational leaders do not wait for a burning platform. They start the fire.

However, we must acknowledge that transformational leaders, in the truest sense of the word, are uncommon. And it is far more likely that a business will want to focus on customer experience when it is in a state of flux than when it is in a comfortable, successful state.

But what if the business is successful, making significant profits, and achieving double digit growth, despite having paid little attention to customer experience to date? Why bother to change? Surely the business needs to be in decline for leadership to look towards customer experience as a way of mitigating risk and differentiating the organisation for future sustainability and growth?

This is one perspective, but not one I necessarily agree with. It is difficult to convince business leaders of the need to change behaviour and mindset if their organisation is hugely successful. Yet just because it is difficult, it does not mean it is impossible. It simply requires a refocus from problem-solving and rebuilding to safeguarding and defending.

Will the customer experience readiness assessment stop you from banging your head against brick walls? Regrettably it will not. But it will give you clarity on where the wall came from, how to knock it down, and which allies in your organisation can help you do that.

“IT WILL GIVE YOU CLARITY ON WHERE THE WALL CAME FROM, HOW TO KNOCK IT DOWN, AND WHICH ALLIES IN YOUR ORGANISATION CAN HELP YOU DO THAT.

NOTES

story

Customer experience commitment - the story of JC Penney

It is possible for brands to lose touch with their customers with alarming speed. The most clear-cut example of all is JC Penney. In 2011, as the new CEO of one of the largest department stores in the US, Ron Johnson (the man who brought Apple stores to the high street) made several strategic decisions without considering employee or customer experience.

Johnson decided change was needed. The logo changed, the pricing policy changed (no more discount sales and coupons), and the layout of stores changed. A new ad campaign heralded the change: “No more jumping through hoops. No coupon clipping. No door busting. Just great prices from the start”.[11]

But the changes were catastrophic for JC Penney.

This is an excerpt from Ron Johnson’s profile on Wikipedia:[12]

Many initiatives that made the Apple Store successful, for instance the “thought that people would show up in stores because they were fun places to hang out, and that they would buy things listed at full-but-fair price” did not work for the JC Penney brand and ended up alienating its aging customers who were used to heavy discounting. By eliminating the thrill of pursuing markdowns, the “fair and square every day” pricing strategy disenfranchised JC Penney’s traditional customer base. Johnson himself was said “to have a disdain for JC Penney’s traditional customer base” When shoppers weren’t reacting positively to the disappearance of coupons and sales, Johnson didn’t blame the new policies. Instead, he offered the assessment that customers needed to be “educated” as to how the new pricing strategy worked. He also likened the coupons beloved by so many core shoppers as drugs that customers needed to be weaned off.

By the time Johnson was fired in 2013, JC Penney had lost over $4 billion during his tenure. The JC Penney executive committee believed that Johnson’s actions might bring the business down. It launched a nationwide TV advertising campaign apologising to customers and begging them to come back: “Recently JC Penney changed. Some changes you liked, and some you didn’t. But what matters with mistakes is what we learn. We learned a very simple thing, to listen to you.”[13]

Just because a company still exists, it does not mean it will continue to be successful without focusing on customer experience. JC Penney lost sight of what it did well. As a result, it stopped doing some of the things that customers loved it for. All good things can come to an end with alarming speed if you do not remain focused on both commercial goals and customer needs.

> " JUST BECAUSE A COMPANY STILL EXISTS, IT DOES NOT MEAN IT WILL CONTINUE TO BE SUCCESSFUL WITHOUT FOCUSING ON CUSTOMER EXPERIENCE.

Key takeaways from Chapter 1 – Readiness

know

Every organisation is different, which means its readiness and ability to change will vary.

do

Take a systematic approach to establishing change readiness. Assess whether the business is backing rhetoric with action.

remember

Customer experience management is just as much about safeguarding strong customer relationships as it is about problem-solving.

CHAPTER 2 - BELIEF

= AUTHORITY (OUTWARD) AND SKILLS (INWARD)

Your assumptions are your windows on the world. Scrub them off every once in a while, or the light won't come in.

ISAAC ASIMOV

theory

Building your authority

Armed with an objective view of your organisation's readiness for change, you might be embarking on this chapter feeling upbeat and confident.

But you are more likely to be facing in to a change-unready organisation. Take heart – transforming the way people think, behave, and act is a monumental aspiration. It's a rollercoaster. If it feels hard, you are doing it right. But for each day when you want to wave the white flag and admit defeat, there will be another ten when you feel like you have conquered Mount Everest.

Customer experience professionals are hardwired to work in the interests of the customer, the employee, and the shareholder, and to keep doing what is right, despite the challenges or resistance put in their path. Adversity makes us stronger and more determined! But very often, doing what is right can be lonely. To stand any chance, our profession and anyone working in it must have resilience and belief.

In the same way that you assessed the change readiness of your organisation, you must develop your own readiness to lead by building your authority and skills.

Who owns customer experience?

This is a simple question with a complicated answer. In most organisations with a customer experience focus, the role is 'owned' by sales, marketing, customer service, or operations. Sometimes it is under the leadership of a customer experience director, usually at least one layer below the executive committee. Many senior leaders responsible for customer experience will also deliver part of the customer journey. Occasionally, the customer experience 'owner' may sit on the executive committee as chief customer officer or chief experience officer.

If that person is you, or their authority has been handed to you, is it your responsibility to deliver and improve the customer journey that drives your customer experience? No.

The customer journey is made up of a series of interactions between customers and the organisation, known as touchpoints. These touchpoints are owned by multiple functions in the business – from sales and marketing, to ecommerce, to customer service, to logistics, etc. These functions are supported by central services like HR, finance, and IT and steered by the executive committee and CEO, who make decisions every day which affect customers. All of these functions are essential to enable the journey to work. The customer journey and the experience that it creates is a collective effort.

Your responsibility, therefore, is to hold the mirror up to the whole organisation to allow it to see itself through customers' eyes. Using facts and data, and eliminating politics, you enable every colleague in the business to clearly understand the customer experience strategy and their role in achieving it. You enable the organisation to deliver and improve the journey by introducing clarity and shared objectives. You lead collaboration across functions and hold others accountable for delivering.

> "HOLD THE MIRROR UP TO THE WHOLE ORGANISATION TO ALLOW IT TO SEE ITSELF THROUGH CUSTOMERS' EYES.

I am responsible for customer experience, so you have to listen to me!

When we take on a role, it would be wonderful if others took note of the job title bestowed upon us and took it as a given that they should listen. I have heard the words "I am responsible for customer experience, so you have to listen to me!" uttered in real life. Not surprisingly, nobody was listening. It does not matter who we are, where we have come from, how prominent our education was, what job title we are given, how much we are paid, or who we report to – we must all earn authority in our roles.

In a customer experience role, your scope of responsibility is wide and deep, but you will frequently find yourself in an environment where very few understand what you do or why you are necessary, let alone allow you to lead. Earning authority needs to be a core element of your personal strategy. It will be the difference between doing your job by continually bashing in to brick walls and fulfilling your purpose with the support and collaboration of others.

Three types of authority

I once had the pleasure of listening to a keynote presentation by Curtis Bingham, CEO of the Chief Customer Officer Council.[14] He described three types of authority necessary for a chief customer officer (or any customer experience professional), which have stuck with me.

Positional authority – the position that you hold in your organisation. Most of us do not benefit from sitting on the executive committee, so it is difficult to influence from our position alone. In my first customer experience role, I was four levels below the executive – who was going to listen to me?

Borrowed authority – if you cannot benefit from positional authority, you must borrow authority from someone with influence. It may be the CEO, it may be another senior manager – ultimately it does not matter as long as they can give customer experience the platform needed at senior level.

Earned authority – the problem with borrowing authority is that you cannot do so for ever because the impact wanes over time. You must grow your earned authority before your borrowed authority either runs out or leaves the business.

Figure 2-1 Chief Customer Officer Authority Model

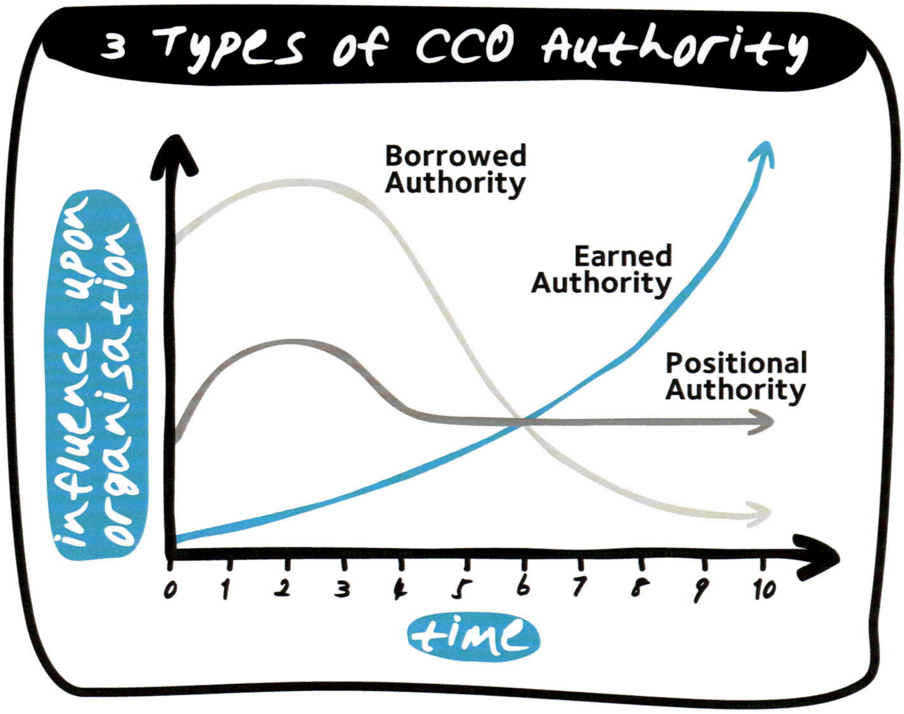

Source: Curtis Bingham, Chief Customer Officer Council[14]

Borrowed authority will get you started. But earned authority will liberate you. It allows you to speak truth to people at all levels from a position of trust. It is essential currency for your role, so make sure you are taking action to build earned authority from day one.

Find out how decisions get made and how work gets done

The first step towards earned authority is to learn how the business works. Your organisation is an ecosystem made up of people, skills, relationships, beliefs, environments, processes, technology, and data. Study it – go out into the organisation and learn what it's like to be a customer and an employee, how decisions get made, and how work gets done.

Not only will this give you a fantastic overview of the customer journey and how it gets delivered, but it will give you a genuine appreciation of what your colleagues do and how you can best collaborate.

You will also collect stories, ideas, and inspiration. Customer experience theory will be of little practical use to most of the people in your organisation, but if you can bring it to life with a sprinkling of anecdotes and examples, others will be able to appreciate this fresh perspective and 'get' how it applies to your organisation.

Ask yourself three questions

NOTES

1. Do you know what other people in your organisation do?
2. Can you articulate how their roles influence the customer experience?
3. Have you ever seen or experienced the customer journey for yourself?

If you have answered "No" to any of these questions, make time to shadow colleagues in other parts of the business. Not only will it help you appreciate your colleagues more, but they will respect you for taking the time to do it.

Assessing your own readiness

Enabling an organisation to change the way it thinks about, and acts towards customers is underpinned by a unique set of skills.

You need understanding and practice in the following six subject areas:

- Customer-centric culture – creating and nurturing a culture through behaviours, practices, and standards that encourages all employees to focus on delivering outstanding customer experiences.
- Voice of the Customer, customer insight and understanding – building collective insight into customer needs, wants, perceptions, and preferences through the capture and analysis of the Voice of the Customer.
- Organisational adoption and accountability – driving change and developing cross-company experience accountability from the executive committee to the front line.
- Customer experience strategy – developing a strategy that articulates a clear vision of the experience that a company seeks to create in support of the company's brand values, including its direct linkage to customer experience activities, resources, and investments.
- Experience design, improvement, and innovation – implementing practices and approaches to continuously improve, design, and differentiate customer experiences.
- Metrics, measurement, and return on investment (ROI) – creating and reporting measures of customer experience success, including their use in business cases, to illustrate the ROI and business value of customer experience.

These are the core competencies of customer experience recognised by the Customer Experience Professionals Association (CXPA). You can read more about them at ccxp.org.[15] Recognising your own level of competency in each of the skills is an essential step to building both credibility and authority.

Rate yourself against each of the above competencies on a scale of 1–10. 1 is the lowest level of knowledge; 10 is the highest. It's important to rate yourself objectively and honestly.

Figure 2-2 Customer experience competencies

Competency	1	2	3	4	5	6	7	8	9	10
Customer-centric culture										
Voice of the Customer, customer insight and understanding										
Organisational adoption and accountability										
Customer experience strategy										
Experience design, improvement, and innovation										
Metrics, measurement, and return on investment (ROI)										
1 = very low level of knowledge ⟷ 10 = very high level of knowledge										

Download a blank template at ijgolding.com[16]

Customer experience professionals are specialists by virtue of their very broad skill set and the ability to apply it to effect culture change. Those of us who hold the CCXP qualification have honed and sharpened our skills through practical application over many years. CCXPs have a strong level of knowledge in all these competencies, but will usually score a 9 or maybe a 10 in only two or three areas. There are specialisms even among the specialists.

If you are scoring 7 and above in all the competencies, you may be eligible to take the CCXP qualification soon. If you are not there yet, what's important is that you have a clear view on where to invest time in developing your skills and where you might need more specialist support.

For example, Voice of the Customer data provides you with concrete evidence about the quality of your customer experience and what is driving customer behaviour. Getting your facts right will ensure that you identify the right priorities for improvement. Get them wrong and your customer experience improvement plan will not align correctly with what matters to customers and will therefore not deliver the business outcomes you predict. Creating an unbiased, robust measurement may require you to outsource the work to an independent specialist.

The CEO who waits on tables

NOTES

Every time I work with a new business, there are three things I insist on doing to find out what is happening. Meeting key stakeholders is one. Learning how the business works is another. Finding and befriending long-serving employees is another – they are among the most knowledgeable and influential people in any organisation.

Undercover Boss is a Channel 4 series in the UK.[17] The idea is to watch senior business leaders as they go undercover to find out what is happening in their businesses.

One memorable episode featured the former chief operating officer of a UK energy company as he went undercover in his contact centre.

I found it remarkable that this was the first time the man responsible for this organisation's contact centres was walking into one. The fact that a member of the executive committee has to go undercover to find out what is really going on is pretty shocking to me. But what's even more remarkable is that no one in the contact centre had any idea who he was! He found out what his customers thought of his company. And how hard it was to do the job of a customer service agent. He had never fully understood and appreciated these things before. But what a shame he felt he needed to take the unusual step of going on national TV to figure it out.

He is not the only executive to be guilty of failing to appreciate what his colleagues in the business do. And it is not only people at a very senior level who operate in a vacuum. Often whole businesses operate in silos, where each function settles into a comfortable pattern in which they operate largely independently of other functions in the business, and just get on with it. The silos are often measured differently, work towards different goals, and have no appreciation of what the other functions do, or how they do it.

Businesses like this are very unlikely to offer their customers a seamless customer journey. A customer journey is delivered by multiple functions, so if each one does not understand and appreciate the other, how can they possibly expect the customer to get what they want?

Some years ago, I had the pleasure of being a judge at the Customer Service Training Awards. One of the entries was from Pizza Hut. I remember it because of the remarkable behaviour of their CEO, Jens Hofma. Jens was the only CEO who accompanied his team to the awards day. The question is why?

Because Jens is a rare example of a senior executive who genuinely appreciates his people. He understands how his business works and what the people in it do each day.

He is a leader who puts himself in his people's shoes. Literally. Jens regularly works as a waiter in his Oxford Street restaurant.[18] Not only does this enable him to see and speak to customers, but it allows him to see and speak to fellow employees and observe the business in action. There is little chance of Jens walking into one of his restaurants and his team not knowing who he is.

In the early days, not everything Jens saw and experienced on the front line was positive. There were many challenges to address.

But being an authority on customers and employees allowed Jens and his executive committee to make the right decisions, collectively, to drive improvement.

Key takeaways from Chapter 2 – Belief

know

You don't own customer experience. You do own the strategy and must hold others accountable for delivering.

do

Build your authority. Develop your customer experience competencies and get to know your organisation intimately.

remember

The CEO who waits on tables – experience what your people do every day and see for yourself what it's like to be a customer.

CHAPTER 3 - STRATEGY

True simplicity is derived from so much more than just the absence of clutter and ornamentation. It's about bringing order to complexity.

JONATHAN IVE

theory

Customer experience strategy – the missing link

Now you have spent time understanding your organisation and the perceptions of colleagues around you, it's time to start bringing structure to your work.

Embedding customer experience management in your organisation requires you to move from delivering random experiences to acting consistently and intentionally. Some organisations are able to go even further and become famous for customer experience by developing a distinctive personality and sophisticated delivery capability which allows them to deliver flexible, personalised journeys – they are continually adapting to customer behaviour. An idea summed up perfectly in this diagram, once again by the brilliant Jerry Angrave.[9]

Figure 3-1 Evolutionary phases of customer experience

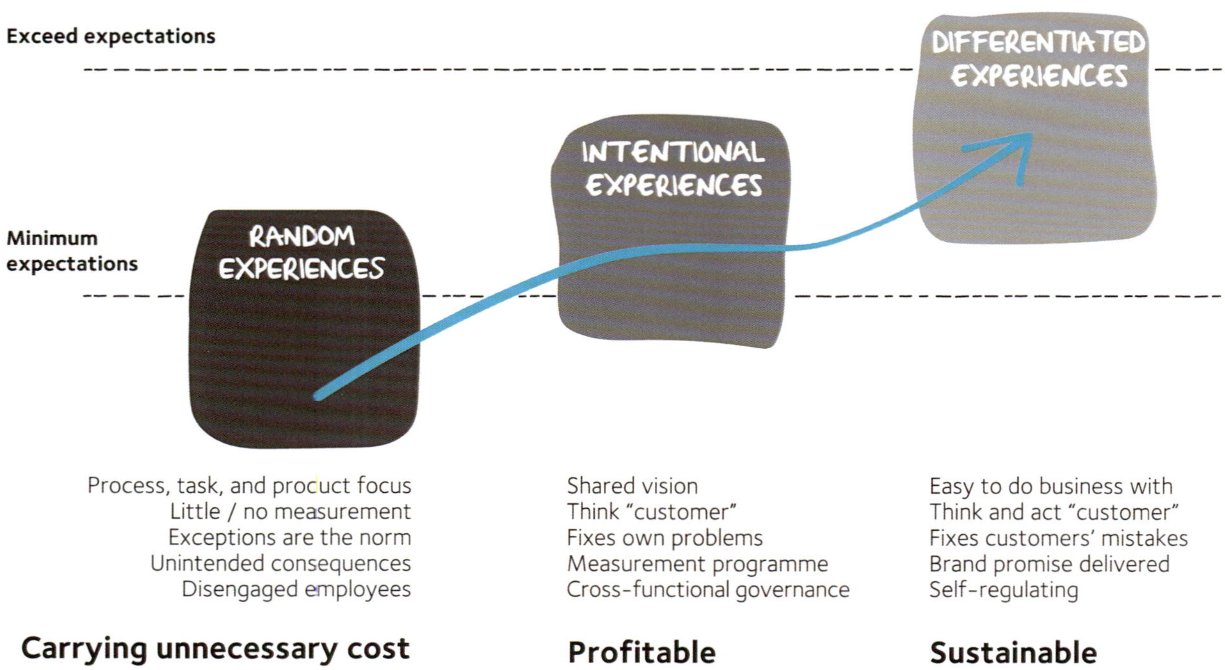

Source: Jerry Angrave, Empathyce[9]

I'm going to make a bold statement: 95% of customer experiences are random. What we're really good at is executing responsive tactics – quick, efficient, and sometimes engaging responses to customer demand. The organisations I work with are often very proficient at delivering and managing transactions, but looking across their end-to-end journeys, I find waste, cost, and missed opportunities.

Going from random to differentiated is not easy. It will take you six to eight years to get there, and as such is a long-term strategy which requires sustained commitment from the whole business. It's impossible even to get to the middle 'intentional' state unless everyone in your organisation is aligned and contributing to the experience. Whether 95% is the correct figure or not remains unknown; it may even be too high. What I do know is that very few businesses are able to make it all the way to differentiated, because very few businesses are able to think long term or achieve the level of alignment needed.

NOTES

> **IT'S IMPOSSIBLE EVEN TO GET TO THE MIDDLE 'INTENTIONAL' STATE UNLESS EVERYONE IN YOUR ORGANISATION IS ALIGNED AND CONTRIBUTING TO THE EXPERIENCE.**

The link between customers and the business has to be explicit

Strategy, people, and measurement are at the core of customer experience. You need absolute clarity on the experience you intend to deliver, you need to be able to connect your people to it, and you need to be able to measure how good your business is at delivering it. There is no right order in which to tackle these elements, because they are totally interdependent. You cannot have one without the others.

But I recommend that you tackle them one at a time, strategy first. The greatest gift that you, as a customer experience professional, can give to your organisation is clarity – creating a bridge between business strategy and customer experience strategy allows leadership to understand how meeting, or exceeding, customer expectation drives financial performance.

> THE GREATEST GIFT THAT YOU, AS A CUSTOMER EXPERIENCE PROFESSIONAL, CAN GIVE TO YOUR ORGANISATION IS CLARITY.

But strategy is often missing, or is poorly integrated.

The most important thing is to be clear about what the aspiration is. You may simply aspire to be a business that will reduce waste and increase profitability. You may not aspire to be world famous for customer experience, preferring to focus your energies on delivering a straightforward, dependable service which gets it right first time.

Starting with strategy aligns your activity to the day-to-day workings of the business from day one, and helps key influencers 'get' customer experience in the context of business objectives. In fact, you need to help each of your stakeholders undergo their own personal epiphany so they are truly change ready.

The change-ready leader

- Understands that investing in customer experience management is not a nice to have; it is not a fluffy thing with no substance;
- Acknowledges that achieving your customer experience objectives is in fact integral to the business strategy and contributes directly to business KPIs;
- Commits, in words and deeds, to the strategy and sees themselves as accountable for delivering.

But if there is no clarity on the proposition, how can you articulate what you want people to do or measure how well you are delivering against it? And how can you turn employees into 'fans' of your brand if they do not quite know what the brand exists to do?

Articulating this connection, clearly and explicitly, is the only way to create engaged and committed stakeholders and to unlock the people, resources, and focus needed to deliver the strategy.

Creating a strategy statement

practice

Communicating business strategy is an art. Frequently it is not communicated well. Often it is positioned in a way which is overly complex and difficult to engage with. And people – customers and employees – are absent or treated as a given. This all amounts to something uninspiring and forgettable. Making this link is your next critical step in developing your authority. Use the template in Figure 3-2 to build a simple message, which makes the implicit explicit.

A simple strategy statement

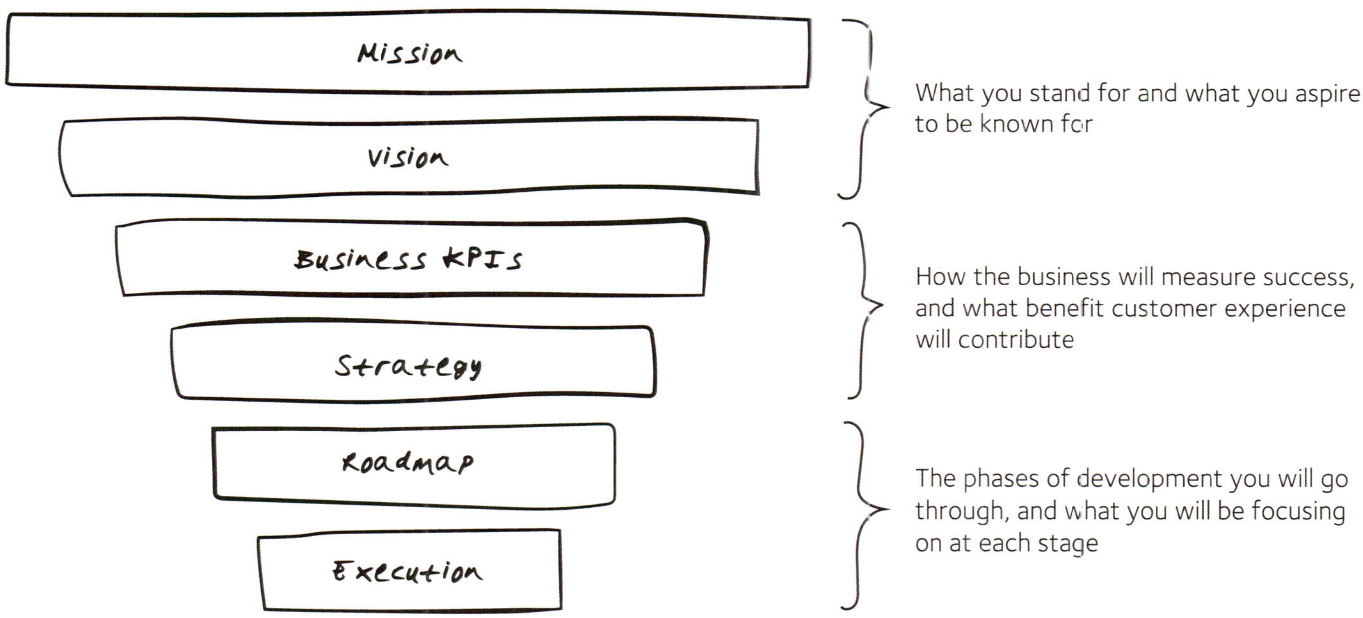

> A SIMPLE MESSAGE, WHICH MAKES THE IMPLICIT EXPLICIT.

Figure 3-2 Strategy template

Strategy layers	Description	Example (an energy technology business)
Mission	What is the purpose of your business? What does it exist to do?	To give customers control over their energy bills and level the playing field between utility suppliers and customers.
Vision	How are you going to fulfil your purpose? What will your brand be famous for and why will customers choose you?	We will develop the most intuitive and affordable energy technology in the market.
Business KPIs	How will you measure success as a business? Where will you outperform your competition?	Reputation - product performance, reliability, and ease of use. Reach - number of homes using our meters. Profitability - control production cost to keep the solution affordable. Measuring: coverage, installation cycle time; meter uptime; savings per customer; cost to serve; referrals; sentiment.
Experience strategy	This is all about your customers and what it will feel like to deal with you. Who are your core customer segments? Given your brand positioning, what does the experience need to be?	The cost conscious; the environmentally aware; technophiles; housing providers; small-to medium-sized business users. Transparent - you know what to expect. Easy - intuitive controls. Responsive - we're always here.
Roadmap	What key interactions (Moments of Truth) will you focus on?	You will complete this later
Execution	What action are you taking to build those components in the near, medium, and long term?	You will complete this later

Download a blank template at ijgolding.com[19]

Only complete the first four layers at this point. The bottom two layers require you to understand more about your capability and the quality of the experience being delivered today – those are the subject of future chapters.

The first three layers – mission, vision, and business KPIs – need to be taken from existing business strategy. If this information does not exist, you will need to make room in your own scope to create it; all the elements of the strategy need to be stated explicitly. If they are not clearly articulated, easy to find, and known by everybody, you need to make them so.

From here on in, your mantra is to *COLLABORATE IN ALL THINGS!* Bring your stakeholders in to work on this with you. You have spent time understanding the business, shadowing employees, and interviewing stakeholders, so you will know the right people to involve.

As a group, work through and validate the top three layers, then create the experience strategy layer together. At this stage you are not setting targets, or even trying to evaluate where you are now. You are simply stating what will be.

Here are some examples to help you (Figure 3-3). Retail and commercial vehicle rental are two very different businesses, but both have articulated basic experience principles and how they relate to business strategy. Both examples are simple and memorable. This is as complex as it needs to be.

Mantra No.1
Collaborate in all things

NOTES

Figure 3-3 Example strategy statements

A RETAILER

Our vision	We make it easy				
KPIs	Grow customer numbers, retain customer business, reduce cost to acquire new customers				
Our target customers	Families	Young adults	Mature		
What they want	Simple shopping	Everything in stock	Control delivery time/cost	Fix issues fast	Speak to a human being when I need to
Target experience	Easy shopping	Consistent delivery	Brilliant recovery		

VEHICLE HIRE

Our mission	Make vehicle hire easy, flexible, and affordable				
Our vision	When people think about car hire, we're the *first* business they think of and the *only* business they want to deal with				
KPIs	Grow customer numbers, retain customer business, reduce cost to aquire new customers				
Our target customers	Business travellers	UK holidaymakers	Urbanites		
Principles	Good availability	Seamless delivery and collection	Clean, modern, well-maintained vehicles	24–7, local response	No hidden costs

Authenticity, the key to unlocking the greatest customer experiences

Authenticity is a characteristic which differentiates the individuals or organisations which I believe are best placed to differentiate on customer experience.

What makes an individual or organisation authentic is having the integrity to be true to who they are; being trustworthy in everything they do; and being genuine about what they do and how they do it.

Authenticity is being able to say truthfully that the decisions you make each day – small or large – would not have been made differently if your customer was standing beside you.

We're never far from a colourful newspaper headline relating to a failure to act authentically – whether it is car manufacturers, supermarket supply chains, banks, or large corporates and their tax affairs. It is difficult to think of a sector that has not been tarnished. Each new incident adds to the consumer's growing sense of mistrust of 'big business'.

The bad behaviour trend started in financial services.[20] The global banking crisis and the enormity of the PPI mis-selling scandal[21] revealed an underlying toxic culture and a casual disregard for both employees and customers.

Is it possible for an organisation which is not acting authentically to deliver great customer experiences? No. Not in a sustainable way. Because the motivation is money, and money alone.

These organisations have lost sight of the reason why they exist. They have forgotten their purpose, and are thinking and acting as though their primary reason for being is to make money. That is a fundamental issue for customer experience – all businesses exist to fulfil a purpose. Truly authentic businesses understand that purpose, and know that the better able they are to fulfil it, the more money they will make – a subtle, yet very significant difference.

It is not a right to have customers. Continuing to have customers willing to interact with you is not something that should ever be taken for granted. Just talking about purpose means nothing.

> “AUTHENTICITY IS BEING ABLE TO SAY TRUTHFULLY THAT THE DECISIONS YOU MAKE EACH DAY - SMALL OR LARGE - WOULD NOT HAVE BEEN MADE DIFFERENTLY IF YOUR CUSTOMER WAS STANDING BESIDE YOU.

Weleda

Weleda was founded in 1921 by an Austrian philosopher and natural scientist, Rudolf Steiner; Dutch doctor Ita Wegman; and Oskar Schmiedel, a chemist and pharmacist from Munich in Germany. The company was, and still is, founded on the philosophy of anthroposophy: "the wisdom of man".[22] As a modern day business, this philosophy translates to a principled organisation which cares deeply about creating harmony with its people, its partners, and the natural environment.

I can testify that this business quite literally lives and breathes what it does. In 2015, I was invited to address a conference attended by over 100 Weleda brand ambassadors. Every individual I met was passionately; overwhelmingly; hook, line, and sinker; and madly, truly, deeply in love with what they do!

I have never been in a room where it was so clear how much every single person in the room believed in their purpose – not just in the quality of the product, but in the purpose of the brand. It is usually me trying to inspire the people I am invited to address. In this case, I was inspired by them.

" I HAVE NEVER BEEN IN A ROOM WHERE IT WAS SO CLEAR HOW MUCH EVERY SINGLE PERSON IN THE ROOM BELIEVED IN THEIR PURPOSE.

Photograph: Ian Golding

What defined their unshakeable belief in what they were doing was a set of values[23] that actually meant something to every individual within, or connected to, the organisation:

1. Fair treatment of customers, partners, and suppliers
2. Management–employee relations in a spirit of partnership
3. Extensive quality
4. Combining natural and spiritual sciences in research and development
5. High environmental standards
6. Ethical and value–creating business practices
7. Cultural diversity as an inspiring force

NOTES

These values are all genuine. They can all be trusted. This puts Weleda in pole position when it comes to delivering great customer experiences. It absolutely does not guarantee that this company will always get it right, but the underlying culture will mean that employees and customers are far more likely to forgive when things do not quite go to plan.

What makes Weleda an even greater example of authenticity is its amazing humility. The business almost struggles to recognise quite how good its brand is – making money is just an added bonus!

Old Mutual Zimbabwe

The second example comes from a very different part of the world and from an unexpected industry. It is a business devoted to helping customers achieve something that may feel impossible, in a country that continues to battle with a struggling economy.

Old Mutual Zimbabwe is part of a global financial services giant – Old Mutual Group. If you are not up to speed with your Zimbabwean economics history, you may not know that the financial situation in the country can be described as challenging at best. In April 2009, the Zimbabwean dollar was effectively abandoned. By the end of 2015, it had been demonetised and replaced by the US dollar.

Rather than falling apart, everyone I met seemed to be truly appreciative of what they have, and Zimbabwe has turned into a country where people genuinely seem to want to help each other.

And that is where Old Mutual Zimbabwe comes in. In 2013, the organisation launched a new concept. Called the Green Zone, it is a one-stop shop for all the financial needs a Zimbabwean citizen may have. Whether a customer is renewing car insurance, getting a life insurance policy, depositing money, or obtaining a mortgage, the Green Zone exists to help Zimbabweans in a way that no other financial services organisation can.

Outside the shop front is a sign that says, "Every need; every day; every step of the way". The shop is a place where anyone, existing customer or not, can just walk in off the street and ask for help with any financial service under the sun. What immediately struck me was how this is the opposite of what is happening in the UK, where banks and post offices are withdrawing from the high street.

Like Weleda, Old Mutual launched the Green Zone in order to be better at fulfilling a core purpose, which is 'to enable positive futures'. The Green Zone has not only delivered a great customer experience but it has also delivered higher revenues.

Photograph: Ian Golding

> BY BEING BETTER AT FULFILLING ITS PURPOSE, A BUSINESS WILL MAKE MORE MONEY.

Two more Green Zones have since opened their doors to customers,[24] most recently in a small mining town – not a city or large urban centre, a small mining town. The location was chosen in recognition of the support Old Mutual has consistently received from this community, to say thank you for its loyalty and commitment to Old Mutual. To me this is an extraordinary example which proves that by being better at fulfilling its purpose, a business will make more money.

As soon as an organisation loses faith and puts profit and shareholders before anything else, the principle of authenticity fades. It takes guts to be authentic. It takes wanting to do the right thing – for employees, customers, and shareholders – truly, trustingly, and genuinely.

Key takeaways from Chapter 3 – Strategy

know

This journey will be measured in years, not months. Organisational alignment behind a clear purpose is critical to staying the course.

do

Align customer experience strategy and business strategy. Be explicit about how meeting, or exceeding, customer expectation will drive financial performance.

remember

Truly authentic businesses understand their purpose and know that the better able they are to fulfil it, the more money they will make. Always collaborate – it must be a shared purpose.

PART 2. CULTURE: CONNECTING PEOPLE TO THE STRATEGY

100% of customers are people.

100% of employees are people.

If you don't understand people,

you don't understand business.

SIMON SINEK

Employees, customers, and leadership – in that order!

theory

If you have ever heard me speak in public, it is very likely you will have heard me recount this quote from inspirational business author Simon Sinek.

For me it encapsulates the idea that to reach your full potential as a business, you must nurture and cherish all the people who interact with you, inside and outside your business. It is my favourite quote about culture, partly because it doesn't use the word culture!

That is why this chapter introduction has a very long title. In the original manuscript for this book, I simply called it 'culture'. But that didn't quite work for me, or encompass its significance or the complexities and nuances I wanted to express. Culture is a catch-all term for so much. It is your people, your belief systems, and your behaviours. And you can have all the tools and methodologies in the world, but if the culture of your organisation does not align with your strategy, transforming your customer experience is impossible.

The next challenge was separating the elements – employees, customers, and leaders. Putting them in individual chapters implies you can discuss them one at a time – but you can't. So, which do I talk about first? Surely in a book about customer experience it should be customers themselves? But the truth is, truly customer-centric organisations do not put customers first. They put employees first.

"THE TRUTH IS, TRULY CUSTOMER-CENTRIC ORGANISATIONS DO NOT PUT CUSTOMERS FIRST. THEY PUT EMPLOYEES FIRST.

Customer experience reflects how people feel about their work

Whether the experience is delivered in a real-time human interaction – face to face, over the phone, or by web chat – or indirectly through a document, or a smartphone app, or an artificial intelligence interface, all interactions between your organisation and customers are delivered or designed by people. Most often these people are employees of your business. The way those interactions feel for customers is an extension of how the people delivering or designing them feel about their work.

If a business cares for its people, and they feel engaged and empowered, in turn they will care for the customers of that business. If your business does not care for its people, your customers will interact with disengaged, unhappy employees, and disengagement and unhappiness is what they will remember about the experience.

This sounds obvious, perhaps. But it often doesn't feel that way inside a business. Doesn't it often feel as if it's more about spreadsheets, targets, and rules? Despite being an adult, proficient in what I do, and unfailingly polite and affable to the people I meet, as a customer I quite often feel as if I am being told off: "You are in the wrong queue", or "Please stand behind the line", or "You can't travel on this train, you have a super-saver ticket so you need to wait". I find this infuriating, and it provides an endless supply of material on how *not* to do it for my blog.

Sadly, I occasionally find myself, or see others, being treated this way in a work context: "Oh you can't use that here" (Blu-Tack)), or "We're not normally allowed" (encouraging people to leave the room for a break whenever they need to). You quickly learn these subtle, unwritten rules and conventions on joining an organisation and then slowly stop noticing them: "Oh, I don't know why but we always have to do it that way".

Are these, let's call them protocols, a necessary aspect of organisational culture that are created to make sure the right things happen, at the right time? Or is this just a way of working that has insidiously crept in to organisations almost unnoticed, quietly and steadily exerting control and destroying the experiences that we have as employees and as customers?

"THERE IS NOTHING BETTER AT CREATING A NEGATIVE CULTURE THAN BUREAUCRACY.

I don't sit on the fence when it comes to this question. There is nothing better at creating a negative culture than bureaucracy. It wastes time – the time of the people who create it and the people who are subjected to it. As a Six Sigma practitioner, I believe waste serves no useful purpose and needs to be eliminated – this saves time; improves efficiency; improves morale; improves customer perception; and saves money.

The smallest biggest change

Mary Barra is Chairman and CEO of US car giant General Motors. When she became CEO, she set out to make General Motors lean and efficient. If you think this sounds like a mandate for more control and more bureaucracy, you could not be more wrong. In fact, what Mary Barra did was something that many have failed to do – that many have not had the courage to do. Mary Barra tackled bureaucracy head-on by drawing power away from the top of the hierarchy and handing it back to managers.

Mary referred to this as her "smallest biggest change".[25] First, she signalled her intent by changing the General Motors dress code. Over the years, the GE bureaucrats had managed to produce a dress code which ran to 10 pages. What a fantastic waste of time – a weighty document advising employees what they could and could not wear. Why did the business feel the need to mandate what people wear to work? What Mary did was simple, but so powerful. She scrapped the epic and over-engineered policy, and replaced it with just two words: dress appropriately.

In an interview about the change, Mary explained her motivation as follows: "It really became a window into the change that we needed to make at General Motors, because I'd have managers sending me emails or calling me saying, 'I need you to write it down.' So, I would take them through and say, 'OK, what do you do?' You know, 'I run a group of 20 people. I'm responsible for $10 million of budget, etc.' And I said, 'I can trust you with $10 million of budget and supervising 20 people, but I can't trust you to dress appropriately, to figure that out?' It was kind of a step in empowering. Because we found that sometimes people hid behind the rules and didn't like them, but didn't necessarily step up. So, this really encouraged people to step up."

Consistency vs control

Business leaders are constantly telling me that they do not have enough people to do the things they need to do to deliver great customer experiences. I believe they have more than enough people, it's just that they are so bogged down in dealing with bureaucracy that they do not have time to do the things that would add value. While the motivation behind bureaucracy may start well, that is, to create order and consistency, it's a path that inevitably leads to far greater issues. When bureaucracy takes hold, thinking, accountability, and initiative go unrewarded. Eventually they become a thing of the past, having been displaced and replaced by rules, procedures, policies, and controls. People lose the ability to think, and eventually they lose the ability to feel.

> "WHEN BUREAUCRACY TAKES HOLD, THINKING, ACCOUNTABILITY, AND INITIATIVE GO UNREWARDED. EVENTUALLY THEY BECOME A THING OF THE PAST.

As human beings, we possess a unique set of qualities that make us capable of achieving wonderful things, draw us towards each other, and make us want to join forces to achieve them. One of them is imagination: our ability to think creatively and experiment. Another is humour: the ability to laugh and enjoy ourselves.

As customer experience leaders, part of our mission has to be to help the businesses we work in to trust their people again. And to enable them to bring their whole, colourful, interesting, clever, quirky, individual selves to work.

All organisations need to have a sense of how it feels to work there. Gallup pioneered the employee engagement movement, which helps organisations track how employees are feeling. Rather than seeing engagement as a binary 'yes' or 'no' state, they identify three levels:

Engaged. Highly involved in, and enthusiastic about, their work and workplaces. These employees psychologically 'own' their work, helping move their organisations forward by driving performance and innovation.

Not engaged. Psychologically unattached and putting little energy or passion into their work.

Actively disengaged. Resentful that their workplace needs aren't being met and likely to be acting out their unhappiness on the job.

Gallup estimates that 85% of employees worldwide are either not engaged or are actively disengaged.[26] In the UK this figure is even higher, at 92%,[27] and is rising year on year.

This is worrying news for customer experience. Do organisations know this about their people? What have organisations done, or not done, to make them feel this way?

And where are all the engaged employees? Working in the most customer-centric organisations! Engaged employees are the ones who enable those organisations to deliver fantastic customer experiences through their own efforts and their ability to inspire others. As a customer experience professional, it's important that you make it your business to understand the picture of engagement in your organisation. And help maintain or build it.

You can take action in three ways:

1. Talk about why employee experience is important in your organisation.
2. Help employees connect to customers, starting with the practical exercises in this chapter.
3. Help your leaders understand their role in trusting employees to deliver.

Hence, employees, customers, and leadership – in that order! The three chapters in Part 2 look at each of these in turn.

CHAPTER 4 - EMPLOYEES

If you're not serving the customer, your job is to be serving someone who is.

JAN CARLZON

theory

The importance of employee experience

Delivering a joined-up customer journey is dependent on the connectivity of a human chain that is enabled by engagement, technology, and processes. If one link in that chain breaks, it will show in your customer experience.

Remember Jens Hofma from an earlier chapter? He is the CEO who waits on tables. He does this partly because he wants to see for himself what his customers see, but he also believes he cannot truly understand his business, or run it, without knowing what his people experience every day.

If you took my advice in Chapter 2, you will already have completed your own fact-finding mission and will have a sense of how things are. Whether you are leading on customer experience in your organisation or someone else is leading, you can help your business understand what it feels like to be an employee and how investing in employees will help deliver and sustain your customer experience.

Think about it – what happened when you last contacted your IT help desk? Did the person you spoke to help you? Did you feel that the person you interacted with had an understanding of your role and why addressing your issue was important? I am not intentionally picking on IT, but this is a good example of the consequence of not understanding who your colleagues are and what they do.

The fire drill effect

A whole new industry is springing up around engineering positive employee experiences. Is the work environment welcoming; are people getting the right work–life balance; is someone noticing when they do things well, and thanking them every day for their contribution; do people have the right tools and skills to do their job in the way they think it should be done; do they have a sense of how they contribute?

The last point is often a challenging one. If you are sitting in an office right now, reading this book, just stop for a second. Sit up and have a look around you. Do you know everyone you see? Do you know what they do? Do you know how they contribute to delivering your customer journey?

A friend once shared an observation with me about what happened to her during a company fire drill. She left the building, along with everyone else, and made her way to the evacuation point. When she looked around her, she noticed two things. Firstly, she saw several people she had not seen for years, who she thought had left the business or retired. And secondly, she noticed a large number of people she didn't recognise at all.

She could have passed them in the street without knowing they worked in the same organisation.

My experience in workshops is the same. I can have a group of people who have worked in the same business for many years but it's the first time they have ever met in person! These are colleagues working in relative proximity, serving the same customers, and contributing to the delivery of the same customer journey. Yet they do not really know each other. They have not had enough opportunity to understand who everyone else is and what they do.

practice

Customer-centric role profiles – creating a direct connection to customers

Organisations are so afflicted by impenetrable silos, I believe we have to make a conscious effort to help our people meet and network with colleagues. This is just as important as knowing our customers.

> SHE COULD HAVE PASSED THEM IN THE STREET WITHOUT KNOWING THEY WORKED IN THE SAME ORGANISATION.

Role profiles are rarely shared in an organisation, and when they are it sometimes feels as if they are written in a different language. So, this exercise is designed to create a common language to help colleagues understand what the people around them do, and to replicate and sustain the buzz and energy you get following a workshop.

The idea is to translate your role profile into customer-centric language by answering the following five questions:

1. Who are your customers (internal and external)?
2. What do you do for your customers?
3. What is the balance between internal and external customer interaction?
4. What is your role in the end-to-end delivery chain to external customers, i.e. how does your role relate to the purpose of the business?
5. How is your performance measured?

Getting colleagues to create these profiles together is extremely valuable and insightful. It is not always straightforward, particularly if you are not interacting with external customers. It is wonderful to watch colleagues helping each other, and to see lightbulbs illuminating all around the room as people find their connection to the purpose and each other.

Often clients make these questions part of company intranet profiles, which is a great way to make it a useful tool for everyone. And wouldn't it be wonderful if role profiles started life this way, before the first interview!

story

The curious case of the business that lived up to its name

If you have children, it is highly likely you are familiar with the brands owned by United Biscuits. They make Jaffa cakes, Hobnobs, Cream Crackers, and Mini Cheddars to name but four.

This wonderful story concerns a packet of Mini Cheddars, a little boy named Tyler, and his mum Helen.

Tyler loves Mini Cheddars. One day during the school holidays, he was enjoying his usual packet when he found something extra inside: a piece of string.

Mum was concerned. Tyler was only four years old, so she called United Biscuits. The customer services team were very understanding and apologetic. They asked her to return the packet and contents to a freepost address and, strangely, asked what Tyler's favourite animal was.

A few days later, Helen received a letter. The team at United Biscuits were on the case and asked her to pass something on to Tyler. With the letter was a branded box. Inside Tyler found a cuddly monkey, about eight inches high, along with a Jaffa cake ruler. He was delighted with this. And so was Helen.

Five days later, Helen received a second letter from United Biscuits explaining that the manufacturing team had discovered that the string was a piece of webbing from the conveyor system that had broken free. They explained that these are checked regularly but they would be putting extra checks in place to make sure it didn't happen again. They also sent some vouchers.

Getting a great response from a customer services team isn't so unusual. But getting a response like this, which demonstrates absolute clarity of purpose is unusual. No reference to terms and conditions, no back-covering, and no fobbing off. All they wanted to do was engage and retain a valued customer.

"NO REFERENCE TO TERMS AND CONDITIONS, NO BACK-COVERING, AND NO FOBBING OFF. ALL THEY WANTED TO DO WAS ENGAGE AND RETAIN A VALUED CUSTOMER.

What's even more extraordinary is the backing and support the customer services team received from their colleagues in manufacturing. They were genuinely concerned, investigated the issue, and bothered to communicate their response in plain English. Not only do they exist to manufacture fabulous Mini Cheddars, but also they consider it part of their job to deliver a fabulous service.

United Biscuits lived up to their name! They delivered a masterclass in united, customer-centric teamwork. The whole team appeared to be focused on wanting to create and sustain long-term relationships between their brands and their customers. They took a complaint extremely seriously, making the customer feel listened to and cared for.

The result is not just a customer whose complaint has been dealt with, but a customer who has become an advocate of the brand and everything it stands for. She even called to thank them for the way they handled the whole thing and for making both her and her son feel incredibly valued.

Helen will never forget what United Biscuits did. And nor will Tyler, who thinks about Mini Cheddars every time he looks at his cuddly monkey! I guarantee both of them will continue to be customers and will tell many people about this story in the years to come.

Key takeaways from Chapter 4 – Employees

know

Employee experience drives customer experience. Make it your business to understand the picture of engagement in your organisation. And help maintain or build it.

do

Use customer-centric role profiles to create and maintain a connection between employees and the purpose of your business.

remember

Every contribution counts. If even one link in your organisational chain is broken, it will show in your customer experience.

NOTES

CHAPTER 5 - CUSTOMERS

When dealing with people, remember you are not dealing with creatures of logic, but creatures of emotion.

DALE CARNEGIE

Walking in customers' shoes – something we do, not something we say

NOTES

theory

Can you describe a day in the life of your customers? Do you know what keeps them up at night? Knowing what you want and expect as a customer is not the same thing. I am talking about getting close enough, and picking up a clear enough signal, to appreciate someone else's perspective and motivations without judgement or reference to your own point of view.

But if you think you know your customers, you are probably wrong. Even front-line employees can find it remarkably difficult to describe their customers, or what matters to them objectively. Organisations often make the mistake of thinking that customers spend time thinking about them. Most of the time they don't. I rarely, if ever, stop to think about what my electricity provider is doing for me. Or whether the packaging on that pair of shoes I just bought was the right colour or thickness.

I have lost count of the number of times people have asked me to tell them who their customers are and what they want. I have developed a useful phrase to respond to this: "I don't know, but we're going to find out". It took me a while to feel comfortable saying that, because people expect me to know! But the truth is, none of us – even customer experience professionals – are born with an extra well-developed part of our brain which helps us to be naturally insightful.

Being comfortable to not know something, and admit it with an "I don't know" gives us the freedom to seek insight. Having insight helps us to be objective and make good decisions. Together with the right culture, insight helps us develop empathy and make customer-focused decisions.

One of my clients is a major supplier of delivery services for eBay. This company is very committed to customer experience and absolutely understands what is required, but the majority of employees don't use eBay. They don't understand how it feels to be an eBay trader and how important it is to a trader's reputation and future sales for the delivery to go to the right place at the right time. As a result, it's very difficult for them to empathise with the customer, or understand the best course of action when things don't go to plan.

Early in my career, I was employed by an online retailer. We sold mainly clothing, and I noticed that very few of my colleagues chose to wear the clothes we sold. Consequently, very few of them, particularly senior managers, actually knew what it felt like to be a customer. We set about changing this, with a very generous staff discount and a request for help by trying the shopping experience, trying our products, and helping us improve.

There was never a three-line whip, or even an expectation that our people would automatically become customers, but uptake was huge. And before long my inbox, as Head of Customer Experience, was overflowing with comments, suggestions, and requests from colleagues. I will never forget the glow of satisfaction I felt hearing a colleague discussing a dress with a customer, saying she had one just like it and was confident the customer was going to love it.

'Walking in customers' shoes' is a horribly overused phrase. But if a business wants to transform its culture, it is vitally important that it becomes a practice, not just something that is said. It means understanding what customers' day-to-day lives are like, and appreciating the context of what we do for them and how we fit in. We need to understand their life to serve their life.

There are situations where it is not possible for just anyone to become a customer, for example in the pharmaceuticals industry, or business-to-business organisations. In these scenarios customer research and insight must act as a bridge between people and customers.

I'm not about to launch into a thesis on customer insight methodologies. That's a specialism in its own right, and one for a book on market research to cover. But I want to make an important point. Human beings are complex, fickle, irrational, and often inarticulate. They come in all shapes, sizes, and emotional states which defy being neatly labelled and filed away.

Market researchers do an incredible job of making insight digestible and succinct for senior executives. In fact, they sometimes do too good a job. Unstructured data gets passed through many different filters and lenses, structuring, justifying, and intellectualising until a single number pops out the other end. But by that stage the humanity has been smothered by over-engineering, and the insight has lost all of its power to engage us on an emotional level.

“WE NEED RICH, MEMORABLE STORYTELLING INSIGHTS. WE NEED AN OPPORTUNITY TO GET TO KNOW CUSTOMERS, IN THEIR NATURAL HABITAT, IN THE WILD.

The reality is that insight is a nuanced, rambling, and messy affair, so while robust quantitative data has a place in this book (in Chapter 8 in fact), right here and now we need rich, memorable storytelling insights. We need an opportunity to get to know customers, in their natural habitat, in the wild – not by reading a report on how they scored when they answered 20 questions about our website, or by finding out whether they would recommend our product to friends and family.

One of my clients, a pharmaceutical business in India, recognised that it didn't know very much about its customers. Selling over-the-counter products to pharmacies, the business rarely encountered its customers at all, or felt it understood the customer journey. In fact, the organisation tended to see customers as a collection of ailments to be treated.

Having recognised this gap in its knowledge, the business decided to go about addressing it. Each member of the leadership team committed to spending one day a month in the home of one of their customers. By doing this, they were able to observe customers in every aspect of their lives. What they learned not only transformed the way they communicated with each other and their people. It changed their decision-making. The business is still driven by the business strategy and an understanding of shareholder expectations, but it is now balanced by the confidence that comes from having authentic, personal insight into what its customers want from the business and an ability to make conscious choices around when and how it will meet, or exceed, those needs.

NOTES

Getting comfortable with getting close

practice

The first step is to state the research objective – which is to help your organisation understand. This means, firstly, losing any preconceptions. And secondly, entering the process with an open mind. At this stage, you are not helping the business test a hypothesis or validate assumptions. You just want to help it understand.

The second step is to find a method which works for people. This is where having a physical product and a physical store gives you an advantage. But if your organisation is selling a service, or working remotely from customers, it is still possible to make it happen.

1. Be a customer
Encourage and help your people to walk your journeys and try out your products and services. It is likely this will involve a cost to them, and so you will need to support them financially.

2. Work-shadowing
Help your non-customer-facing people get close to colleagues who are interacting with customers every day. If most of your interactions happen on the phone, arrange for people to sit and listen to calls in sales and service. Or if possible, take calls themselves.

3. Ethnography
A long word, which means learning about people in their own environment. This means stepping into the customer's world and observing them making decisions in a natural setting – among the stresses and competing priorities of real life. Do people usually buy the weekly online shopping in laboratory conditions? No, they do it while watching TV, sitting on a train, chatting to the family, painting their nails, or musing about health/weight/fridge space. Context is everything!

4. Technology
Technology has transformed, and democratised, research. There are some wonderful tools which can help you get very close to customers without leaving your seat. They cost a little more money than the other methods, but allow you to gather fascinating insights, at scale, in a sustainable way. >

- Video diary or ethnography apps – a quick search online will connect you with dozens of providers. Customers use smartphones to capture activities, thoughts, photographs, and video clips.

- Online community – this takes a lot of commitment, but many businesses are setting up large customer / consumer groups online to hold a conversation and help them tap into the day-to-day life and priorities of the people they serve.

Dos and don'ts

- DO make this something that is easy to do, and encourage people to commit to doing it regularly. It's not a royal visit that is only done once. It is a great investment of time that will pay for itself many times over.

- DO encourage people to make themselves known to customers, talk to them about what they are doing, and engage them in a conversation. Encourage them not to use job titles but just to talk to customers as one human being to another.

- DO make notes, capture stories, find souvenirs, and take photographs.

- DO help people share the stories they collect. They will want to share, and you will get more value from the exercise if you can start to draw out themes and tie the work in to your internal communications strategy. You are starting the process of bringing customers inside your business!

- DON'T be surprised if you meet resistance. Start with the low effort activities and work upwards. Perhaps use the video diary approach to get people used to the idea and help them see the value.

- DON'T confuse this exercise with the practice of segmentation or developing personas as design tools. This is about closeness, getting comfortable, and seeing another perspective.

story

Clear and direct communication – how O2 turned employees into fans

Communication is an essential element of your activity to connect your people with your purpose. If you want your people to buy in to your purpose, to support it, and to advocate it, they need to know what it is, what it means for them, and what you want/need them to do. You need to tell people, not once, in a poster on a wall that quickly becomes a dust gatherer, but continuously and indefinitely.

I am a huge admirer of one particular communication strategy developed by O2, known as the O2 Fanbook. Following a takeover and rebrand, O2 battled to turn its business around. It not only needed to help its people get to know and love its customers, it needed them to become fans of its purpose and commit to it emotionally. If you have never seen the O2 Fanbook video, I urge you to watch it.[28]

The business turnaround was a success, and this remains my favourite example, from anywhere in the world, in any sector, of what can happen when a business wakes up to the fact that its people hold all the keys to success. The Fanbook delivered the corporate message with clarity and directness, but there's also an implicit message when a business respects and cares about its people to such a degree that it wants to produce something so beautifully crafted and uplifting to watch.

> “THERE'S ALSO AN IMPLICIT MESSAGE WHEN A BUSINESS RESPECTS AND CARES ABOUT ITS PEOPLE TO SUCH A DEGREE THAT IT WANTS TO PRODUCE SOMETHING SO BEAUTIFULLY CRAFTED AND UPLIFTING TO WATCH.

Key takeaways from Chapter 5 – Customers

know

Employees can find it remarkably difficult to describe their customers or what matters to them objectively.

do

Help your colleagues step into your customers' world and develop personal insight into what life is like for the people your business exists to serve.

remember

If you want to transform your culture, walking in customers' shoes needs to become something employees do. And it needs to happen at all levels of the organisation.

CHAPTER 6 - LEADERS

Technology is nothing. What's important is that you have a faith in people, that they're basically good and smart, and if you give them tools, they'll do wonderful things with them.

STEVE JOBS

Helping your leaders trust their people

theory

I dream of many things when it comes to the world of customer experience. Filling the world full of people who get it is one. Another is to ban avoidable use of the word 'no'. Or at least redefine it.

'No' can have serious ramifications for the behaviour of your employees and your relationship with customers. When a customer contacts your organisation to ask for help, hearing the words "I am sorry, but no, we cannot help you with that", leaves them feeling let down, or treated like a child.

"Why can't you do that?", they will ask. The answer? "It is not company policy", or "It's in the terms and conditions which you signed up for".

It's the equivalent of telling a child "because I said so". Even "I might be able to, but I will need to refer to a supervisor", feels like a lack of commitment to the customer. Almost as though we're doing them a favour.

The sad truth is, you can have empathy by the bucketload and still find yourself saying "No". Empathy is not enough to deliver action. Understanding your customer and appreciating their perspective is an essential component, but will not improve customer experience on its own.

> "THE SAD TRUTH IS, YOU CAN HAVE EMPATHY BY THE BUCKETLOAD AND STILL FIND YOURSELF SAYING "NO".

You also need the desire and capability to act in a customer's best interests in the moment, together with the confidence to challenge the status quo and improve customer experience in the long term.

In the 1980s, two psychology professors called Peter Salovey and John Mayer[29] were researching the effectiveness of health promotion messages relating to cancer and HIV/AIDS. They discovered that a person's emotional state directly affected their ability to act, for example to stop smoking.

The theory was developed into a model by Daniel Goleman,[30] who identified a set of 12 skills and abilities which he described as emotional intelligence. These 12 competencies profoundly affect people's thinking and action, and can be measured as an emotional quotient (or EQ-i).

Empathy is indeed one of the competencies, but alongside it you need to be able to recognise and manage your own emotions, and have the right relationships to get things done. In other words, your head must be connected to your heart, and your environment must support action.

Where empathy exists, a failure to act is a failure of culture. The role of good, old-fashioned teamwork and leadership in creating the right conditions for action cannot be underestimated.

> YOUR HEAD MUST BE CONNECTED TO YOUR HEART, AND YOUR ENVIRONMENT MUST SUPPORT ACTION.

Your people will be unable to act to unless they feel safe to do so. Without that bias towards action, your people will be deeply empathetic towards customers, but unable to do anything about it.

The EQ framework[31]

Self-awareness
Emotional self-awareness: the ability to understand our own emotions and their effects on our performance.

Self-management
- Emotional self-control: the ability to keep disruptive emotions and impulses in check and maintain our effectiveness under stressful or hostile conditions.
- Achievement orientation: striving to meet or exceed a standard of excellence; looking for ways to do things better, set challenging goals and take calculated risks.
- Positive outlook: the ability to see the positive in people, situations and events and our persistence in pursuing goals despite obstacles and setbacks.
- Adaptability: flexibility in handling change, juggling multiple demands and adapting our ideas or approaches.

Social awareness
- Empathy: the ability to sense others' feelings and perspectives, taking an active interest in their concerns and picking up cues to what is being felt and thought.
- Organisational awareness: the ability to read a group's emotional currents and power relationships, identifying influencers, networks and dynamics.

Relationship management
- Influence: the ability to have a positive impact on others, persuading or convincing others in order to gain their support.
- Coach and mentor: the ability to foster the long-term learning or development of others by giving feedback and support.
- Conflict management: the ability to help others through emotional or tense situations, tactfully bringing disagreements into the open and finding solutions all can endorse.
- Inspirational leadership: the ability to inspire and guide individuals and groups to get the job done, and to bring out the best in others.
- Teamwork: the ability to work with others towards a shared goal; participating actively, sharing responsibility and rewards and contributing to the capability of the team.

'No': one of the most overused words in the English language

It is also one of the shortest words. We use it dozens of times a day without thinking about it. In a way, it is an expression of control, of power.

Being customer centric means letting your people know you trust them, giving them permission to do whatever it takes to help your customer, and never allowing rigid application of rules and processes to get in the way.

What if your business banned the word 'no'? What if it were to mandate that all employees will say "Yes" and that it will become the job of leadership to find a way to support them. If your organisation adopted this practice, you would not only breathe life into your people engagement, you would be ensuring that your customers are able to interact with a business that will do whatever it takes.

If the word 'no' is being used a lot in your organisation, it is very unlikely you are ready to suggest such a bold step. Persuading your people to change the words they use would be easy. But persuading your organisation to embrace the new word would be very challenging.

In fact, your head might be telling you to wait until you have the right data and can buy in to a full roadmap before you start trying to change things. But don't wait. The data and roadmap will take time to build, and you need to start taking small steps now to win the hearts and energy of the people in the organisation and get them behind you.

Choose one thing, and say "Yes!"

Remember that mantra number one is to collaborate in all things? Here's a second mantra for you. *Act*. Choose one thing, and engage your business in finding a way to say "Yes". Position it as an experiment – a way of desensitising your business to change and a step towards proving your strategy of enabling people.

Mantra No. 2
Act

Use the role profiles exercise, and make your people and leaders part of it by encouraging them to suggest areas for change. Involve them in designing the solution and trying it out.

You will be delivering rewards to your organisation early in the transformation journey as well as building their belief. This will be a remarkably empowering and enjoyable first step on the road to transforming organisational culture.

The British Airways pilot who got out of his seat

Here's a great example of a very small shift in behaviour which had a big impact on me.

Very early one Friday morning, I boarded a British Airways flight from Paris Orly airport to London Heathrow. Everything was going to plan and we were scheduled to arrive five minutes early. It was only on our descent into London that the pilot advised that there was a problem – thick fog. He asked us to turn off our electronic devices to comply with an order from air traffic control in London. Although the landing was a little bumpy, we arrived without issue and on time.

story

I was due to take a connecting flight from Heathrow to Manchester. The gate was announced as normal and people walked to the gate, but ten minutes after the scheduled departure time, we were still seated at the gate. Then came an announcement. The flight would be leaving half an hour late because the incoming aircraft had been delayed. We assumed this was down to the fog.

Eventually we started boarding, then we sat and waited for the aircraft to leave. Five minutes or so later, the pilot started to make an announcement. Nothing unusual about that. However, as I looked up, I saw that he was not making the announcement from the security and safety of the cockpit, he was standing in the middle of the cabin at the front of the aircraft.

The captain proceeded to explain exactly what was going on. The flight had indeed been delayed by fog, but also one of the tyres had a tear in it, and needed to be replaced. Boarding was delayed because the tyre could not be changed with passengers on the plane – "You wouldn't change a tyre on a car with passengers in the vehicle either," he told us.

He apologised for the delay and inconvenience, gave us an idea of how long we would have to wait for the flight to leave, and completed the usual announcements he would normally have made from the comfort of the cockpit.

I fly a lot, as regular readers of my blog are fully aware. And to me this was extraordinary. A pilot getting out of his seat and addressing his customers in person? And in plain English?

This had a dramatic effect on what could have been perceived as a negative experience. He treated us as people, showing us the courtesy that he would like someone to show him. He made the experience memorable for the right reasons. I completely trusted his explanation, felt extremely well looked after, and in fact completely forgave British Airways for the inconvenience the delay caused me. And here I am recounting the story to this day.

It wasn't just me who was impressed. I could hear murmurings of approval from the passengers around me. And the cabin manager told me how lovely it is when a captain is brave enough to do that kind of thing.

What an interesting comment. That it should be seen as an act of bravery to come out of the cockpit and talk to people like that. What are they afraid of? Is it fear of disapproval? Fear of treading on the toes of the cabin crew? Fear of public speaking?

We do things we are comfortable with, and without really noticing it we can easily fall into regular patterns of behaviour which don't force us to think too much or experience discomfort. When it comes to customers, this regularly translates into as little personal interaction as possible. I regularly meet with senior leaders who are not only afraid of meeting and talking to customers but also avoid talking to their own people. They will say they are too busy, or that they trust their line managers to do it, or that their door is always open.

I am sure all those things are true, or that they truly believe them. But the trouble is, they become excuses. They become the norm. But to make an impact on people and create a memorable experience you sometimes need to step out of the comfort zone. What this British Airways pilot did was just that – he showed personal leadership in breaking an unwritten rule that pilots don't come out of the cockpit. In doing so he delivered a little bit of magic which transformed the experience for his customers and fellow crew.

Bringing it all together

By now you have one or two plates spinning. Possibly a lot of plates! But you don't have a roadmap and deliverables because the heavy lifting has yet to be done. But you must follow through, so you need a way to sustain the culture and maintain belief while you do that heavy lifting. The plates must keep on spinning.

> "YOU NEED A WAY TO SUSTAIN THE CULTURE AND MAINTAIN BELIEF WHILE YOU DO THAT HEAVY LIFTING. THE PLATES MUST KEEP ON SPINNING.

If you look back at your earlier assessment of customer experience readiness in Chapter 1, I hope you can now see where you have moved things on. People should be starting to do the following:

- understand clearly what you do and why the business needs you;
- respect your methods and trust that you will work with them, not do things to them;
- feel a sense of curiosity about customers and a desire to be personally involved in your strategy;
- recognise their purpose in the organisation, whether it is to serve customers or to serve the people who serve customers.

What you need from your peers in the organisation is active support and sponsorship for the work done to date. You need them to role model the new practices you have instilled to sustain the conditions and culture that will enable your customer experience strategy to flourish.

Start talking to them about the next phase of your work, which is to embed customer experience management. Tell them the hardest, steepest part of the journey is done, and thank them for walking it with you. And ask them, explicitly, to help you with the next part of the journey. It's not steep, but it is long and painstaking!

Ask them to do the following things for you:

- always make time for conversations with their people about customers;
- make direct contact with customers, regularly;
- cross boundaries and break down silos to enable customer experiences;
- facilitate true empowerment and provide air cover for their people;
- share your bold ambition, but help their people to deliver in increments;
- stand by you when faced with decisions which look unprofitable in the short term but are right for the customer.

That's a short list of big commitments, rather like a list of New Year's resolutions. When did you last commence a health kick on the 1st January, only to slip back to normality by the 1st February? If not sooner?

Human beings, as well as the organisations we work for, find it very easy to make a promise or commitment to ourselves and others. Yet the realities of who we are and the world we live in often make it extremely difficult to stand by these promises and commitments.

Before moving on, make sure you are as confident as you can be that your organisation is ready. If there are any question marks or obvious gaps, it's essential to resolve them before you embark on the next chapter.

If you have worked methodically and successfully built your foundations, you have given yourself the very best chance of being able to realise that commitment. You will have a ring of belief, strategy, and culture to sustain and protect you.

Key takeaways from Chapter 6 – Leaders

know

Your people will be unable to act to unless they feel safe to do so.

do

Act now to enable your people. Choose one thing and engage your business in finding a way to say "Yes".

remember

Deliver benefit early in the transformation journey. This will build belief and get the organisation behind you.

PART 3.
MAKING IT HAPPEN IN PRACTICE

When one has finished building one's house, one suddenly realises that in the process one has learned something that one really needed to know in the worst way – before one began.

FRIEDRICH NIETZSCHE

The tools of the trade – knowing how (and when) to apply them

theory

Now you have everyone's attention, from the front line to the boardroom and everything in between. You are ready to get hands-on with measuring, designing, and improving your organisation's customer experience.

Congratulations, you have reached a tipping point. What you do next will determine whether you start the business of change, or disappear into a black hole of analysis which leads you away from the action.

Build on the good work you have already done in creating a desire to get closer to customers and a bias towards action by communicating a very simple message about where you want that action to be directed, i.e. where the greatest return on investment (ROI) can be found.

Where should you start? By establishing the facts about your customer experience today. At this point, it is far too easy to get sucked into a constant hamster wheel of journey mapping, reporting, and analysis. Do not fall into this trap. You need to see the end-to-end journey in its entirety before you can start adjusting your focus to zoom in on the detail.

> "YOU NEED TO SEE THE END-TO-END JOURNEY IN ITS ENTIRETY BEFORE YOU CAN START ADJUSTING YOUR FOCUS TO ZOOM IN ON THE DETAIL.

There are many practice models, tools, and techniques to help you do this. All professions come with a host of them, and customer experience is no different. It's very unlikely you will ever meet a customer experience professional who is not accompanied by a flurry of sticky notes, persona templates, and journey maps! But, as with all professions, you do need to know how and when to deploy them. There is often a temptation to follow a prescribed process and use them like a checklist. Every tool, technique, and method is used and 'ticked off' in the name of consulting, whether appropriate or not. So, please allow me to briefly impart some wisdom to help you with the job of determining what tools are used, and when, to best achieve an outcome.

When I was plying my trade as a Lean Six Sigma Master Black Belt, I witnessed a gold rush. The desire to embed process improvement methodology led to millions of people worldwide being trained in the Six Sigma technique.[32] To achieve accreditation as a yellow belt, green belt, or black belt, individuals would be encouraged to complete projects demonstrating the use of every tool in the box. The problem was that most of these people never learned when and how to select the right tool for the job, or how to create a strategy and objectives. All their training pointed towards tactics – using every tool, every time. This inevitably led to the one thing they were brought in to remove – waste! They used the tools and produced the analysis, but had no way of operationalising their findings, so nothing changed as a result of their efforts. This had the unfortunate effect of seriously undermining credibility, not only of the practitioner themselves but of the whole philosophy behind Six Sigma.

Customer experience, sadly, is at risk of suffering the same fate. As I often say, "If I was given £1 for every time someone told me they had created a customer journey map but did nothing with it, I would be comfortably retired by now!" Ask any of the many hundreds of my fellow CCXPs and they will say exactly the same thing. Customer experience is not a methodology that can be deployed as a checklist or an off-the-shelf standard set of tasks to be applied in every situation. It relies on the competence and judgement of the practitioner to know what tools, techniques, and methods to deploy at the right time to land a strategy and drive change.

So, with that in mind, we will look at the three main tools you will use and how to deploy them effectively – the CX strategy statement, journey maps, and personas.

CX Strategy Statement

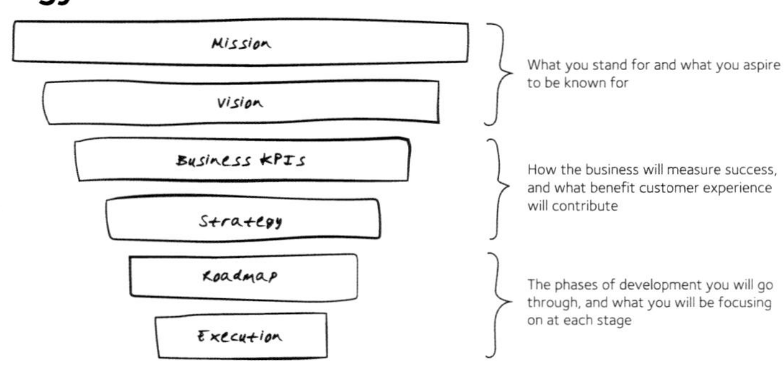

Rather than falling foul of the 'checklist effect', the opposite seems to be true of strategy statements – they are often absent, or sitting in a drawer, or even on a wall hiding in plain sight. Your strategy statement is essential, regardless of the environment you are in. It states what you are there to do for your customers; why they should choose your business over another; which business metrics will improve as a result of delivering the strategy; which customers are your priority; and which points in their journey you will focus on. And how it will feel for them when they are dealing with you.

And, unless your business rebrands or gets disrupted so violently that the business strategy is altered substantially, it will not change. Your strategy is a constant – your North Star.

In this next phase of activity, you will complete the strategy you began building in Chapter 3 by adding your change roadmap and a set of tactics to execute it. The other tools listed here will help you do this.

This will become your blueprint for change, and forms the basis of all your communication. And depending on how far your organisation has departed from the basic human values of 1904, you will probably need to keep on communicating, reinforcing, demonstrating, and delivering on your strategy for many years to come until people really start to get it.

Journey maps and personas

What is a journey map? It's a visualisation of the customer journey. Combined with a set of personas, maps become a strategic tool to drive action. Where things go wrong is when the act of mapping is seen as a one-off exercise.

Mapping is not a one-off task.

Good maps take time to build – requiring input from every function in your business to create them, and careful measurement.

They also require frequent updating – at least annually, and preferably in line with your business planning cycle, whether that is monthly, quarterly, bi-annual, or annual.

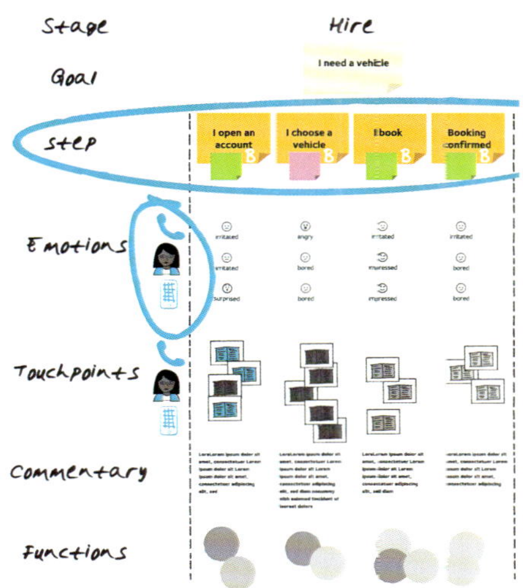

Next, we have the good old customer, or buyer, persona.

What is a persona? It's a fictional character who represents a proportion of your customers and is based on validated research data. Personas connect your brand proposition, or purpose, to the needs and wants of the different types of customers who interact with you. They capture the full breadth of different customer requirements your journeys need to meet.

Like journey maps, they take time to build and must be based on robust analysis. Get them right and they afford you a degree of predictive capability by guiding you through the design process again and again without you having to go out and conduct fresh research each time

The whole of the next chapter is devoted to how to create journey maps and what to do with them. We will learn more about creating and using personas in Chapter 10 – Doing / design.

> COMBINED WITH A SET OF PERSONAS, MAPS BECOME A STRATEGIC TOOL TO DRIVE ACTION. WHERE THINGS GO WRONG IS WHEN THE ACT OF MAPPING IS SEEN AS A ONE-OFF EXERCISE.

CHAPTER 7 - DOING /THE JOURNEY MAP

Map-making had never been a precise art on the Discworld. People tended to start off with good intentions and then get so carried away with the spouting whales, monsters, waves and other twiddly bits of cartographic furniture that they often forgot to put the boring mountains and rivers in at all.

TERRY PRATCHETT, *Moving Pictures*[33]

The six functions of your journey map

NOTES

theory

A customer journey map is a hard worker, performing no less than six functions in a customer experience management programme:

1. A record of what the journey is today – do not underestimate the power the simple act of creating a single view of the journey can have. It is common for functions in a business to have no idea what role other functions play in delivering the journey, and seeing an end-to-end journey laid out, showing all the touchpoints, is a great way to start unifying the business.

2. An assessment of scope – you need to be able to firstly measure, then manage, the entirety of your customer relationship, not just a sales or service contact scenario. Your map shows you every touchpoint to be measured and who in your organisation is accountable for delivering it.

3. An indicator of quality – overlaying measurement onto the journey creates a visual representation of how the journey feels for the different types of customers who interact with you and where it is stronger or weaker at enabling those customers to achieve their goals.

4. A place to capture and hold ideas – walking your personas through your journeys helps you to understand why your measurement looks as it does. For every customer or organisational pain point the map highlights, there's going to be a host of ideas, hunches, and inventions that can be used to resolve them. The map acts as a central place to collect and record ideas.

5. A method of prioritising – your map is a diagnostic tool which shows where you need to focus. The moments which matter most to your customers and your business results. Having those overlaid onto the map shows you which improvement ideas to investigate first.

6. A communication tool – maps, or variants of your map, will help you communicate to everyone in the organisation – from the CEO to the front line – what the customer journey is, the role they play in delivering it, and how they will be involved in continuously improving it.

The benefits of keeping it simple and manageable cannot be overstated. Your map will not only carry a record of the journey and report on measures but will also need to be capable of carrying a significant amount of information about the elements of your business ecosystem (people, process, technology, data) which drive the journey.

When you embark on a journey mapping exercise, you might discover the terrain you need to map is vast and there is simply no room for unnecessary decoration. However, a working map may not be fit for consumption by senior stakeholders, or anyone not directly involved in project work. There's › a fine balance to be found between working at a meaningful level of detail and maintaining clarity. It's likely you will need more than one version. Simplified (and potentially 'prettier') versions at varying levels of detail, or focused on particular aspects of the journey, will help you engage and communicate with stakeholders in the different levels and functions of your organisation.

For example, assessing the scope and change impact of a customer experience programme requires a map which depicts the entire customer relationship and shows how the various business functions and processes run behind the scenes to deliver it. Capturing and storing ideas, however, may require a map which focuses tightly on one area of the relationship, or even a single interaction, for example delivery or payment.

A map being used in culture change communications might depict the entire relationship but have most of the detail of metrics and service blueprint stripped away to show only the highest level of detail of touchpoints. This design enables an increased focus on describing the journey in the customers' own words and what emotional states they go through along the way. One of the best resources for learning about the different ways you can apply diagramming techniques to visualise your data through maps is from Jim Kalbach. Jim's book *Mapping Experiences* [34] describes a range of techniques developed throughout his career in information architecture and experience design, and provides valuable guidance on when and how to apply each one.

As Jim says in his book, the ultimate goal is creating an inclusive dialogue within your organisation, not creating the map itself. Many of the designs shared in his book really are works of art, and there's no doubt that a visually arresting map is an asset because it will get people interested and asking questions about your work.

While it's important to generate that level of engagement in your organisation, creating beautiful pictures that become corporate wallpaper is not the primary objective. The objective is accurate and actionable maps which will help you drive change. It's important to start right at the beginning and make sure you get the 'ugly' version right before you get carried away with the twiddly bits!

Map-building step by step

The departure point for your journey mapping work is to go right back to first principles. What is your brand purpose and how does it enable you to create and keep customers? That's the high-level journey you are mapping: the relationship journey. This should be the first element that you express visually.

When a customer first chooses to connect with your business, however they choose to do that, you should consider that first interaction to be the start of a long, prosperous relationship – not just a one-off transaction.

A ring is the perfect analogy for how our relationships with customers should be – never-ending and continuous. You cannot tell where the relationship starts and ends. Like any relationship, the beginning of the journey is important, but we also need to pay close attention to what happens in the middle, so customers do not feel taken for granted. Things will not always go completely smoothly, but if the relationship is strong enough, customers will be sufficiently engaged and willing to work with us to resolve issues as they occur.

This cycle can be expressed as a circular journey which shows the stages in the journey. This is the journey map in its very simplest form. I like to borrow a term from my Six Sigma background to describe this and call it the Level 0 journey map, so-called because it is drawn at the highest level of detail. We start with an overview to avoid getting lost in the detail – the simpler you can make it, the better your chances of keeping your stakeholders (and yourself!) in the circle of understanding. It acts as a permanent reminder that this work is connected to the business purpose and that our role in customer experience is to work out what we need to do to keep customers in the relationship circle and help the business to deliver it.

> “THE DEPARTURE POINT FOR YOUR JOURNEY MAPPING WORK IS TO GO RIGHT BACK TO FIRST PRINCIPLES. WHAT IS YOUR BRAND PURPOSE AND HOW DOES IT ENABLE YOU TO CREATE AND KEEP CUSTOMERS?

NOTES

practice

Examples of Level 0 journey maps

A utilities journey

This journey map could also work for phone or broadband provider relationships.

There's a decision point in each cycle: 'Shall I switch, or stay?' The customer has a choice about whether to remain in this relationship, and can decide to leave at any point.

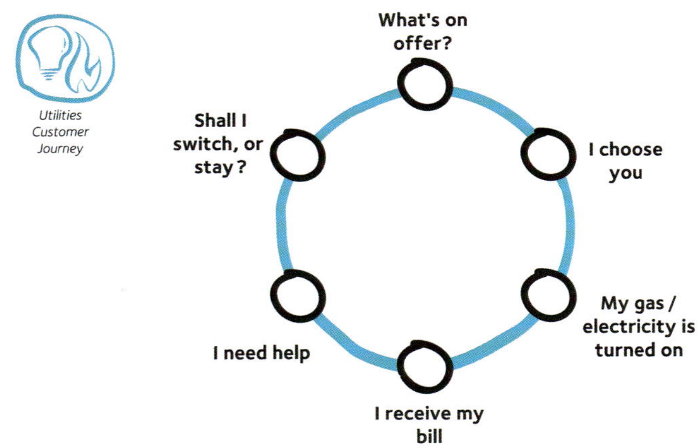

Car hire

A relatively transactional journey in nature, but one which may be repeated if the experience is positive.

The journey from Hire to Return determines whether the customer will hire from this brand again in the future.

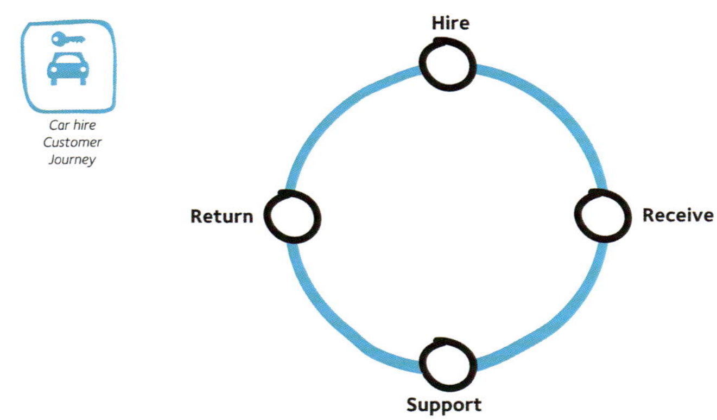

Online shopping

Similar to the car hire journey, customers can choose whether to remain in this relationship.

The customer experience challenge is to help the business complete the circle between Receive and Browse as many times as possible, and retain customers.

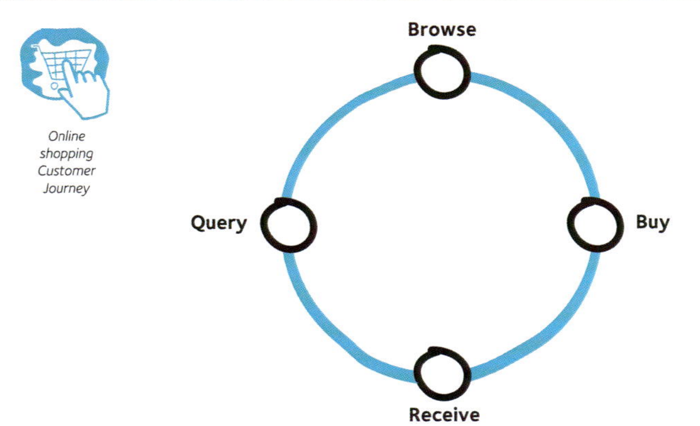

Home delivery

You can also express parts of your journey as circular journeys. For example, this home delivery loop would sit within the online shopping journey. This is useful where there are frequently travelled micro-journeys within the relationship journey, for example 'contact', 'pay', or 'change details'.

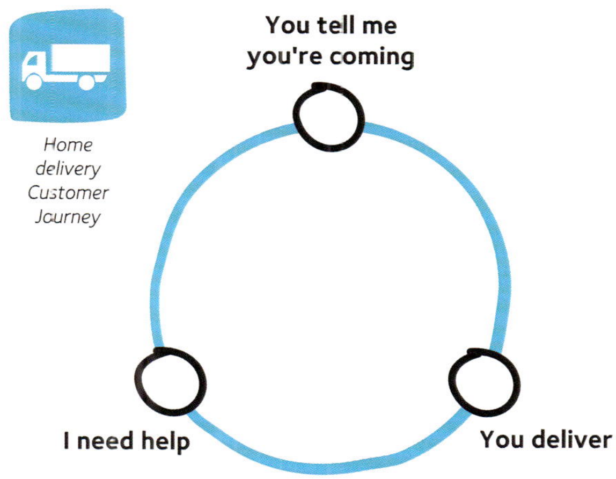

If your journey feels more like a series of transactions, help your business visualise it as a loop, and start talking about it as a cycle. This will help people start to understand how focusing on building the relationship can improve your ability to retain customers and grow the business.

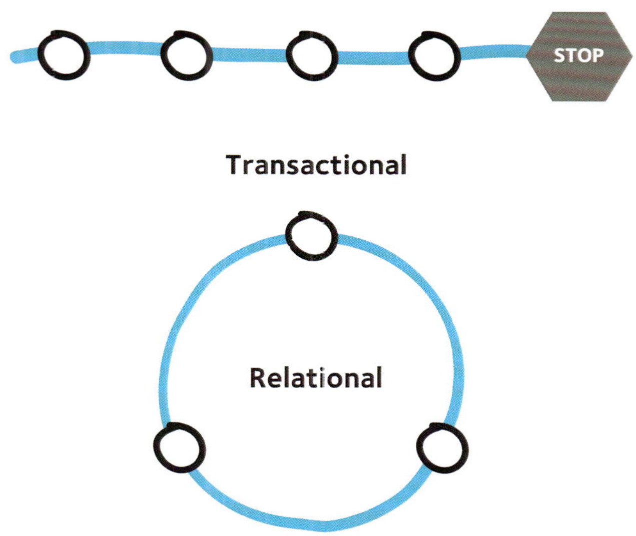

The Level 1 journey map

Each stage in your Level 0 journey contains a series of steps customers take to achieve their goals. These steps make up the Level 1 journey.

How to create the Level 1 map:

1. Break the circular **Level 0** journey into a straight line and add it as a top line. It's still a circle, but we're doing this to make it easier to work with. I use **yellow sticky notes** for this, but you can use any colour you choose.

2. Add your **Level 1** steps underneath, arranged vertically under the yellow sticky note they belong with. I use **orange notes** for this.

Examples of Level 1 journey maps

Here are our example **Level 0** journeys expressed at **Level 1.** Note the steps are described in customer terms, rather than in technical business language.

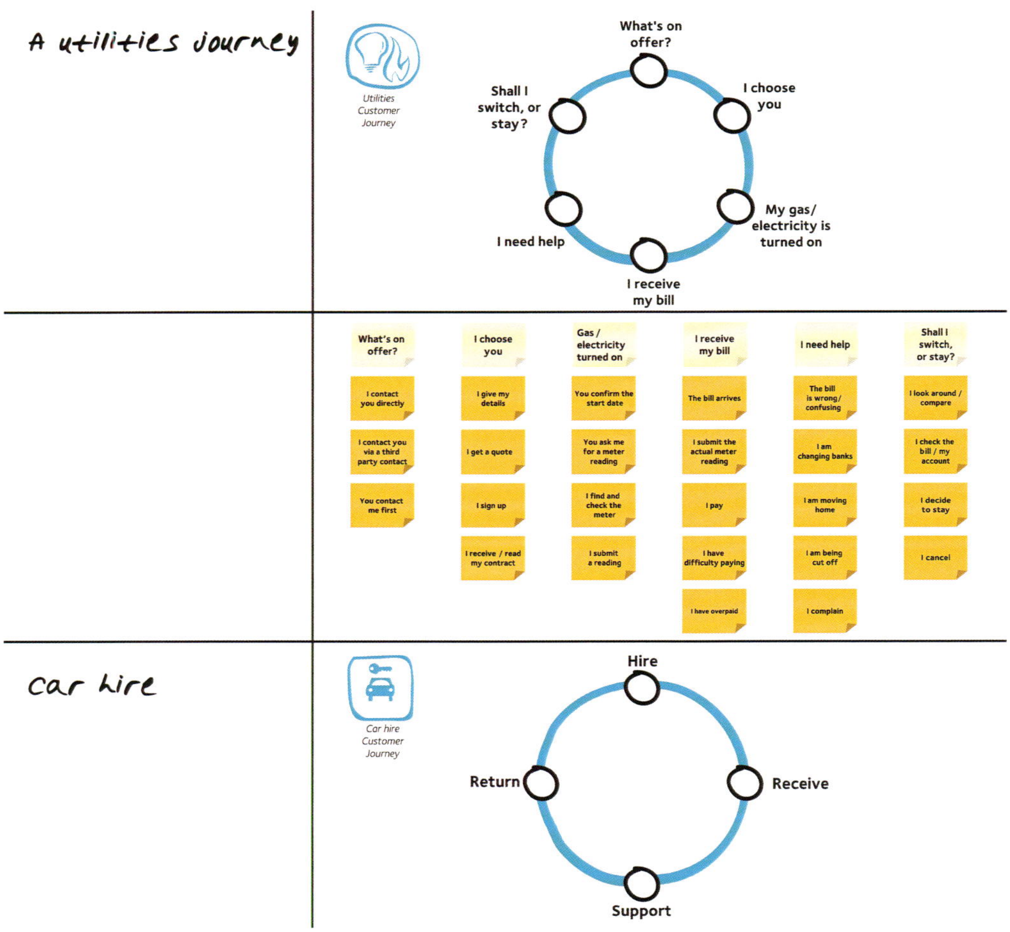

Hire	Receive	Support	Return
I need a vehicle	I need to collect or have my vehicle delivered	Something has happened to my vehicle and I need your help	I do not need my vehicle any more
I open an account	My vehicle is delivered	I report a breakdown or accident	You arrive to collect my vehicle
I choose a vehicle	I check it over	I query my account	We check it over and discuss any issues
I book	I make sure I am comfortable with the controls	I await help	You confirm all is OK
Booking confirmed		I get back on the road	

Online shopping

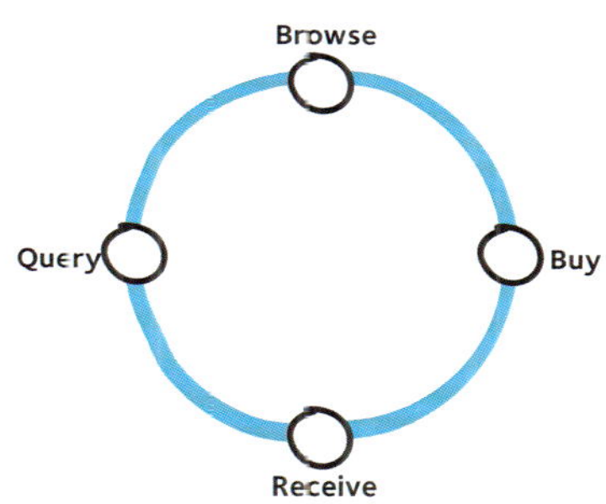

Browse	Buy	Receive	Query
I want to buy something	I buy something	I receive my purchase	I need to query or complain
I look for a product or inspiration	I check whether you have it in stock	I await delivery	I find the return instructions
I check the price / special offers	I add it to my basket	I take delivery	I arrange a return
I check the delivery time and cost	I carry on shopping / save for later / check out	I open the package and try on / use	You collect
	I confirm my details and pay	I keep / return my purchase	I await a refund
	You confirm the order		

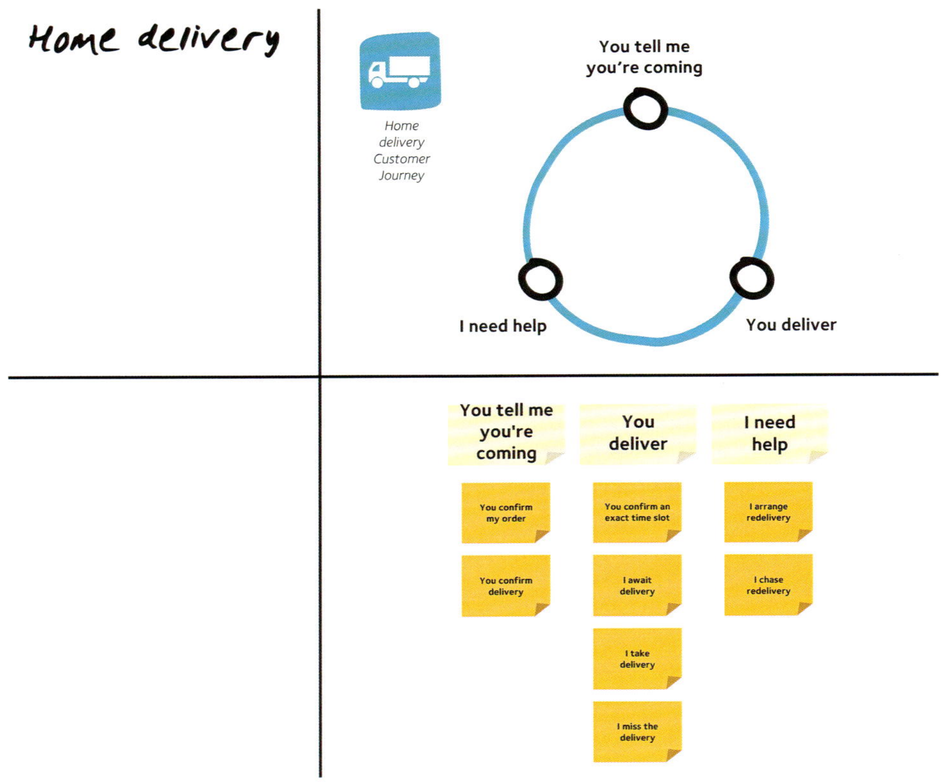

> “A TOUCHPOINT IS EVERYTHING FRONT OF HOUSE THAT YOUR CUSTOMER CAN SEE, HEAR, FEEL, AND TOUCH. NOT THE INTERIOR WORKINGS OF THE BUSINESS.

There are no rules on how many steps a Level 1 journey map can or should contain – it needs to be a complete record, so it will be as broad and deep as the journey. The examples above vary in volume, and even at Level 1, we can see that most of the steps are individual journeys in their own right, which we will eventually want to map in detail. At this point in time, you don't need to be specific about which interaction channel your map is capturing. Stay at a high level of detail for now, and describe the step in general terms. For example, in the home delivery journey, we're not specific about whether the 'arrange redelivery' happens on the phone, or via live chat or mobile application.

The Level 2 journey map

Each step in your Level 1 journey contains a series of touchpoints where customers interact with your brand. A touchpoint is everything front of house that your customer can see, hear, feel, and touch. Not the interior workings of the business behind the scenes – these should not be visible to customers!

How to create the Level 2 journey map:

Bring your functional stakeholders together to help you do this. Choose people with practical knowledge who can help you piece together what your journey looks like. Knowledge is more important than seniority.

1. Create a template to work on.
I normally use flip chart paper, pens, and sticky notes. But use whatever materials you have to hand. Put the flip chart paper on the wall, and add your stages and steps horizontally.

2. Ask the group to validate your stages and steps.
This helps people familiarise themselves with the journey structure, and ensures you are starting with an accurate and complete view.

3. Add touchpoints underneath each step.
For now, work with what you know to be true about your journey and document the touchpoints you directly own or influence – in-store, packaging, signage, websites, adverts, social media accounts, text messages, emails, people. Skip forward to Figure 7-4 to see an example.

Remember the first function of this map is to be a record of your journey in its current state, and as such it is important to be accurate. Try not to make assumptions about the touchpoints you don't own and are outside your control – word-of-mouth, blogs, review sites, competitor websites, and competitor retention activity.

You can monitor indirect touchpoints, and alter or create touchpoints of your own to leverage them, or mitigate their impact, but you cannot control them. Later in this chapter, we will use our customer personas to add some assumptions about these broader touchpoints, and validate our assumptions with customers.

You will also need to guide your stakeholders firmly towards touchpoints which are visible to customers, and not let your mapping efforts get sidetracked with backstage processes. This can be surprisingly difficult for stakeholders to do.

Make notes as you go along and capture the conversations which happen around the mapping activity. Stakeholders won't always agree, or have the answers, so your notes will serve as useful commentary on the questions, observations, and debates which cropped up along the way.

Identify areas of focus

Going back to the Level 1 journey, which steps do your stakeholders think you should be working on first? Go through Level 1 of the map with your working group, and annotate it as follows (see Figure 7-1):

- Steps in the journey which customers will see as a basic requirement (mark them with a B on the sticky note)
- Steps in the journey where your business exceeds customer expectations (mark them with an E on the sticky note)

Figure 7-1 Level 1 journey map annotated with basics (B) and exceeds (E)

Figure 7-2 Level 1 journey map evaluated for experience quality

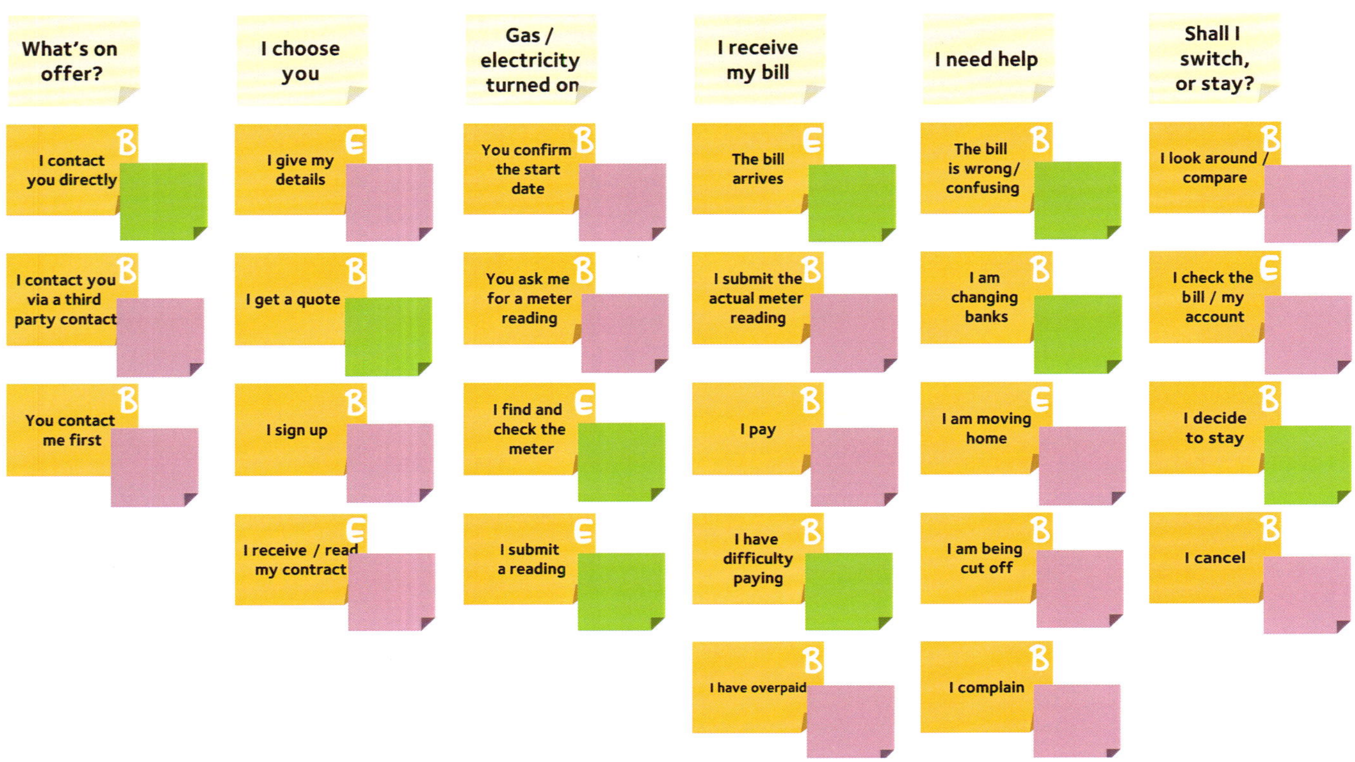

For example, let's take the utilities journey. Providing your customers with accurate, clear billing isn't going to win you a customer experience excellence award. It's a basic requirement. But taking the trouble to include a breakdown of usage by time of day, and present it in a visual format, or in a choice of channels, might be very well received and make your organisation stand out. This may exceed what customers might expect.

Next, evaluate each step in Level 1 of the map for experience quality. Use a green sticky note to identify positive experiences and pink to identify negative experiences (see Figure 7-2).

This activity requires careful facilitation. You have, so far, taken the right actions to enable the group to take an objective view of the journey, including the touchpoints their own functions are responsible for delivering. But having your role in the journey critiqued in this way can really hurt, and you will need to work hard to make people feel safe and supported.

Remind them that you are asking for their view on how customers perceive the journey, and that the next stage of the work is to establish whether that's really the case, and why. Reiterate that the journey is a team effort and that any wins and losses will be shared between you! And a positive or negative experience can be a result of something that happened way upstream in the journey – hours, days, weeks, or months before the customer arrived at the touchpoint in question. Help people to stay as objective as possible and try not to prejudge the outcome.

NOTES

Describe the emotion

One final step to complete with your stakeholders is describing the experience each of the green and pink stickies relates to. Learning to name the emotion generated by an experience helps us understand how the journey needs to respond, for example where customer no.1 is confused and customer no.2 is impatient. Both are associated with negative experiences and will be marked with a pink sticky, but the confused customer needs a different response from the impatient customer.

By now your map will look something like the one in Figure 7-3. You will be starting to appreciate how a visual record of your journey is a useful communication tool. If you have more pink than green on your map, you have stated a case for change! Or at least earned the right to a conversation in your business.

Figure 7-3 Level 1 journey map with emotion descriptors

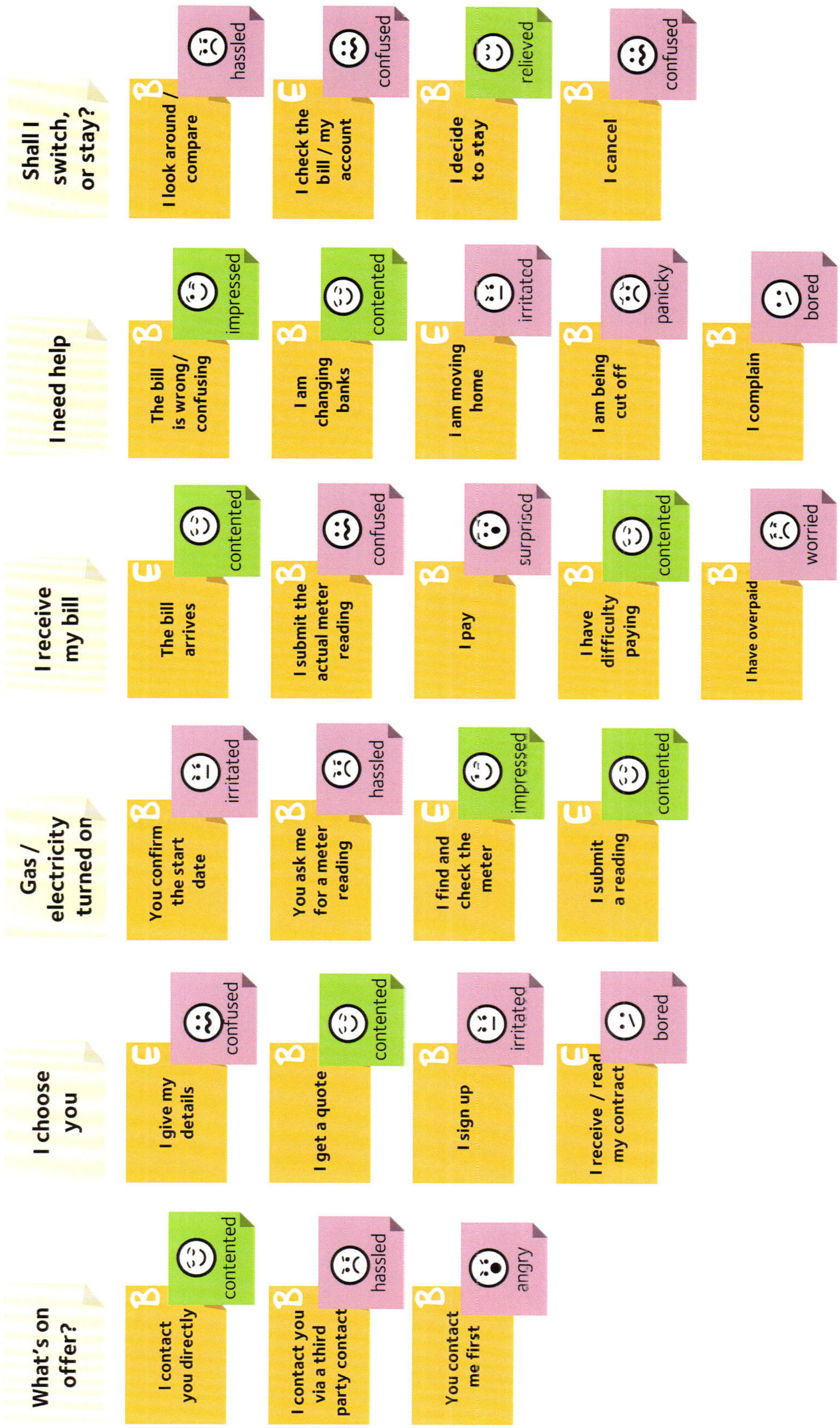

In fact, according to Forrester, the leading customer experience brands average 17 emotionally positive experiences for every negative experience, while the lowest-performing brands provide just two emotionally positive experiences for every negative one.[35]

Creating the 'outside in' journey map

The beauty of keeping your map simple thus far is that you have an overview. You have brought clarity and engagement to what can be a very confusing and divisive process. And brought a large group of cross-functional stakeholders along with you. Do not underestimate the importance of this ability to engage and involve others – it is critical if you want to stay the course on your CX journey.

> YOUR MAP ISN'T A JOURNEY MAP YET - IT'S AN INSIDE OUT VIEW, BECAUSE YOU HAVEN'T OVERLAID CUSTOMER INSIGHT AT THIS POINT.

But you might be thinking your map looks too simple. And wondering whether it should have more 'stuff' on it. In fact, your map isn't a journey map yet – it's an inside out view, because you haven't overlaid customer insight at this point. Now you need to start gathering qualitative insights to establish a true end-to-end view of the journey – including the touchpoints you don't directly control and don't yet understand. And you need to validate your journey map with customers.

This will expand the scope and scale of your map exponentially, so this activity is best broken down into the stages in your Level 0 journey. Let's take our car hire journey as an example to work on. We can break the work into four separate streams: hire; receive; support; return.

The work of gathering insight is best done as a team exercise with your working group – the stakeholders involved in mapping. Using the research techniques outlined in Chapter 5, guide your working group through a process of discovery.

1. Collate and review existing qualitative insights
This may save you some research effort, and will allow you to cast your net wider in terms of finding and engaging supporters.

2. Be a customer
If you have not already walked the journey yourself as a customer, do so now. Have your working group do the same. In our example in Figure 7-4, this would mean walking the end-to-end journey of hiring a car from the organisation. In this example customers can complete parts of the journey online, on the phone, or in person. If your journey is available in multiple interaction channels, you must walk the journey in *all* of them.

Encourage the working group members to take detailed notes at every step:

- What they did and how.
- What worked well, and what didn't.
- How the experience made them feel.

Ask them to take photographs of all the tangible touchpoints, record which functions in the business delivered them, and if possible record pieces to camera explaining what they are seeing.

Bring the group back together to share their findings. Start creating an insight wall alongside your map, collecting all your findings in one place and grouping them by journey stage and step. If you discover new touchpoints while walking the journey, add them to the map.

Then plan out the next stage of your activity together, which will be to spend time work-shadowing in all the functions which deliver the journey.

3. Arrange for working group members to do work-shadowing
Buddy up in pairs and get close to colleagues who are interacting with customers every day. If most of your interactions happen on the phone, arrange for people to spend time listening to, or taking, calls in sales and service. If, like our car hire company, you also have a physical product and in-person touchpoints, you will want to go out on the road with delivery drivers, collection teams, engineers, and cleaners. For digital interactions, seek out your digital analytics specialists. Ask them to talk you through their insights from web analytics and social media.

Again, it's important that everyone takes detailed notes and collects photographs and video. But you are looking for something slightly different this time.

- Observe customers and listen very closely to what they are asking for/curious about/worried about/checking on.
- Identify what customers are trying to achieve through their interaction with you (the goal) and what they want to achieve in each stage of the journey (jobs to be done). Customers may also mention touchpoints visited outside of your journey; be ready to notice these and capture them for the map.
- Observe your colleagues. How easy is it for them to deliver the journey and help customers achieve their goals? What do they feel is working well or not working well? Look for things like shortcuts and workarounds, and ask them which aspects of the job they found most challenging to learn and which aspects they most enjoy or most frustrate them.

NOTES

Figure 7-4 Level 2 journey map showing touchpoints, narrative and the functions which deliver the journey.

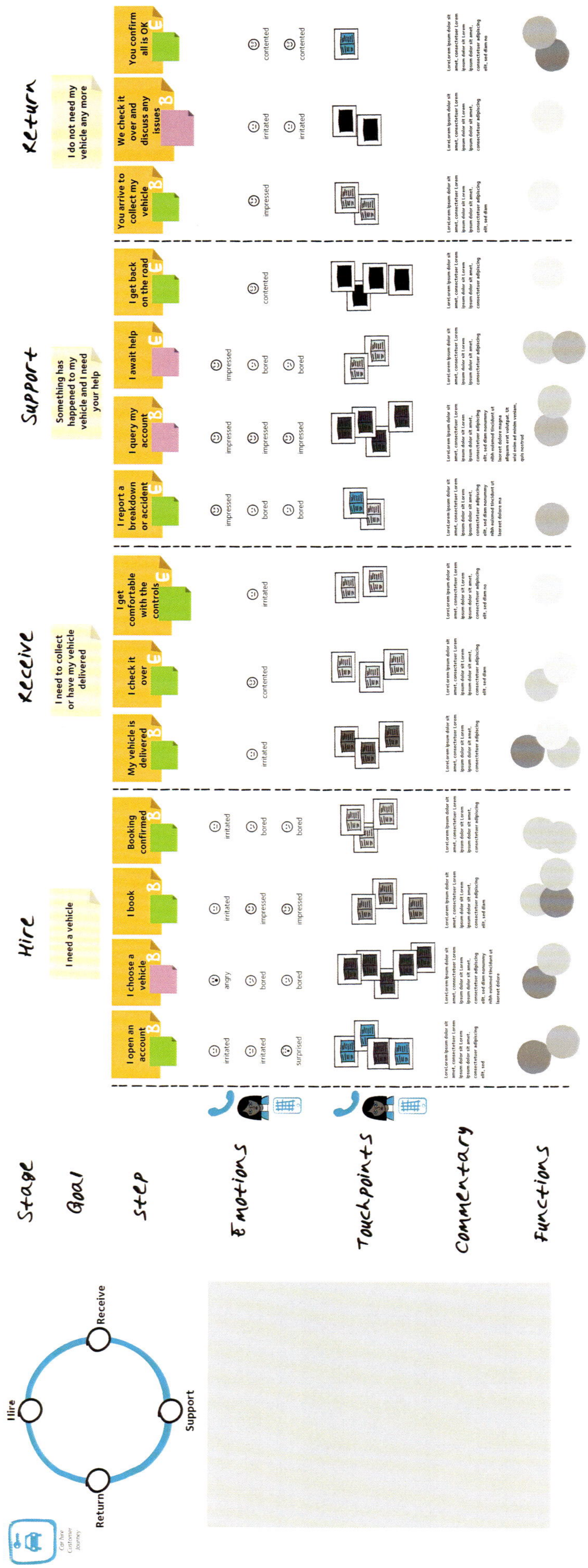

Bring the group back together and add to your insight wall, which by this time should be getting nice and full! At this point you might need to create more space on your map to add the layers of insight you are collecting. It should be starting to look like the journey map in Figure 7-4 .

Keep the some space free on the left-hand side of the map. Later in the process you will develop design personas to help you create the future-state journey. Don't be tempted to fill it with anything yet – just leave it blank so you can use the same format for your future-state map.

4. Observe customers taking your journey (ethnography)
So far, your insights have been based largely on walking the journey yourselves and observing colleague and customer interactions. But you also need to observe customers taking your journey and validate whether your findings to date are accurate.

This might sound like an exhaustive approach, but the validation step is worthwhile. For one motor insurance business, it was ethnography which highlighted that it had effectively lost control of annual customer renewals. The business was contacting customers a few months prior to renewal, with a new quote and terms and conditions, but discovered that price comparison sites were contacting the same customers far earlier. Understanding this aspect of its journey meant that the business could communicate with customers earlier in the renewal cycle, and therefore retain more business, and could communicate more frequently throughout the journey so customers didn't feel as though they were only being contacted once a year when the insurer wanted something from them.

How you collect this data depends on the resources and budget available to you. If you are fortunate enough to be part of a large organisation with its own research and insight team, or a research supplier, consult with them about the best approach.

If your budget is limited, use a video diary or ethnography app which allows your customers to capture activities, thoughts, photographs, and video clips using a smartphone. You will need to select customers and invite them to take part, using as wide a sample of different customer types as you can. They will need a detailed brief to work to – use your own experience of being a customer and work-shadowing to do this. Some app providers offer a managed service and can run the research on your behalf for an additional fee.

NOTES

story

Cost out, experience in – a tale of two banks

Before becoming an independent customer experience specialist, I worked for a range of different organisations of varying shapes and sizes.

I started out with a small independent invoice finance business in 1995 and then moved on to the Royal Bank of Scotland, Deutsche Bank, and GE. Over time, the businesses I worked in got bigger and more diverse. I spent time working for Liberata (outsourcing), Brakes (food service), and Shop Direct (retail).

Although every company I worked for was completely different culturally, behaviourally, and strategically, they all demonstrated a striking commonality. Whether it was food, invoice finance, or a pair of jeans, all of these businesses continually struggled to juggle two balls. The first is cost. Cost control is a consideration for all businesses, and the rearing up of the 'cost-cutting scythe' is a constant threat. The other is revenue or growth and the desire to grow – to get a bigger share of the current market, diversify into new markets and territories, and grow profits in some way.

When I started the GE chapter of my career, it was in the last few years of the Jack Welch era. He was one of the most transformational business leaders of all time, and the influence he exerted on one of the biggest organisations on the planet has very much shaped who I am as a business professional today.

Jack Welch introduced Six Sigma to GE; process improvement methodology was a huge part of his plan to turn the multinational conglomerate into the most efficient customer-focused set of businesses in the world.

The reason why Jack Welch believed in introducing a rigorous process and fact-driven methodology into his business strategy is that he understood that in order to be able to effectively juggle cost and growth together, you need to understand how to take the cost out of your processes while making the experience better for your customers.

When you think about it, this makes perfect sense. But when you remember that he started out on this path in the early 1980s, it was revolutionary at the time. Fast-forward to today, and things are no different – most organisations are still juggling cost and growth. The difference today is that a growing number are adding customer focus into the mix as a means of achieving this. There is no better way to describe my approach to business than cost out, experience in. Removing waste while putting customer experience back in enables growth. If you can solve customers' problems, you will improve their experience, reduce your costs, and be able to win more customers and grow. But when solutions are misjudged and aimed at the wrong areas of the customer journey, or executed poorly, this can have the opposite effect. It can drive up your costs and create issues for customers that did not exist before.

Just as all customers are not created equal, all journeys are not created equal. A basic expectation not met is always going to damage the experience. It's something so intrinsic to your product or service that customers just expect it to happen. But a journey comprising a series of well-executed basics is going to be forgettable, and may even drive a negative experience if your brand promises something more. A great customer experience is a combination of a stable, well-executed journey and a handful of special signature touchpoints which signal clearly to customers that you are different and distinctive.

> **A GREAT CUSTOMER EXPERIENCE IS A COMBINATION OF A STABLE, WELL-EXECUTED JOURNEY AND A HANDFUL OF SPECIAL SIGNATURE TOUCHPOINTS WHICH SIGNAL CLEARLY TO CUSTOMERS THAT YOU ARE DIFFERENT AND DISTINCTIVE.**

I remember feeling very inspired by an advert I once saw on TV. The advert was for an app launched by a UK bank which offered a simple way for customers to transfer money and to pay using their mobile phone. There are many of these types of apps available today, but at the time this was something quite new, and it seemed to me that it was the perfect demonstration of continuous improvement in the bank customer journey and was a differentiator which would set this bank apart from any other. It was not something that customers had necessarily expected from their bank, it was an added bonus.

The advert in question made a very big deal about the fact that you could use the app to transfer money using only a mobile phone number. It made me question why anyone would want to transfer money to someone in this way. But I figured that provided everything else worked seamlessly, it might be an interesting feature.

I checked out online customer reviews for the app, and unfortunately for the bank it appeared that the experience was not 100% seamless and that customers were encountering friction as a result. Differentiators are highlights in your journey that customers will remember for the right reasons. But for the highlights to shine brightly, your customers need to know they can rely on you for the basics. Despite good intentions, in trying to solve one problem for customers, the bank had created another. What should have been an innovative new feature felt clumsily nailed on.

As well as executing seamlessly, differentiators need to fit seamlessly into the journey. Take loyalty schemes, for example. For a while now I have pondered over whether they really work. Are they a valid way of maintaining a relationship between company and customer? Or do they just add up to an annual wallet clear out, aimed at stripping out the flurry of bits of plastic and card which congregate there during the year?

Sometimes they work really well because they do what it says on the tin, for example a coffee shop rewards card which leads to a free drink, or a supermarket points scheme which generates discounts.

But sometimes they involve so much effort to type in numbers online or fill in a form to convert points into vouchers that they start to weigh us down even more and can actually worsen the experience.

One of the most complicated examples I have encountered also comes from the financial services world, this time from a credit card provider. They offered customers like me travel discounts and free coffee every Monday for a month.

This was, in theory, a lovely idea. But in practice it was really complex, with acres of small print. There were time restrictions, payment had to be made via Android Pay, no extras were available in the coffee, and there were warnings about what would happen if you didn't comply with the terms. It went from a really thoughtful offer that recognised my loyalty to something which added to my burden, and even made me feel like a freeloader! As a result, I feel a little less comfortable with this organisation than before – they are not who I thought they were.

> "THE MOST AUTHENTIC PUBLICITY OF ALL - HAPPY CUSTOMERS SHARING THEIR EXPERIENCES ON SOCIAL MEDIA.

A great example of a seamless extra is from Metro Bank, which likes to surprise customers by putting small extra deposits in their account – usually a couple of quid with the reference 'coffee on us'. In Metro Bank's case this simple gesture was executed beautifully. As far as Metro Bank is concerned, it's just an extension of the branch experience, which is so relaxed it doesn't really feel like a bank. There was no 'look at us' fanfare or TV ad needed. Metro Bank earned the most authentic publicity of all – happy customers sharing their experiences on social media.

You will find Metro Bank open seven days a week. Your bank account is opened on the spot, and you can enjoy a coffee while your bank card is being printed.[36] You can even take your dog with you, and Metro Bank will have the dog treats ready and waiting.[37] The 'guerrilla' coffee deposit worked brilliantly, because it fits perfectly with Metro's personality and strategy. Metro Bank is opening 'stores' while other banks are closing 'branches'. Metro is creating an experience where others are bolting on digital channels. If Metro Bank had done what the credit card people had done, and made customers jump through hoops for this, it would have completely undermined its brand.

Metro Bank is still a relatively young company, and arguably it is at an advantage in terms of being customer focused because it was born that way – unlike the aforementioned bank or credit card provider, it has not had to bring a legacy organisational design, systems architecture, or culture through a transformation programme. It is an organisation that was designed with customer service as its number one reason for being. Metro Bank is already very good at delivering the basics. As a result, it can focus on delivering human touches like these that make it stand out very clearly from the crowd and keep customers coming back.

Most businesses are not blessed with this level of capability and agility, and there will not be a bottomless investment pot to fund customer experience development.

In other words, you will need to make choices and help your business understand which basics and which differentiators they should work on first to add genuine value. To do this confidently, you need to be able to measure the journey and know the relative impact of each touchpoint on customer and business metrics and how relevant it is to your customer experience strategy. Making informed choices is the subject of the next chapter.

Key takeaways from Chapter 7 – Doing / the journey map

know

The simple act of creating a single view of the journey is powerful. Seeing an end-to-end journey laid out, showing all the touchpoints, is a great way to start unifying the business.

do

Keep it simple. Start at Level 0 and work down to the detail methodically.

remember

Why you are doing this. The ultimate goal is creating an inclusive dialogue within your organisation, not creating a good-looking bit of wallpaper.

NOTES

CHAPTER 8 - DOING /MEASUREMENT

The great thing about fact-based decisions is that they overrule the hierarchy.

JEFF BEZOS

Establishing the facts

With construction of your journey map well advanced, you know what your customer journey looks like, and you have an initial view on where it is working well and what you need to do to improve it.

Having gathered all this quality insight, and laboured over creating a visual representation, you – along with your working group – will hopefully be feeling exhilarated at the prospect of doing something with it, particularly if you have generated a large number of ideas for change. After all, that's why you embarked on this mapping exercise – to get your hands on the improvement opportunities!

This is the point when you need to create the final two layers in your customer experience strategy statement – the roadmap and execution. And get the business to sign on the dotted line and commit to delivering them.

- → What key interactions (Moments of Truth) will you focus on?
- → What action are you taking to build those components in the near, medium, and long term?

You need to guide your organisation on making the right investment choices to realise the optimum return on investment. Your recommendations may not be in line with what is convenient for the business, though; in fact, you are likely to be asking for changes which not only need financial investment but also involve leaders in the business pushing CX improvement activity to the top of their to-do lists.

This is a critical point in your CX journey, and a point of failure for many programmes. To support your recommendations and secure commitment, you need evidence in the form of data. In other words, you need to take opinion out of it.

NOTES

theory

The three voices of CX measurement

Establishing the facts about how customers perceive your journey and how that affects their behaviour will allow you to demonstrate how improving the experience will improve business performance.

You need to be able to measure three voices.

- Voice of the Customer (VoC) – how customers experience your journey.
- Voice of the Employee (VoE) – colleague perception of your business.
- Voice of the Process (VoP) – which correlates performance inside your business (cause) with the quality of the customer journey (effect).

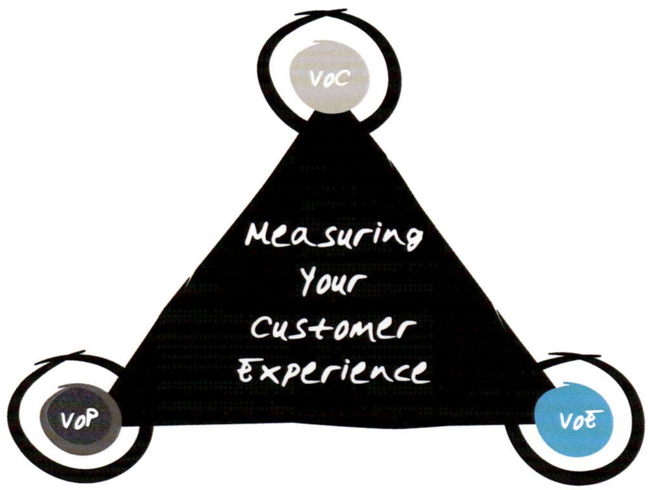

Voice of the Customer (VoC)

Measures of customer perception, commonly referred to as Voice of the Customer (VoC), tell you how your business looks from the outside looking in. You are holding up a mirror to your organisation and enabling it to see itself.

This can be a shock if you are not used to it, so be prepared for defensive behaviour from your organisation. It's important to remember that customer perception is what it is – it is not your role to say whether customers are right or wrong, or explain away their feedback. But it is essential that you measure it accurately, so your methodology needs to be completely robust. Firstly, it will need to withstand the inevitable scrutiny it will attract. And secondly, you will be making recommendations to your business based on what it tells you, so you need to be confident in the findings.

Designing customer experience measurement systems is a specialism within customer experience, and it is not a subject that I can even begin to do justice to in this book. But I will cover some basic principles which are essential to understand before you get into the detail.

> "IT'S IMPORTANT TO REMEMBER THAT CUSTOMER PERCEPTION IS WHAT IT IS - IT IS NOT YOUR ROLE TO SAY WHETHER CUSTOMERS ARE RIGHT OR WRONG.

Choosing a measure

NOTES

Three common mechanisms for measurement are Net Promoter Score® (NPS),[38] customer satisfaction (CSAT), and customer effort (CES).

What is it?	When should you use it?	How does it work?
CSAT asks respondents 'How satisfied were you with X' and invites them to choose a statement which best describes their perception.	CSAT is best suited to measuring the quality of transactions, so it's important to address the question to finding out whether your customer was able to achieve their objective. Did they find what they were looking for in the store? Did they get their query resolved? Or their question answered? CSAT is a granular methodology that can be used to gain a measurable understanding of customer perception across the end-to-end customer journey.	Methods of measuring CSAT vary greatly in terms of the volume and wording of the response options, but the most common method of reporting is top two box scoring. The top two box score counts the number of people selecting the most positive two response options and divides it by the total number of responses to generate a percentage.
NPS measures likelihood to recommend on a scale of 0–10, using score ranges to classify customers as detractors, promoters, or passives.	Coupled with an open-ended question to find out why the rating was given, NPS yields a great deal of useful, unstructured data. It doesn't always make sense to ask about recommendation, for example if you're running an Accident and Emergency Department in a hospital, but if you're aiming above and beyond merely satisfying customers, which I hope you are, NPS is a very useful metric. It's an acid test of whether customers feel 'OK' about your business, or whether you have actually inspired them to talk positively about you to others.	The score is calculated by counting the number of people who scored 6 and below (detractors) and the number who scored 9 and above (promoters), expressing them as a percentage of the overall number of respondents, and finally subtracting the percentage of detractors from the percentage of promoters. The final score is expressed as a number, not a percentage.
CES measures how easy it was to do business with your organisation, or how much effort customers had to put in to dealing with you.	Again, CES is best suited to measuring a specific interaction. The question being asked is how much effort did customers personally have to put in to 'X'? For example, arranging a delivery, or updating address details.	The volume and wording of the response options vary but most organisations calculate a net effort score in a similar way to the way NPS is calculated. The most important thing is that you measure consistently and focus on what the score tells you, not the rights and wrongs of survey design!

I also recommend that you include a measure of how well you are delivering against the intended experience described in your experience strategy statement. It seems obvious, but a surprising number of businesses overlook it. For example, if your experience is intended to be 'welcoming', you will need to ask customers whether they felt welcome. Relaxed, optimistic, happy, safe – whatever your target emotion is, measure it.

All four measures must be accompanied by an open-ended question to generate descriptive data relating to why your customer feels the way they do. A score with no descriptive detail tells you where you are now, but will not offer you any clues about why or how you could have improved the experience for that customer. This generates unstructured data – not a score – so you will need a way of mining the data to pull out trends. For a small business, you can do this manually. But on a larger scale you will need a text-analytics or voice-analytics solution, which can analyse large amounts of unstructured data from social media, phone or web surveys, and emails.

Always measure as close to the interaction as possible; the further away you get from the event itself, the less of the descriptive detail you will capture.

"YOUR MEASUREMENT APPROACH NEEDS TO ALLOW YOU TO SEE HOW CUSTOMER EXPERIENCE QUALITY DRIVES THE BUSINESS METRICS YOU HAVE COMMITTED TO DRIVE.

And remember that asking for and giving feedback constitute touchpoints in your journey. The feedback experience needs to be designed from the customers' perspective. We've all seen those silo-driven abominations, where every function and stakeholder has had their say. There's a raft of questions, usually multiple choice to keep it nice and tight, with very little opportunity for customers to tell us about their experience in their own words. Do not let it become a case of design by committee. You'll just end up with a survey that is so long and has so many irrelevant questions that customers will feel they are being cross-examined and will not finish it.

How to align measurement to your journey

Your objective as a customer experience leader is to change customer behaviour. It's explicitly stated in your customer experience strategy that you will contribute to achieving business KPIs. So, your measurement approach needs to allow you to see how customer experience quality drives the business metrics you have committed to drive – you need to be able to demonstrate how your VoC results correlate with behaviour. For example, showing that promoters are 20 times more likely to repurchase. Or a 2% increase in CSAT drives a 5% improvement in repurchase behaviour.

If you get the alignment right, and you can predict how much an increase in VoC scores will be worth to the business in terms of additional revenue or reduced costs, your measurement framework can be fully adopted by, and embedded in, your business. And customer experience planning, investment, and tracking will become part of the business planning cycle, rather than a peripheral dashboard that nobody looks at.

practice

Which VoC metric should you use? CSAT lends itself readily as a correlation metric that links sentiment to behaviour. And NPS or CES work better as summarising headline scores. But my preference is never to rely on a single metric – they all do different things. None of them in isolation does a good enough job of predicting business outcomes, so use them in combination.

The research and insight professionals in your organisation, or an outsourced agency, will be able to perform regression (or key driver) analysis to establish how VoC scores correlate with, for example, repurchasing, complaints, contact patterns, and so on. And which customer touchpoints have the biggest impact on sentiment – also known as Moments of Truth (MoTs).

> **Moments of Truth (MoTs)** You will hear a lot of talk in customer experience circles about MoTs and how important they are, but surprisingly little useful information about how to pinpoint where they are in your journey. When you start measuring customer sentiment and overlaying data onto your map, you will see a pattern of peaks and troughs emerging in your journey. These are not MoTs. Although they are an important indicator of where your journey is strong or weak, they don't tell you the relative importance of each peak or trough. There's no doubt that you will be able, to some degree, to identify MoTs through the strength of sentiment metrics the peaks and troughs represent, but the only reliable way to discover where they are is by using statistical analysis to correlate which 'Moments' result in customers actually changing their behaviour. For example, operational data can be very revealing, and so can clusters of unsolicited compliments or complaints, or more direct negative action, like closing an account, or positive action, like upgrading.

Spend your time driving scores, not explaining them

You may be feeling confident that you are measuring customer experience already. But most organisations do measurement badly. And I believe that bad measurement is most definitely not preferable to no measurement at all. At best, it will lead you down the path of focusing on the wrong things, which do not deliver the expected return on investment. At worst, poor measurement can give the impression that your organisation is doing very well at delivering the journey and can suggest that the customer experience is world class.

Both of these scenarios will undermine, and probably prove fatal to, your customer experience strategy. And you will find yourself in a situation where your organisation is focusing only on the score and is not committed to driving action. For me, this is the worst possible place for a customer experience professional to find themselves, because it tends to lead to… not very much. Focusing on the number - usually CSAT or NPS - makes organisations introspective.

“FOCUSING ON THE NUMBER - USUALLY CSAT OR NPS - MAKES ORGANISATIONS INTROSPECTIVE.

I have heard CEOs at business networking dinners bragging about their NPS scores. And yes, remarkably, many of them do appear to believe they are outperforming Amazon. This is nothing more than vanity. Unless you can talk passionately and confidently about what you are doing to achieve the number, and how you expect it to change in line with your roadmap, it is pointless. In fact, I might argue that you should stop surveying your customers if you're not driving action – you are doing it for the wrong reasons and possibly wasting money.

Unfortunately, this type of organisational tunnel vision is more common than I care to think about. It is a scenario which is frequently accompanied by an unhealthy tendency towards short-term thinking, where the tiniest downward movement in the score creates bedlam and a flurry of inward focus, diverting attention away from customers. A tiny upward movement creates a flurry of backslapping and zero interest in why the score has changed.

This pattern of behaviour is one you need to break. It diverts attention away from the very reason you started measuring in the first place – to drive forward a customer experience strategy which will differentiate your business and give you a market advantage. Do not feed the beast!! Focus ruthlessly and unrelentingly on the outcome you want to deliver: measurable changes in customer behaviour. Do not fall into the trap of reporting too frequently. All metrics are subject to a level of volatility, and you need to be able to keep people focused on the long-term view or you will find yourself expending excessive amounts of your time and energy on explaining scores rather than driving them.

It's always a good idea to involve the research and insight professionals in your organisation, or an outsourced agency, in the process of aligning measurement with your journey, particularly if you are not confident you have the right data, or that it is being workec as hard as it can be.

In order to align your measurement correctly with the journey you must do three things:

1. Measure the whole customer journey

If the measurement you are capturing is not representative of the entire journey, your data will only be representative of the parts you are measuring.

It's not enough to measure only servicing touchpoints, or only sales, or only customers who make a purchase. The airline which only gathers feedback on the plane will not pick up on insights from customers whose luggage got lost. The retailer which only gathers feedback after delivery will miss out on all the customers who dropped out before checkout because they didn't want to create an account.

You need to measure everything to be able to understand how cause and effect works in your relationship with customers and what improvement activity will have the greatest effect on improving customer perception and, as a result, commercial goals.

I can say with certainty that if your customer metric looks too good to be true – for example your NPS is better than that of Lush or Amazon, or whoever else is topping the CX benchmark league tables – the measurement approach is probably flawed, and it's likely to be because you have not collected data across all your touchpoints.

You will need to be able to measure every stage of your journey by collecting data for every step on all channels.

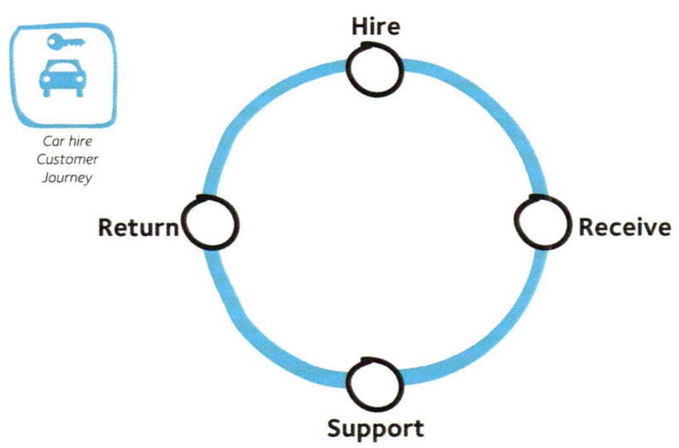

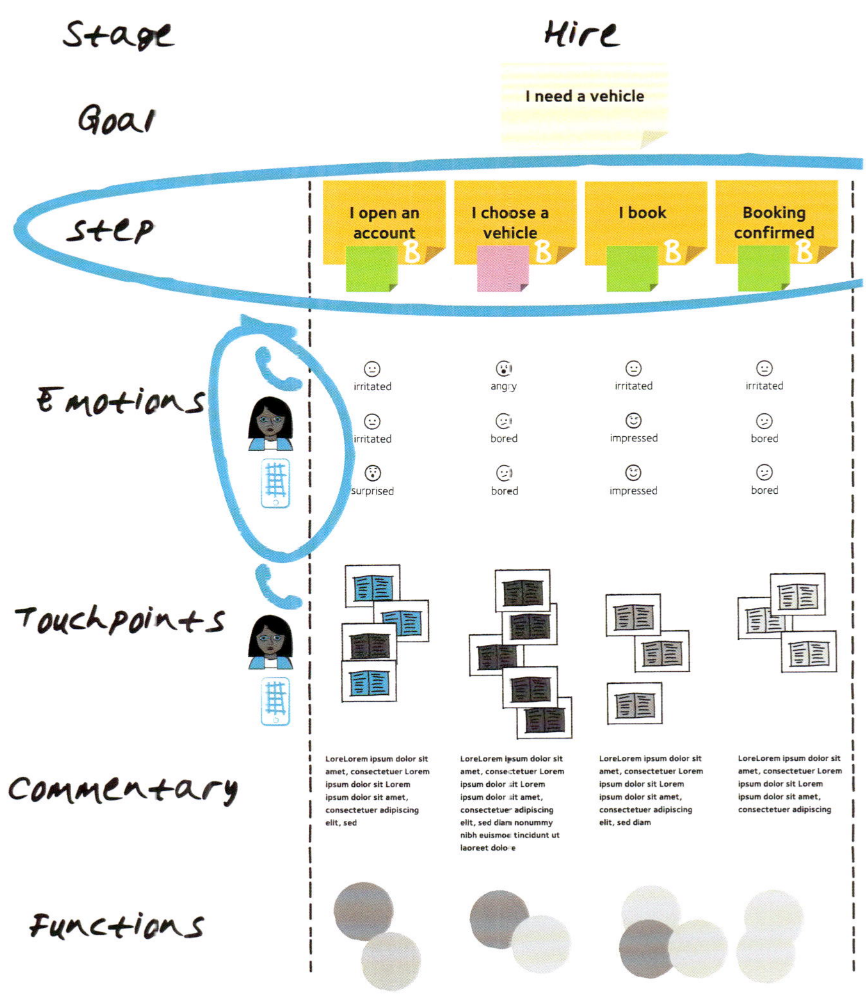

Going to the next level of detail and collecting data for each touchpoint is often not practical or desirable. It will potentially create a level of complexity that makes your measurement less effective – you need to be able to report on measures in a way that people can understand and act on. Instead, use text- and speech-analytics techniques to mine your unstructured data for clues about individual touchpoints.

2. Measure Voice of the Process (VoP)

Think of your organisation as a series of 'layers', very much like a city in cross section. Your customers are walking around at street level, going about their journeys. Go down a level under the street and you will find a service layer, made up of business processes which deliver the journey. Go further still and you will find a second service layer formed by technology that enables the business processes which deliver the customer journey.

When your system of measurement correlates performance in the service layers with the customer journey, you can measure cause and effect (otherwise known as lead and lag indicators). This is important, because your role as a customer experience leader is to influence how the business works to deliver a different effect. So being able to measure the cause gives you the ability to predict the effect.

Figure 8-1 The organisational 'layers' of customer experience

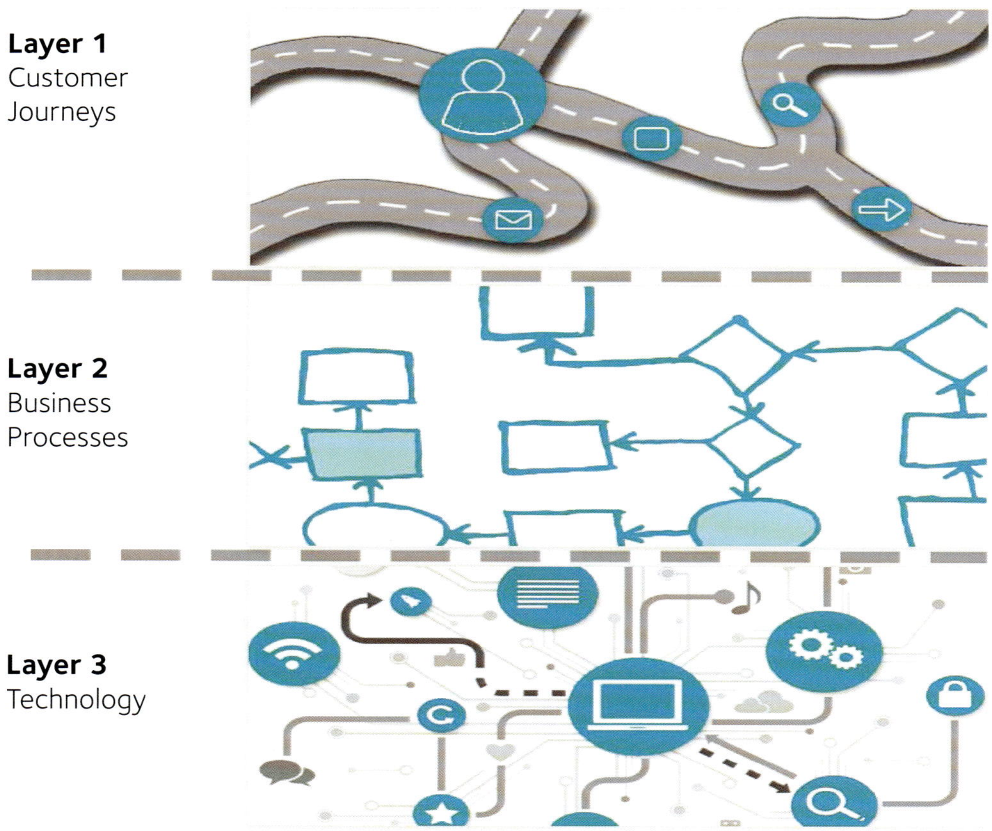

When you have clarity on which processes contribute to which elements of the journey, you can identify an appropriate operational metric for each one – Voice of the Process (VoP). As you change a process, or the way it is delivered, you can predict the measurable effect on the way customers feel about what you do and how likely they are to buy more, stay longer, cost less to serve, and so on.

All too often, this thinking is turned on its head. The customer journey is designed around what's easy or convenient for the business, from a system and process point of view. Then the business congratulates itself on a job well done in delivering a great customer experience. This is not customer experience management, this is process management. In reality, what the business has done is engineered a customer journey around the business infrastructure, with little regard to whether it will produce the desired effect. As a result, it is impossible to correlate a change in the performance of processes with customer feedback.

3. Measure Voice of the Employee (VoE)

Colleague perception of your business is a hugely influential piece of fact, as well as a sign to your people that you value their opinion.

- Do your people use your products and services themselves?
- Do they (or would they) recommend your products and services to others?
- How good do they think the customer experience is?

Knowing whether or not your people would use the organisation's products or services themselves, recommend them to others, or think the organisation is any good at delivering the customer experience is vitally important information. Asking colleagues these questions demonstrates how much their opinion is respected. Acting on what they say demonstrates how much it is valued.

A fellow practitioner discovered through an anonymous colleague survey that not only were employees not buying their company's products and services but they were actively warning friends and family not to buy them either because they felt so strongly that they did not represent good value for money. VoE should always be collected anonymously to ensure people feel safe to be completely truthful and do not dress up their feedback

“COLLEAGUE PERCEPTION OF YOUR BUSINESS IS A HUGELY INFLUENTIAL PIECE OF FACT, AS WELL AS A SIGN TO YOUR PEOPLE THAT YOU VALUE THEIR OPINION.

story

Feedback as a touchpoint – a lesson in how *not* to do it

Having been involved in the world of customer experience for so many years, I shouldn't be surprised by anything. I have witnessed the full spectrum of good, bad, and ugly business behaviour. But every now and then, something happens to me, or someone I know, that still has the power to shock me.

One such event involved a customer feedback survey invitation which was sent to my wife, Naomi, by our digital TV provider. We pay a significant amount of money each month for a variety of TV channels, and have been doing so for over 15 years. That should make us valuable customers. But we have not been satisfied customers for a while. Not only is the provider's offering not particularly good value for money, but our digital TV receiver regularly fails. In all honesty, we should have cancelled our contract a while ago, but have just not got around to it.

So, let me get back to the story of the survey request. Feeling as unsatisfied as she did, Naomi decided to take the opportunity to let the provider know by completing the online survey. As she went to open the survey, the following message was returned:

> *Survey Completed – Thank You*
>
> *Thank you for your interest in our survey – customer feedback is extremely important to us, however unfortunately on this occasion, we have reached our target number of participants in your grouping and so we are unable to continue with the survey at this time.*
>
> *We regularly run research studies, so please look out for these in the future as we'd love to know your thoughts. You will be redirected in 5 seconds.*

Where do I start? If a customer is willing to take time out of their day to complete your feedback request, you'd better be listening.

- Do not say customer feedback is extremely important, then slam the door in a customer's face.
- Do not refer to target numbers, participants, and groupings. The mechanics of your research are of no interest or relevance to customers.
- Do not ask your customers to 'look out for' future studies. They do not work for you.
- Do not tell them you'd love to know their thoughts before immediately redirecting them away from an opportunity to feed back.

This has to be one of the most appalling customer communications I have ever seen. Yes, that's right, customer feedback requests are communication, and as such they constitute a touchpoint which needs to be designed and managed with as much care and attention as the rest of your journey! What this particular touchpoint communicated was a casual disregard for customers.

A good friend of mine, and a fellow customer experience professional, received a similar response from the same business. But in his case, it was in response to a complaint. His complaint related to a terrible service experience. I won't go into the details but he got fobbed off and handed over to multiple teams in different locations, none of which seemed to be able to agree on how to resolve his query, and all of which were very much more interested in their own internal processes than in his well-being as a customer.

This went on for months, and inevitably, he ended up making a complaint. To compound the issues, the complaint was handled in a similar fashion but the focus had switched to placing blame rather than reaching a resolution, which is what complaint escalation is for.

Several months into the saga, he got desperate and wrote to the CEO, expecting at least some form of acknowledgement and preferably an apology. What he got in return was quite different:

We are writing to advise that the complaint you made to us and currently being managed by us has now been open for 8 weeks.

We want to re-assure you that our priority is to resolve your complaint as quickly as possible and we are continuing to work to find a satisfactory resolution and update you regularly on the progress of your case.

It may be that you would wish to seek independent advice in respect of your complaint. We are a member of Ombudsman Services: Communications, an independent alternative dispute resolution scheme and the service is free for you to use, their contact details are set out below.

In the interim, if you have confirmed with us that your complaint has been resolved, please disregard this letter.

Yours sincerely

NOTES

> TAKING FEEDBACK FOR GRANTED OR FAILING TO LISTEN AND ACT EFFECTIVELY MEANS YOUR ORGANISATION IS RELYING ON CUSTOMERS' INERTIA LEADING THEM TO STAY WITH YOU.

This organisation, like any other organisation in the world, relies on the feedback of its customers to know what works and what does not work in the customer journey. Taking feedback for granted or failing to listen and act effectively means your organisation is relying on customers' inertia leading them to stay with you. This is a foolish approach, which could ultimately be fatal.

The priority of my digital TV provider most certainly is not to resolve complaints as quickly as possible. These are empty words. And as a result of the provider's actions, I was finally motivated to do what I should have done years ago – I ended my 15-year association with them and went to a competitor.

Key takeaways from Chapter 8 – Doing/measurement

know

Designing customer experience measurement systems is a specialism – bad measurement is most definitely not preferable to having no measurement at all, so bring in help if you need to.

do

Make sure your data is representative. Measure your whole journey – from end to end. And measure all three voices – customer, process, and employee.

remember

Asking for and giving feedback constitute touchpoints in your journey. The feedback experience needs to be designed from the customers' perspective.

CHAPTER 9 - DOING /PRIORITIES

You have freedom, so you have to make choices – and at the point when I make a choice, the building starts to look like a Frank Gehry building. It's a signature.

FRANK GEHRY

theory

Constructing your roadmap

Now that you have established the facts about your journey, it's back to the following choices:

- What key interactions (Moments of Truth) will you focus on?
- What action are you taking to develop those interactions in the near, medium, and long term?

Prioritising customer experience change is not always easy. It sometimes involves difficult choices – do you fix the basics or create differentiation first? What if you find yourself dealing with conflicting customer experience requirements?

Overcrowded trains are a real issue for commuters in the UK. Trains on some routes are estimated to be carrying passengers at over 200% capacity – imagine 1,366 people squeezed in to 12 carriages designed to carry just 640.

In response, train companies are redesigning carriages to accommodate more people. Which makes perfect sense. The new carriages have wider aisles, wider doors, and more grab rails. And – you guessed it – fewer seats; they are designed for standing. In some cases, even if you do get a seat, there are no tables to work at, or even put your coffee on – they have been removed.

Standing is OK on short journeys. But these are not necessarily short journeys. Passengers can find themselves standing for up to 90 minutes. If you are a regular commuter, you may find yourself standing for up to three hours a day, and paying large sums of money each year for the privilege of doing so. Add to this the delays and cancellations passengers so often encounter on the overcrowded sections of the rail network, and it makes for a very frustrating experience.

A cynical person might say that the train companies are taking a shortcut to higher profits – more passengers mean more revenue. But in reality, it seems to me that they are having to make choices. And sometimes those choices are challenging to make. Do we fix the basics and create more capacity on our trains to get people from A to B? Or do we meet their expectations of comfort and serve fewer passengers? The ideal solution fixes a broken basic while meeting expectations. But it's not always possible to find that ideal solution, and you will often find yourself weighing competing priorities.

The vital five – completing your strategy statement

practice

Your list of priorities should be short. Remember you are not ruling anything out or taking it off the list, you are just choosing what to do *first*. You will refresh your priorities every year as part of the business planning cycle.

Create a table. List all your areas for improvement in the first column, then score them. Be guided by your metrics and identify interactions which correlate most closely with the business KPIs captured in your strategy statement.

- Which improvements will benefit your people or make the transformation journey fun and engaging for them?
- Which steps in the journey matter most to your customers? This can be a functional basic which is broken or an opportunity to exceed expectation and make your brand experience memorable.

In the final column, list any new organisational capabilities that will be needed to build or support each improvement opportunity.

> YOUR LIST OF PRIORITIES SHOULD BE SHORT. REMEMBER YOU ARE NOT RULING ANYTHING OUT OR TAKING IT OFF THE LIST, YOU ARE JUST CHOOSING WHAT TO DO FIRST.

A	B	C	D
Stage and step (descriptive)	Matters to our people low – medium – high	Matters to customers low – medium – high	Capability needs (descriptive)

The vital five

The improvements which score highest in columns B and C are the ones you need to focus on. Pick your 'vital five' deliverables. Mantra number three is *KEEP IT SIMPLE*. Remember, even a relatively small change to the customer journey can involve a significant proportion of your business ecosystem. The change required to deliver each of your vital five will be like a small iceberg, so five will be more than enough.

Mantra No.3
Keep it simple

Your vital five deliverables are not necessarily the top five in your rating table, because you want to create a balanced change portfolio. You do not need to exceed customer expectation on everything, as your journey map should demonstrate. And, unless you are at a very mature stage in your CX journey, you will normally have at least one basic which requires fixing.

But be strategic and smart with your budget – I recommend that you distribute your vital five across all three categories. Remember this is a long-term strategy, and you are going to be on this transformation journey for at least six years. A strategy devoted entirely to fixing the basics may be less successful at maintaining the sustained business engagement and commitment you need. Assign your vital five to the table below.

Figure 8-2 The vital five priorities

The vital five					
Thoughtful touches making it memorable					
Exceeding expectation turning people into fans of our brand					
Fixing the basics – the things customers take as a given					

The vital five					
Thoughtful touches making it memorable	Leafy ♥ Love – we plant a tree for every £100 you save				
Exceeding expectation turning people into fans of our brand	One-touch controls with remote access.	1-step installation. 24–7 support.			
Fixing the basics – the things customers take as a given	No hidden costs billing.	Plain English everywhere.			

This will help you communicate them to the business, and align them with the final two layers of your strategy statement, which now looks like this:

<table>
<tr><td>Our mission</td><td colspan="5">To give customers control over their energy bills and level the playing field between suppliers and customers.</td></tr>
<tr><td>Our vision</td><td colspan="5">To develop the most intuitive and affordable energy technology in the market to grow our reputation, reach, and profitability.</td></tr>
<tr><td>KPIs</td><td colspan="5">Geographical coverage; installation cycle time; meter uptime; savings per customer; cost to serve; referrals; and sentiment.</td></tr>
<tr><td>Our target customers</td><td>Cost conscious</td><td>Environmentally aware</td><td>Technophiles</td><td>Housing providers</td><td>Small to medium-sized business users</td></tr>
<tr><td rowspan="3">Roadmap</td><td colspan="2">Fixing the basics</td><td colspan="2">Exceeding expectation</td><td>Thoughtful touches</td></tr>
<tr><td colspan="2">No hidden costs billing.
Plain English everywhere.</td><td colspan="2">One-touch controls with remote access.
1-step installation.
24–7 support.</td><td>Leafy ♥ Love – we plant a tree for every £100 you save.</td></tr>
<tr><td colspan="2">Billing system upgrade.
Plain English rewrite, inside and out.</td><td colspan="2">Control unit redesign.
Remote access app.
Field service workflow.
Support team resource model.</td><td>Tree-planting facility and team-building opportunities.</td></tr>
</table>

When you look at your roadmap now, and can see your own vital five customer experience investments set out in black and white, the reference in the opening paragraphs of this book to hardcore change management will be vividly coming to life.

Part of your role as a customer experience leader is to help the organisation develop capability in the six customer experience management competencies.

1. Customer-centric culture
2. Voice of the Customer, customer insight and understanding
3. Organisational adoption and accountability
4. Customer experience strategy
5. Experience design, improvement, and innovation
6. Metrics, measurement, and return on investment (ROI)

But your organisation also needs delivery capability. The capabilities required to deliver the roadmap are not purely customer experience strategy capabilities, they are the wider organisational capabilities which underpin the customer journey and make up the business ecosystem.

You need change managers, training professionals, data analysts, designers, and researchers. Delivering the roadmap is a collective effort. The customer experience roadmap and the business roadmap need to be one and the same. If your organisation does not yet have these capabilities, developing them must also go onto your roadmap. If capability levels are very low, it may be that you will need to gear your business roadmap around building capability for the first two to three years, before you can start the work of improving the journey.

" THE CAPABILITIES REQUIRED TO DELIVER THE ROADMAP ARE NOT PURELY CUSTOMER EXPERIENCE STRATEGY CAPABILITIES, THEY ARE THE WIDER ORGANISATIONAL CAPABILITIES WHICH UNDERPIN THE CUSTOMER JOURNEY AND MAKE UP THE BUSINESS ECOSYSTEM.

theory

Random to intentional. Right skills, right priorities

Despite the emergence of customer experience as a core strategic priority for organisations in recent years, customers are yet to see a seismic shift in their daily experiences. The more companies seem to talk about customer experience and customer centricity, and brag about their NPS scores, the more arbitrary our experiences as customers seem to become.

Throughout this book I have described an approach which is very much like creating and piecing together a jigsaw puzzle. While many companies have successfully created the pieces of the puzzle, they are finding it more and more difficult to figure out how to connect the pieces together – and therefore they never actually realise the vision that the completed puzzle would create.

One critical piece of the jigsaw puzzle is skilled people. In my experience, aside from culture, a lack of skilled people in organisations who can actually fix the customer journey is one of the main reasons why experiences do not seem to be improving. In the context of customer experience, "Can we do this?" is often followed by "No, we don't know how!", or "We're too busy", or "No, we need another business case".

A great deal of the theory behind customer experience is actually very simple. And at the risk of stating the unbelievably obvious, until you actually change, amend, replace, redesign, or improve a touchpoint in your customer journey, nothing will change for your customer. In fact, the longer you take to make changes, the more likely it is that customer expectations will rise and customer perception will decline.

The three most significant issues underlying this apparent inertia are as follows:

1. Lack of specialist skills – experience design and process improvement are deep, vertical skill sets in their own right. Many business people just do not have the capability to do these things. Investing in bringing in specialist resources is essential if you want to see measurable progress towards improving customer perception and commercial performance.

2. Failure to deploy these specialist resources in the right places – there are still far too many organisations using the specialist resources they do have for the wrong reasons. Focusing all of your resource on driving sales or reducing cost is not the same as delivering a customer experience strategy. If you are lucky, there might be some overlap, and you might accidentally fix the right stuff, but it's just as likely that in driving sales or cost reductions hard, you will eliminate or break some of the strengths in your customer journey and make the customer experience worse.

3. Procrastination – perhaps the biggest frustration of all are those organisations that know full well what the opportunities are, but do nothing. Instead they continually defer change, either through a desire to gather more facts or data, or because everyone is too busy doing 'other things'. This is a failure of culture and commitment.

So, once again, can you do this? Yes, you can. If you have resources that can drive change and improve things, you must use them to do that. If not, you need to invest in growing your capabilities. It really isn't complicated.

> "IF YOU HAVE RESOURCES THAT CAN DRIVE CHANGE AND IMPROVE THINGS, YOU MUST USE THEM TO DO THAT. IF NOT, YOU NEED TO INVEST IN GROWING YOUR CAPABILITIES.

Key takeaways from Chapter 9 – Doing/priorities

know

Changes to the customer journey can involve a significant proportion of your business ecosystem. The change required to deliver each of your vital five will be like a small iceberg, so five will be more than enough.

do

Keep it simple. Your list of priorities should be short. You are not ruling anything out or taking it off the list, you are just choosing what to do first.

remember

This is a long-term strategy, and you are going to be on this transformation journey for at least six years. A strategy devoted entirely to fixing the basics may be less successful at maintaining the sustained business engagement and commitment you need.

NOTES

CHAPTER 10 - DOING/DESIGN

I think one's feelings waste themselves in words; they ought all to be distilled into actions which bring results.

FLORENCE NIGHTINGALE

Start with the customer goal, and work from there

theory

Your journey map is coming together, the measurement programme is under way, and you have identified improvement priorities. But what exactly is an 'experience', and how do you go about changing it?

Firstly, keep in mind that your customers are not just buying your product or service – they are filling a need, which your product or service enables. The design process always, always needs to start by understanding what your customers are trying to achieve (their goal) and what your customers expect to have to do to achieve it. Once you know what it is, enable it – don't ever get between customers and their goal.

Secondly, remember that customer needs go beyond what they can articulate or rationalise – they include things like trust, confidence, and happiness. It will be your role, through careful research, measurement, and collaboration, to uncover and articulate deeper customer needs and to help your organisation understand how you can meet them.

Your organisation's brand becomes very important at this stage in your customer experience journey. It is part of the reason why customers choose you – it sets their expectations about what the experience is going to be like and how it will make them feel. If the experience does not live up to your brand, it creates a gap. A gap between a promise and reality is rhetoric, and it's a really big problem.

- If you're claiming to be Britain's most helpful bank, and your customers find you so awkward to deal with that they have given you a score of 1.8 out of 10 on trustpilot.co.uk, there's a problem.
- If you are the airline that's telling customers to expect a big smile and friendly service, and your customers constantly comment on tripadvisor.co.uk about how rude your staff are, there's a problem.
- If you are the energy provider which claims to treat customers like individuals and make them smile, but that only seems to last for the first year of the contract before you hike prices up and your customers find they can't contact you, there's a problem.

You need to be honest about who you are. Do not try and be all things to all people.

Until recently, Ryanair was a great example of this. I was never a big fan, but I did respect Ryanair as a brand for being up front and delivering what it promised – guaranteed low fares. Whether I liked the company or not, I could never argue that I didn't know what I would be getting if I chose to fly with it.

In September and October 2017, however, Ryanair cancelled 40,000 flights.[39] This was a severely disruptive event which was compounded by Ryanair failing to properly communicate with customers and help them through the resulting disruption. Not only was the company unable to fly customers from point A to point B, but it actively avoided its responsibilities to its customers and the Civil Aviation Authority had to step in. Ryanair fundamentally broke its promise.[40]

Customer experience = brand

Remember the intended experience described in your customer experience strategy statement? Look at it right now – that's what is going to deliver your brand promise. Your customer experience is your brand. Your journey transmits signals which tell customers a whole lot more than the words in a slogan or marketing campaign.

When designing, or improving, customer journeys, you must consider both the quality of individual interactions and the tone of the wider relationship.

> "WHETHER YOU CUT IT VERTICALLY, HORIZONTALLY, OR DIAGONALLY, IT NEEDS TO LOOK, SOUND, AND FEEL COHESIVE.

- The experience must match your brand personality, whatever that is.
- Interactions need to work standalone and as components in a connected journey from marketing through sales, fulfilment, and service.
- The journey needs to be seamless between interaction channels – what the customer sees must be completely consistent and connected, whether you are online, offline, or both!

Not only must each touchpoint deliver the intended experience, but the entire journey needs to hang together and do what it says on the tin. Whether you cut it vertically, horizontally, or diagonally, it must look, sound, and feel cohesive. My tip is always keep your Level 0 map in sight so you don't lose sight of the customer mission.

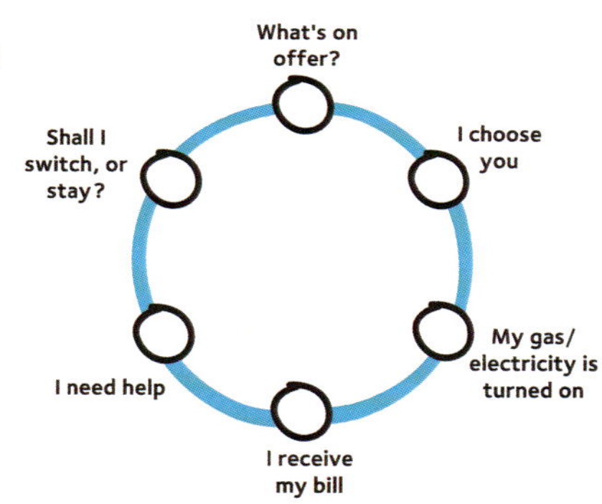

Experiences are built in layers

If you take any experience and break it down into its constituent parts, you will be able to identify a number of different components.

There are plenty of models which have been created in an attempt to describe this, starting with Abraham Maslow in the 1940s, who described a set of needs arranged in a hierarchy.[41]

NOTES

The theory is that needs at the base of the pyramid need to be met first, before we can move upwards. The drive to meet an unmet need grows stronger the longer it remains unmet, but once satisfied it may even become stronger as expectations grow.

Sound familiar? As a profession, we're certainly coming to terms with the fact that customer expectations do not stand still and largely continue to outpace what organisations choose to deliver.

In the 1980s, Noriaki Kano created a model to help product designers prioritise customer requirements.[42] The model organises needs into three categories:

Basic needs. These are typically unspoken, such as safety or cleanliness. Customers don't specify when they buy a car that they want it to be safe – it's a given. If it is safe, customers won't thank you for it; they only notice when it is not.

Performance needs. These relate to the proposition – what your business purports to be. If the proposition is delivered, your customers will be happy. If it isn't, they won't be. The higher the performance attribute, the more customers will pay for your product. If a shampoo, for example, claims to make hair thicker and is shown to work, you can charge a premium. If it doesn't, you will struggle to sell it at all.

Excitement needs. This means meeting unspoken or unknown needs to engage customers. Think Metro Bank and the surprise deposit. A product which meets basic needs and the performance needs stated in your proposition is fine. But the little quirks and unexpected touches are what customers will remember and keep coming back for.

Kano also described **'indifferent' qualities** which, whether delivered or not, make no difference to customers. If they are not delivering value, they are surplus to requirements.

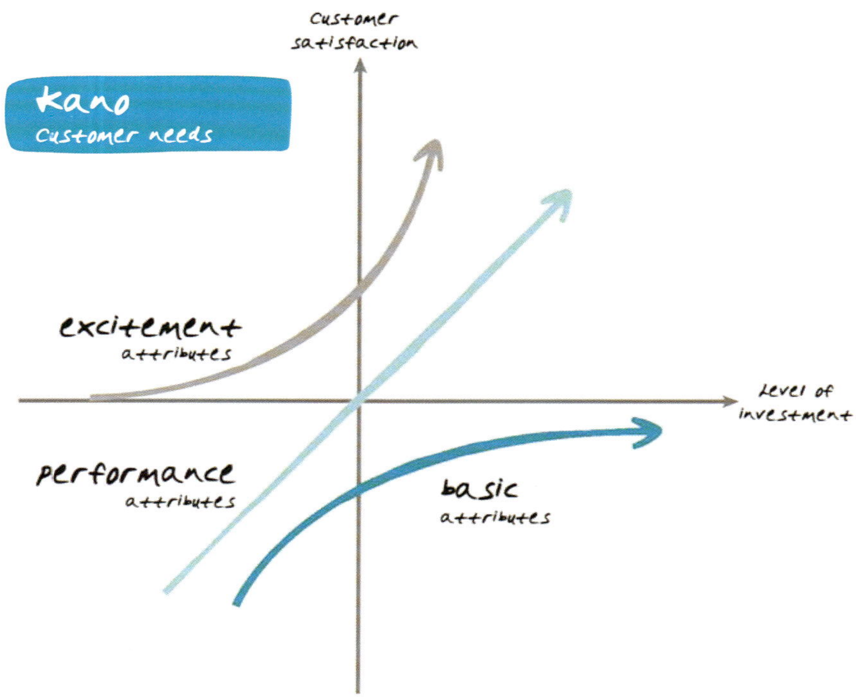

Right up to the present day, we're using similar models to explain or design products, services, and journeys, including the Forrester[43] and Temkin[44] experience models. In fact, you will find them in use in any profession which designs things for human beings, whether it's service design, user experience design, architecture, or transport planning.

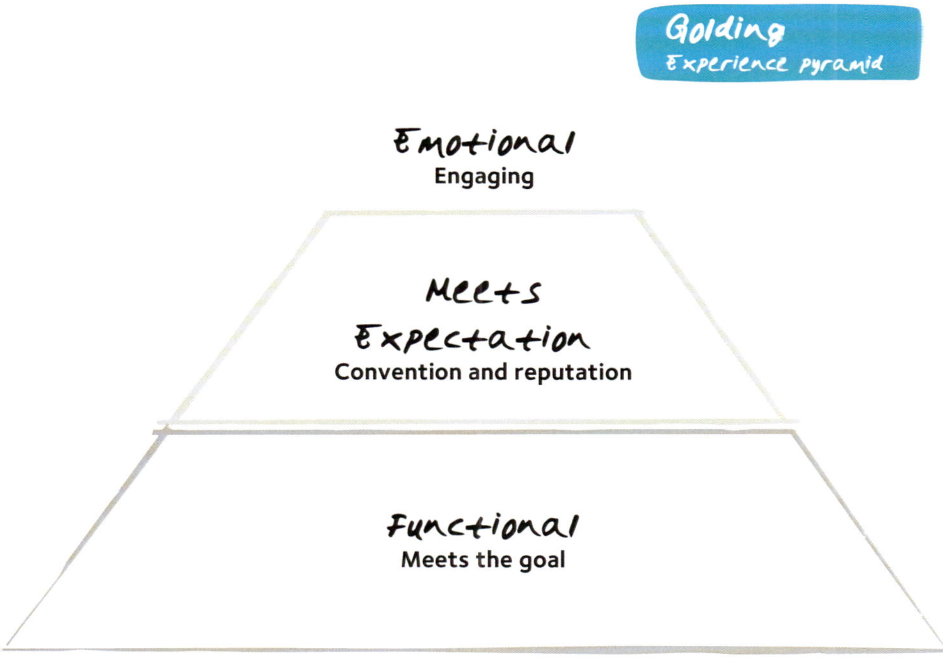

I am no exception to the rule. I like to keep things simple, though, as you know, so my model is very simple too, with just three layers to consider:

- whether the experience does what customers need it to do.
- whether it works as expected.
- how t makes people feel.

The table below describes how each of the layers work and what happens when they are absent or broken.

	Present	Absent
Functional (meets the goal)	This layer is fundamental to the experience and must always be present. It's one of those things like air, gravity, and daylight that you don't notice unless it is absent.	If this layer is absent or broken, the experience is dysfunctional and customers will tell you so, loud and clear. Nothing you do in the expectation or emotion layers will help!
Meets expectation (convention and reputation)	This layer is sometimes described as 'easy'. Easy is part of it, but for me it's more than that. As customers, we do adjust our expectations – what I might expect to pay and my experience of a discount brand is very different to what I expect from a premium brand.	If this layer is absent or broken, you will create friction: increased effort, including cognitive effort driven by complexity, disappointment, or distrust. This creates a perception of having received less value for money, and potentially a feeling of being let down in some way.
Emotional (engaging)	And finally, at the top of the pyramid is emotion, the humanity in the experience! Quirks, thoughtful details, and spontaneous acts of kindness that differentiate the experience, make it engaging and memorable, and give it your 'signature'.	If this layer is absent or broken and the other layers are intact, that's going to equal satisfied customers – no more, no less. But using this layer to mask a dysfunctional experience can make customers question your integrity – it will feel like an empty gesture.

> QUIRKS, THOUGHTFUL DETAILS, AND SPONTANEOUS ACTS OF KINDNESS THAT DIFFERENTIATE THE EXPERIENCE, MAKE IT ENGAGING AND MEMORABLE.

story

Let's try that again, with feeling!

A few years back I wrote about my experiences on a family trip. We had a great time visiting London and seeing the sights. But the reason I wrote about it was because, outside of the sightseeing, so many of our experiences were so spectacularly forgettable!

There was the train journey that did what it said on the tin. A slightly overpriced but good enough hotel. A meal in a restaurant that was not special, but OK. If I hadn't written about it that same week I would have forgotten most of it in a heartbeat.

But when we got back home, we encountered a customer experience hero at the train station in Chester. He displayed so much pride in and passion for his job that I not only remember to this day what he did and how it made me feel, but also what he looked like.

He took the time to stop what he was doing and engage. He chatted to my children about the cacophony of grinding metal and other noise that had distracted them as two trains were uncoupled. He told me how important it was to engage children who showed an interest. "If you explain it to them when they are little, they may show an interest when they are older," he said. This is a man who understands people.

Emotional engagement can be designed into any experience, in any category or market. A certain person who has been heavily involved in producing this book was bitterly disappointed to find the logo on her new MacBook pro doesn't light up. Apple discarded this feature in favour of a lighter machine. Is it rational to feel sad about that? Not in the least! But customers are people, and all of us have the same need for an emotional connection on some level. Here are some other examples of connecting emotionally via a product or service:

NOTES

MailChimp – a hairy chimp's hand appears and gives you an engaging high five[45] when you successfully launch your email campaign.

Ocado – after their first few orders, customers are sent a tea towel bearing the recipe for the Ocado experience.[46]

Any kids' menu – cappuccinos with no coffee, pizzas with bunny ears,[47] alcohol-free kids' cocktails with cute names (and big price tags!), crayons, and colouring books – being a father of three I have seen them all!

A functional experience which meets expectation is perfectly acceptable. It gets the job done with minimal waste and customers will probably be very satisfied with that. A functional experience which meets expectations, without emotion, is not by any means a burning platform for change. But it is forgettable, and means you may miss out on repeat business, new business attracted to a strong brand reputation, and forgiveness from your customers if something goes wrong. And it does make your business that little bit less engaging for your people too.

And be warned... if your brand positioning, or proposition, leads customers to expect an emotional connection and you don't deliver it, they will be disappointed. And if your competitors are delivering the same journey with personality, you can expect your customers, and potentially your people, to defect!

> **“A FUNCTIONAL EXPERIENCE WHICH MEETS EXPECTATIONS, WITHOUT EMOTION, IS NOT BY ANY MEANS A BURNING PLATFORM FOR CHANGE. BUT IT IS FORGETTABLE.**

theory

Designing for value

I am a big advocate of any form of design thinking which focuses on creating value for customers and the business. This is mantra number four – *DESIGN FOR VALUE.*

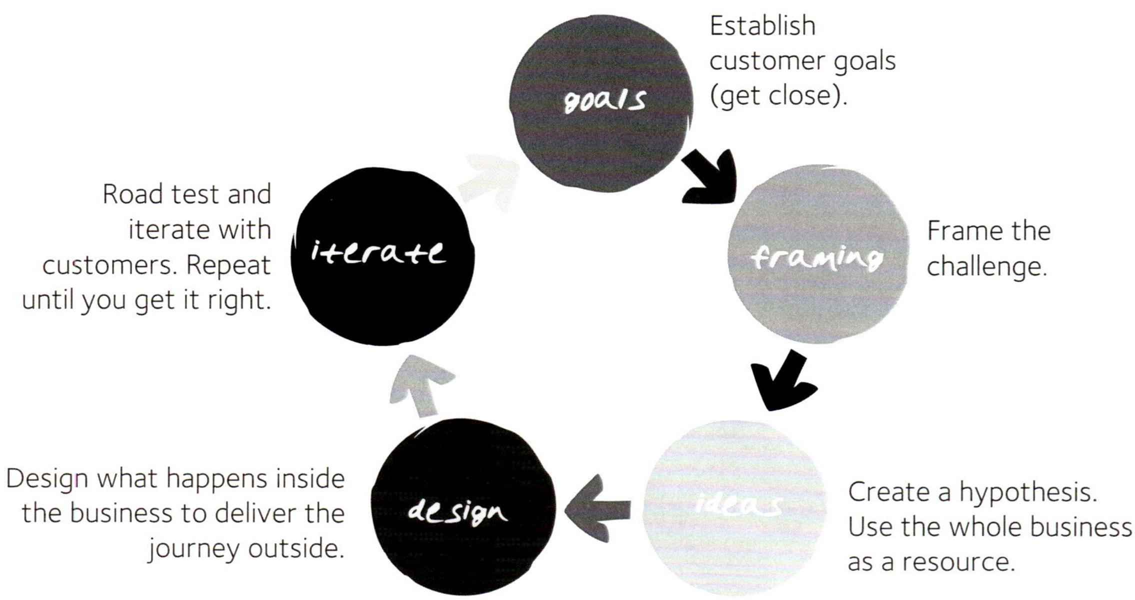

Back in the day, when I first started out as a Six Sigma professional, we used a framework called Lean. Lean thinking is about identifying exactly what customers value and how your business needs to align to deliver it, and it eliminates waste along the way. Unfortunately, it was abused and was presented as a way of reducing cost. It is a way of reducing waste in order to make sustainable improvements – which is not the same thing.

Mantra No.4
Design for value

But designing for value has never gone out of fashion. With Kano's warning about 'indifferent' product qualities still ringing in our ears, we now have a range of practices to choose from, including agile and lean agile, as well as a range of flexible, value-focused change methodologies to support them, like Scrum and Kanban.

NOTES

The important principles to remember are as follows:

1. Always put customers at the centre of the design process. It starts and ends with them. Your personas can help.

2. Establish customer goals and correctly frame the challenge first.

3. Don't try to establish those goals in a focus group – you need to get close enough to see the unarticulated and unknown needs and for long enough to develop cognitive empathy (think ethnography).

4. Be clear on how you will create value for the business by helping customers meet a need or solve a problem.

5. Employ the wisdom of the crowd to solve the problem. This means involving people from different disciplines right across your business.

6. Design the inside to match the outside – the skills, processes, data, and systems your people will need to enable them to deliver the journey.

7. Design and iterate. Again and again until you get it right. This isn't a linear process. And it needs to be driven by the customers who will be using the product or service.

I want to expand on the second point and to retrace our steps a little to ponder on the cultural competencies required for design thinking to work.

> “DESIGNING FOR VALUE HAS NEVER GONE OUT OF FASHION.

practice

Correctly framing the challenge

This is a very short sentence, but encompasses an awful lot. Establishing customer goals requires the level of open-mindedness described in Chapter 5. If you think you know what customers want, you are already off course. Stop and validate your assumptions!

Correctly framing the challenge is an art. And the better the challenge statement, the more easily the design process will flow. A good challenge statement creates a balanced viewpoint which takes in the customer and the business goal. It is specific, but not narrow. It describes the problem without solving it or imposing unnecessary constraints. If you have never written a challenge statement before, you will discover when you sit down to write your first one that it is harder than it looks – it does constitute a fairly heavy brain workout!

I prefer to work on challenge statements with other people. If you can start out with a shared objective and a common understanding of why you are doing it, it makes for a stronger team and a better result.

How can we ____ ?

Your statement needs to contain a question, an action, a description of the customer goal or job to be done, and who you are aiming the solution at. How can we [action] to help [who the solution is aimed at] achieve [goal]. Here are a couple of examples of challenge statements:

1. How can we provide the right information and tools to help customers make choices so they feel confident about switching to a new deal?

2. How can we remove hurdles at sign-up so customers can use their account immediately?

Something you should know at this point, if you don't already, is that there are a large number of occupational hobbyists in the world. They think what you do looks simple, and are always ready with tips to 'help' you.

These tips are often completely unrelated to the challenge at hand, or plainly irrelevant, such as the fact that there's this really cool feature on such and such website that you should include. This is suggested even though the feature in question confirms waiting times for tables in a restaurant, when your design challenge is about solving the problem of customers being put off by excessive small print. There might be merit in the idea, somehow, some day. But not today!

Sometimes the 'help' comes from a very senior person. It turns out the CEO is a big Apple fan and wants everything to be 'like Apple do it'. I even had one executive committee member recommend a colour palette for a customer communication campaign, despite it being completely different to the organisation's brand palette.

My advice? Invite them to your challenge statement writing session. If they are keen on being involved, they will probably really enjoy it!

> CHALLENGE STATEMENTS ARE YOUR DESIGN GUIDELINE. THEY NEED TO BE VISIBLE THROUGHOUT THE DESIGN PROJECT AND RESTATED FREQUENTLY.

Challenge statements are your design guideline. They need to be visible throughout the design project and restated frequently. Your challenge statements do not contain solutions. In fact, they are an explicit acknowledgement that you do not know what is desirable or possible yet.

From the challenge statement, you can start working up hypothesis statements to guide prototyping and testing. Again, this is best done with the group. The more hypothesis statements you can produce, the more chances you have of finding an effective and elegant solution.

For challenge statement number one, hypothesis statements might look like this:

1a. We believe a proactive communication highlighting our most popular deals will help customers determine whether they are getting value and will prompt more customers to proactively switch deals.

1b. We believe upskilling front-line teams will enable them to better communicate what's on offer and prompt more customers to proactively switch deals.

A good set of challenge and hypothesis statements can be carried through to measurement. In both the examples above, you will know you have been successful when you are able to measure a demonstrable improvement in both customer sentiment and customer behaviour. Customers will report feeling more informed or confident, and more of them will take action as a result.

Where do personas fit in? Between your challenge statement and your hypothesis statement. The purpose of a persona is to help you make informed assumptions to generate hypotheses from, which you will later test with customers.

practice

Personas

Not all customers are created equal, and personas can be a very effective way to help businesses understand why the journey might not look the same to everyone. For example, a journey always feels different if it's the first time you've taken it. Remember the first time you filled your car up with fuel? A persona which takes on the role of a 'new customer' will help you see that journey from the right perspective and understand your role as a business in guiding them through it.

I find it amusing to see people's faces contort when I talk about personas. There is generally eye-rolling involved, and sometimes muttering. They really do divide opinion! It's common to find they exist, but are not being used. If you have created them to tick a box, or have forced them onto your people rather than created them with your people, you have completely missed the point. They will simply be gathering dust, which is a shame because personas can, in fact, be a useful way to bring your customers to life inside your business.

But there is a right (and a wrong) way to create and use them. Personas can go badly wrong when they are poorly informed, developed in a silo, or applied beyond their scope of usefulness. They must be 1. informed by data and insights, 2. created by the cross-functional team, and 3. used at the right time in the right way. If you are going to create them properly, based on fact (there's that word again!), it takes time and effort, but they pay you back a hundred times over.

> " A WELL-CRAFTED CUSTOMER PERSONA IS ONE THAT IS BASED ON A QUANTITATIVELY VALIDATED VIEW OF YOUR CUSTOMERS, WHICH ITSELF IS BASED ON THEIR BELIEFS, ATTITUDES, AND BEHAVIOURS AND NOT ON THEIR AGE, SHOE SIZE, OR GENDER.

1. Informed by data and insights
The issue people often have with personas is that they look like stereotypes. If you group people purely on demographic data, without understanding what drives their decision-making, you will create a stereotype.

A well-crafted customer persona is one that is based on a quantitatively validated view of your customers, which itself is based on their beliefs, attitudes, and behaviours and not on their age, shoe size, or gender. Basing it on the latter would create a stereotype, not a persona. Stereotypes are not helpful to you.

Take age as an example. Assuming the characteristics of a whole generation on the basis that they were born in the same decade is laziness! We are all products of our experience to some extent, and generations growing up in the same era will have shared characteristics, but we will also vary widely in our tendency to exhibit those characteristics – you will get both ends of a spectrum and everything in between. And when you look at it in this way, you will start to see that in fact there is massive overlap between generations. So if you hear statements like "Millennials are disloyal", particularly when prefaced with "Everyone knows...", tell the speaker there may be an element of truth in that, but we're going to use research to understand how relevant that could be to our relationship with customers and to what extent that changes what they want and need from us.

The correct method of creating a set of personas is to base them on attitudinal segmentation. Segments are created by surveying a representative sample of your 'audience' in order to understand their beliefs, attitudes, and behaviours.

Your audience is not just existing customers, but should also include ex-customers, people who are not yet your customers but in your target market, and people who took a step towards becoming a customer, but fell out of the journey before completing it.

Segments are formed from analysis of survey responses to identify clusters of common beliefs, attitudes, and behaviours. Those clusters are your segments. Using the qualitative methods outlined in the customer closeness work in Chapter 5, research your segments. This creates a supply of descriptive themes and stories to make your personas relatable. You are essentially creating a fictional character by building on known beliefs, attitudes, and behaviours with demographic detail – never the other way around!!

Things you need to know first

- What are potential customers' goals in the short and long term?
- What are their key motivators?
- Which organisations are they loyal to, and what do they value in those relationships?
- What are their dreams and aspirations? And what aspect of them can your organisation solve, answer, or satisfy?
- What is their attitude towards your category, brand, product, or service?
- Are they conservative or innovative?
- And to inform design decisions, there are practical considerations. What is their level of knowledge about your products and services? What is your organisation's relationship with them today? What interaction channels do they prefer to use?

Making it relatable

Add a name, lifestyle, and interests. If it's a business persona, you'd want to know their role in the relationship – as a decision maker or organiser, for example.

You can hopefully see that if you start with the demographics, you're not going to produce anything actionable. Knowing someone's age, gender, or ethnicity might be relevant in your organisation, but most of the time it really isn't – it's just a shortcut to lazy thinking and false assumptions.

If this is all starting to sound quite technical, that's because it is. This is

NOTES

complex and skilled work which needs to be methodologically robust. It may be part of your skill set, but if it's beyond the boundary, a market research team or agency should handle this for you.

2. Created by the cross-functional team

Remember mantra number one – collaborate in all things? Creating personas needs to be a team sport. You need your stakeholders to embrace the output and befriend and champion your cast of persona characters. Slow down and take them with you.

A colleague of mine told me a story about a teaching workshop on journey mapping in which her client showed her the most impressive set of customer personas she had ever seen. She was very excited to see them, and launched into gushing praise. But there was a stony silence around the room. The other stakeholders didn't believe them. They had not been part of the process and didn't trust the content, or accept the people and attitudes described in the personas.

Make it a team sport; involve everyone in the work of bringing your personas into the world. Involve them before, during, and after the quantitative work by asking them to help you develop your research questions and taking them through the analysis and results. Then give them a role to play in gathering qualitative insights.

Follow up with a persona-creation workshop:

- Each person in the team shares their findings, including photographs, interesting facts, and memorable details.
- Collate insights for each 'segment' into one or two persona templates.
- Give each one a back story – a name, a face, and things they value.

3. Used at the right time in the right way

If you have this kind of clarity on who your customers are, and the confidence of stakeholders across functions that the information can be trusted, your personas start to take on a presence in your business. They become part of your decision-making approach and are valued members of the team who can help you do important work, like crafting targeted value propositions, lowering cost to serve for the different personas, retaining or winning back business by addressing dissatisfaction, or improving general engagement.

They are great at getting the design process started and particularly good at diagnosing common experience ailments. These are sometimes so blindingly obvious you don't see them. For example, missing steps in the journey, clunky handovers, complex language, or long periods of radio silence when the internal process is working fine, but you forget to communicate outwards to customers.

But personas are not your customers. They are a proxy, a way to describe what your customers might need to help you make informed assumptions. Unchallenged assumptions lead to unintended consequences, so make sure

"UNCHALLENGED ASSUMPTIONS LEAD TO UNINTENDED CONSEQUENCES, SO MAKE SURE YOUR ASSUMPTIONS ARE ONLY GRANTED A SHORT SHELF LIFE BEFORE YOU VALIDATE THEM WITH REAL CUSTOMERS.

NOTES

your assumptions are only granted a short shelf life before you validate them with real customers. Do not fall into the trap of designing journeys to fit personas like a bespoke glove. Or limiting the scope of requirements to the largest persona group, to the detriment of others. Always remember that you are designing journeys to cover the breadth of requirements your personas demand. And that customers are constantly shifting and changing in response to circumstances – I might be in business traveller mode one day, then in family of five mode the next. I will want different things in each scenario, and flexibility and choice in the journey remain critical.

Do not let the time and effort involved put you off! Personas pay you back many times over. What you will end up with is a set of personas which resemble this example created for an art and design museum. Charlotte's persona tells the museum what percentage of its market she represents, what's most important to her, and what the museum can do to create value for her. Charlotte will help the museum identify touchpoints to be mapped, and make decisions about where to focus its attention first.

Name and photograph

Descriptor (what's their personality in the context of your business relationship)

Segment size and value

Interests and brand loyalty (or if business-to-business, their role in the relationship, e.g. decision maker/organiser)

What are their goals in the short and long term?

- **Confidence – conservative/innovative**
- **Knowledge – low/very savvy**
- **Status – interested/customer/ex-customer**
- **Digital preference – low/high**

- What are their key motivators?
- What do they value in a brand relationship?
- What are their dreams and aspirations? And what aspects of that can your organisation solve, answer, or satisfy?
- What is their attitude towards your category, brand, product, or service?

Charlotte
Frequent Daytripper

Segment size – 10%
Visits – 10 -15 times a year
Value – £400 a year

Interested in design, and design history (she works as a theatre production assistant, and volunteers with a theatre restoration charity). Blogs about her life and work.

LUSH · CONVERSE ALL STAR · MAC

Charlotte visits to find inspiration for her work. She would like to expand her knowledge of set design.

Confidence	Conservative	★ (towards innovative)	Innovative
Knowledge	Low	★ (towards low)	High
Digital	Dislike	★	Prefer
Status	Interested ☐	Customer ☑	Ex-customer ☐

- I want to be inspired and learn.
- I value beautiful product design, heritage, and quality.
- I need to find a way to learn more about set design while working full-time.
- I like to stay in touch with what you are doing, and visit often.
- Would be good to see you doing more to shape the future of design.

Photographs: Beth Richardson, Bil Strohacker

practice

Collaborating with customers

A good set of personas like these puts the power of your entire market behind your customer experience strategy. It's like having an (unpaid!) expert in the room every time you want to answer a question or mediate in a debate about what the journey should do, or how. It means never having to say "I don't know". And you can achieve all of this without having to commission more market research, which means you make better decisions, faster.

If you want to take it one step further, some organisations have real-life representatives for each segment pulled from their marketing database or online community. Having a real customer in the room representing a segment makes them very hard to ignore in a meeting!

While I place a lot of emphasis on certain research methods, I should state that I don't have anything against focus groups. I am just not convinced that using them is always the best way to generate the intimate insights which are useful for customer experience work. I prefer to work with insight derived from individual customers in the natural context in which they would use a product or service. If one big personality in a focus group takes the conversation down a particular route and dominates the conversation, you don't get to hear the other, smaller voices in the room, and their needs and wants remain hidden. I have seen this happen too many times, even with very skilled facilitators.

However, focus groups can work well at the very outset of your project to generate broad themes as a precursor to doing more contextual research. They can also be successful at prototype stage, by bringing customers together as a group to meet the design team, feed back on ideas, and try out prototypes. Once you have something to show focus groups, and can put structure around the discussion, they can work very well.

Collaborating across functions

> "COLLABORATION NEEDS CLARITY ON SCOPE OF OWNERSHIP AND ROLES AND RESPONSIBILITIES.

Where does your function end and the other functions begin? In this book, I have often made reference to collaboration and cross-functional teamwork. Being able to bring a range of knowledge, skills, perspectives, and expertise together from across your business is what fuels your work. But collaboration needs clarity on scope of ownership and roles and responsibilities.

It's not your role to get hands-on with the detailed design of what a communication looks like, or a web journey, or a system specification, or a process change. It is your role to synthesise and make sense of a vast amount of data gathered from inside and outside the business and to unify the functions to respond to it in the right way. You then need to measure and report on the outcome and return on investment.

If your business is building a house, for example, you are the person who will help the business understand who will be living in the house and what their goals are. You will also help decide where the house should be built (which means considering the environment) and how it will be used (for example, hosting lots of parties, working from home in, or to retire in).

Designing the functional specification to make sure the house has walls, a roof and a floor, and has running water and heating and generally functions properly as a dwelling, is something you will enlist help with from colleagues with business- and process-analysis skills.

How the house is organised and how the rooms flow is a decision for user experience or service design teams. For example, most of us like to see the dining room next to the kitchen. We might need everything on one level or perhaps want extra bathrooms because we have four teenagers in the house!

And finally, your interaction design, branding, and communications colleagues make the house feel like home, with natural light, pleasant furnishings, and landscaping.

What's important is that you engage and involve all of the above skills, and maintain everyone's focus on who will live in the house and what they want to achieve: the challenge statement. Otherwise, what tends to happen is that you get carried away and build the house and then have the difficult job of finding someone to fit it. It should always be the other way around – this is the essence of design thinking.

You can also work with this same group to define a set of standards and design principles to stop issues from arising in the first place, for example always putting in the extra bathrooms as standard!

“AND FINALLY, YOUR INTERACTION DESIGN, BRANDING, AND COMMUNICATIONS COLLEAGUES MAKE THE HOUSE FEEL LIKE HOME, WITH NATURAL LIGHT, PLEASANT FURNISHINGS, AND LANDSCAPING.

story

One customer, three hotel experiences

I am a frequent business traveller. So frequent, in fact, that I have a 'jumbo' passport, which is 30% larger than the standard one so that it has room for all the exit and entry stamps of various countries. My habits are very consistent, and my requirements are very straightforward – and probably very similar to the many other people who travel a lot in the course of their work: to get a good night's sleep and be refreshed and ready for the next day, which is normally a combination of meetings or conferences, and then more travel.

My 'persona' is probably fairly typical of many. My basic functional requirements are to be able to sleep, wash, and eat. I need a bed, a bathroom, and a restaurant. I take for granted that they will be in good order. I might also want to be able to work, and maybe to visit a gym if possible.

The next layer is expectation. So if I am going to be able to sleep, I will probably need a quiet, dark room with a door that locks. I am going to need a bathroom which is well laid out, and a selection of toiletries waiting for me. I will need to be able to visit the restaurant at a time that suits me, probably having checked a menu or maybe even pre-ordered room service. I will want half decent Wi-Fi, a desk, and a power source. Having all these things makes for a satisfactory experience, and if I have them I will be very likely to feel I have received value for money.

The top layer is emotional. This is where the intent becomes very important. It requires organisations, and the people in them, to be conscious and thoughtful in the way they think about their interactions with customers. This layer is entirely discretionary and closely aligned to an organisation's purpose and what it stands for. It's a matter of personality, and is the difference between a forgettable transaction and a memorable experience which makes me want to repeat it.

Here are three real-life examples of how this particular business traveller got on in three different hotels.

Hotel number one – the 'new breed'

One of the most frustrating and embarrassing hotel experiences I have ever had was on a trip to Glasgow, staying in a 'new breed' of hotel designed to welcome the mobile citizens of the world.

Well, that's definitely me. I am a frequent business traveller. I fly at least once a week, and have probably flown with every airline to every major city in the world. I must be the ideal target customer!

I also stay in a lot of hotels, and I have a very clear idea in my own mind of what makes a functional, friction-free, engaging experience for me. And on first impressions, I felt very at home. It was a really nice-looking hotel, with bright colours, gadgets, and fantastic furniture and lighting. It looked as though the 1960s had crashed into the present day and created a whole new style. I actually became quite excited at the prospect of staying the night. This is not how I usually feel on turning up at a hotel when on business, so the signs were very promising that this was going to be a memorable experience.

Regrettably my first impression would not turn out to be representative of the end-to-end experience.

Reception looked rather like the check-in area at an airport – a series of self-service computer terminals. The reception staff did not say hello with a wide beaming smile and did not give me a warm feeling. I was asked by the computer to enter my name or reservation number. I could not retrieve my reservation number from my phone because I could not get a signal and had not yet logged on to the hotel's Wi-Fi, so I entered my name.

The response came back: name not recognised. I tried again a total of three times before scratching my head. "Help," I muttered meekly. Despite reception being a bank of computer terminals, there were two friendly human members of staff on hand. They could not understand what the problem was either.

Eventually, one of the friendly humans discovered that my name had been entered incorrectly into the system – they had missed the 'g' off the end of Golding. This nice, helpful person asked me to re-enter my name, missing off the 'g'. It worked. I was to be known as Mr Goldin for the remainder of my stay.

“I WAS TO BE KNOWN AS MR GOLDIN FOR THE REMAINDER OF MY STAY.

I eventually made it to my room. And what a sight it was. Not the biggest room in the world, but definitely one of the quirkiest. In the bedroom was an enormous bed, literally filling the space wall to wall. In the bathroom there was a huge shower that had a floor-to-ceiling glass wall into the bedroom area. Strangely, the sink was not in the bathroom, but located in the bedroom instead, almost like an afterthought.

I had been told at reception (by a human, not a computer) that everything in the room was controlled by a tablet. I found it sitting in a cradle by the enormous bed, like an oversized remote control.

Now, I have no issue with using a remote control – I have been using them for years to control my TV and I am highly proficient! But when the remote control will only work when it is in its cradle, which is nailed to the table by a bed, it can be problematic.

Every time I lifted the tablet out of the cradle, I was met with a 'low battery' warning. I was completely dependent on it to operate everything in the room – and I mean everything – so I had no choice but to contort my body or get on the bed to do the simplest of things.

The low battery was only the first issue. I wanted to do something quite dramatic – I wanted to turn on the lights. Now, in the good old days, we were able to turn on the lights by pressing a switch. I have never had an issue with the experience of turning a light on or off; I have always found the system perfectly good as it is. However, the designers in this hotel felt it was an experience that needed innovating.

Once I had figured out where on the tablet to turn on the light, what I got was not white light. Instead, the entire room was illuminated with coloured light – all the colours of the rainbow – fading in and out of various parts of the room. My shower was green. Above the bed it was blue. I thought I was either dreaming or hallucinating. All I wanted was a light on – to see. I did not want a disco. Could I figure out how to get the simplest of things, like white light? No.

Next, I wanted to close the curtains, or blinds in this case. In my house, the way this works is that I walk up to my window, reach out my arms, grab the curtains, and pull them together. It takes milliseconds and is very straightforward. But our friends at the hotel felt that this experience needed innovating too.

I could close the blinds by using the tablet or by pressing two buttons on the wall. The problem was that to close the blinds, I had to keep my finger on the button until they had reached their final destination – I could not press the button and watch as the blinds closed automatically like you would a car window. It took 15 seconds! 15 seconds wasted on a completely pointless bit of innovation.

At this point I was starting to think longingly about Premier Inn and Travelodge – they may not be fancy, but at least I know turning on the lights and closing the curtains will happen without any bother. And don't get me started on the lack of luggage space, or the small flood when I used the 'innovative in-room sink', or the fact that I completely failed to work out how to make breakfast appear, and ended up not having any. When I eventually checked out, I only had a computer terminal for company once again. There was no one to ask me how my stay had been or to wish me a safe trip.

There were some positives – the bed was amazing and I had a great night's sleep. I also had a wonderful shower. Yet the whole thing didn't hang together as a hotel experience.

TripAdvisor was polarised on the subject – many people loved the disco lights and the tablet thing. And, if I had been travelling with the kids, they would have absolutely loved it – I would have earned infinite 'cool Dad' points.

But I was there as a business traveller, and the experience was not designed in a way that allowed me to use the product effectively. It had been over-engineered to a point where it was detrimental to me. And because of that I won't go back. The experience design team at that hotel need to experience their journey not as themselves, but as their guests. If they had picked up a properly researched business traveller persona and walked through the journey with them, they would have lived through some of the emotions I felt along the way: from excitement to confusion, embarrassment, frustration, rejection, and resignation. Was that the target emotional response? I certainly didn't feel like a 'welcome mobile citizen of the world'.

They would also have seen the obvious, small tweaks they could have made, such as some extra storage, flexibility around technology (to be able to take a shortcut and turn the lights on and off with a switch!), and a brief communication about breakfast, perhaps from a human being. That's probably all it would have taken to convert me into an advocate.

Hotel number two – 'inspirational, luxury'

In this example, the hotel had been chosen for me by the client, as well as for the 40 conference delegates I was scheduled to deliver a keynote speech to the following day. The hotel belongs to a group, which describes itself as a collection of truly individual and inspirational spaces that is known for quality, service, and attention to every last detail. Something publicly stated like this constitutes a customer promise, and that's an ambitious collection of commitments, so my expectations were set very high.

Arriving at the hotel was like being transported onto the set of *Downton Abbey*. The hotel is in the most stunning setting, found at the end of a driveway half a mile long, and the building itself is beautiful. I was not disappointed, this was a 10/10 first impression.

Walking through the front door of the hotel, I was full of optimism about my two-night stay. But within seconds this optimism started to erode. As I approached reception, I noticed that the receptionist was on the phone. We were the only two people in the reception area. Without making eye contact, she continued her telephone conversation. This went on for three minutes. I know because I timed it. The conversation she was having (and making no attempt to hide), was with a colleague.

> “IF THEY HAD PICKED UP A PROPERLY RESEARCHED BUSINESS TRAVELLER PERSONA AND WALKED THROUGH THE JOURNEY WITH THEM, THEY WOULD HAVE LIVED THROUGH SOME OF THE EMOTIONS I FELT ALONG THE WAY: FROM EXCITEMENT TO CONFUSION, EMBARRASSMENT, FRUSTRATION, REJECTION, AND RESIGNATION.

They were discussing why they were continually booking customers staying for more than one night into different rooms for each night of their stay. From the tone of the conversation, they both found this rather amusing.

To keep a customer waiting for three minutes is not great. Stand still for three minutes and tell me if it does not seem like a very long time! To do so while continuing a conversation with a colleague is rude. To have a conversation highlighting how your hotel gets things wrong in front of a customer is unprofessional. When the phone call was brought to a conclusion, I did not even receive an apology for being kept waiting.

Once I was checked in, the receptionist pointed me in the direction of my room. What she failed to tell me was that I would be walking through a building site to get to it. As I rounded a corner, I was met with dust sheets, rubble, and workmen. I thought I had gone the wrong way. Someone should have mentioned this at booking stage, and at check-in.

Having finally found my bedroom (which took a few minutes due to poor signage), I could feel my disappointment growing. The room was by no means the worst I have ever stayed in, but it was a million miles away from the expectation set by the grandeur of the building and the publicly stated promise of quality. The room was dated in terms of decor, furniture, and equipment. I have not seen a television like it since 1995.

The bathroom light flickered, and had not been cleaned thoroughly for a while. For a hotel group that claims it pays attention to every last detail, it was surprising to find that more flaws quickly became apparent. The hotel is largely used by business people during the week, and it's likely they would use the desk to work at. This means using a laptop that will need to be powered by electricity. This detail was obviously not factored into the hotel's thinking, because the only sockets by the desk were already in use! Add to this the bad mattress, broken lift, and inconvenient gym opening hours, and you start to form a picture.

The unacceptable welcome when I arrived was not a one-off. The lack of engagement was consistent. During my three-day stay, not one member of the hotel team offered me a 'good morning' or 'good afternoon', or even a 'hello'. Everyone I came into contact with looked sad. A lack of visible leadership will have contributed to that – I did not see anyone who looked like a manager in reception, the restaurant, the conference rooms, or anywhere else.

I was so disappointed. An experience that promises so much had me feeling deflated from the minute I walked through the door. The promise of quality, service, and attention to detail was not kept – it was not even close. Making management spend time as customers would be a good start to help them see for themselves how the hotel brand's customer promise was falling short.

I would not want to go back to this hotel again because it made me feel sad to see such a beautiful building going to waste and the people in it being so badly treated. These are not the feelings any organisation wants its customers to have.

Hotel number three – the mid-range chain

On the third occasion, I was visiting Malaysia to deliver a customer experience masterclass, and again the accommodation was selected for me by my client. The hotel in question was part of a large group of hotel brands famous for differentiating on customer experience. My expectations were definitely even higher than usual.

The hotel was very well-appointed, with a spa, a 24-hour gym, and a lovely swimming pool. The bedroom was very nice – not the best room I have ever stayed in, but very good. It was well furnished, with an incredibly comfortable bed, different types of pillow to choose from, and a fabulous bathroom. The hotel had a dining room and room service, but guests were not restricted, because they were offered a 10% guest discount at many of the restaurants nearby. The hotel had chosen to put guest comfort and choice ahead of its own revenue.

The hotel wasn't perfect by any means – for example the free guest Wi-Fi was so slow it took me a full 30 minutes to open an email! But the people were delightful. From the minute I approached the front door of the hotel to the second I got in my taxi to return to the airport, I was met with smiling, polite, friendly, helpful people. Every employee I came across made eye contact with me – from the cleaning team to the concierge to the receptionists. If their mission was to make me feel welcome, they succeeded with flying colours.

> **"EVERY EMPLOYEE I CAME ACROSS MADE EYE CONTACT WITH ME - FROM THE CLEANING TEAM TO THE CONCIERGE TO THE RECEPTIONISTS. IF THEIR MISSION WAS TO MAKE ME FEEL WELCOME, THEY SUCCEEDED WITH FLYING COLOURS.**

It felt like I was staying in a hotel that knew what it was doing. My high expectations of the hotel brand had been met, and when I go back to Kuala Lumpur, I choose to stay at this hotel. And if friends or colleagues were to ask me for hotel recommendations in Kuala Lumpur, I would have no hesitation in recommending it.

A vital component of any customer experience is to feel valued. For ANY customer experience – it doesn't matter who you are – where there's a commercial transaction taking place which involves a customer paying for a product or service, you must show them that you value their business. I only felt valued in one of the examples above.

The first example was, in my view, well intentioned. But it felt as though the intent was to impress customers, not to welcome them. At times, I was certainly impressed. But the design process was so narrow that the experience was very poorly aligned with my needs, and became less welcoming in the process. At times the experience became a confusing and frustrating one for a business traveller, and that is what I remember about the experience. If I am not the target market that's OK, but make it clear to me in the way you position your proposition so I can make a choice.

In the second example, the intent behind the experience was either absent or misguided. I didn't get a particularly welcoming interaction from anyone in the hotel throughout my stay, so I believe the role of customers in the business had not been articulated clearly for employees. And the intent was not clear either. In common with the hotel's employees, I appeared to be part of a process – a swim lane on a process map. I had been dehumanised and was reduced to being a variable to be controlled to make sure I did the right things at the right time to fit around the workings of the business, including building maintenance. What I remember about the experience is the sadness of the environment and the people in it.

In the third example, it felt to me as though the intent was to make me feel welcome. That 10% dining discount was not only thoughtful but was tangible evidence of a desire to put customer needs ahead of profit. It was not the perfect experience, and certainly wasn't quirky or overly luxuriant, but thoughtful touches like this, and the personal warmth I encountered from the hotel team, are what I remember.

Key takeaways from Chapter 10 – Doing/design

know

The design process must always start with what your customers are trying to achieve (their goal).

do

Design for value. Including customer needs which go beyond what they can articulate or rationalise - trust, confidence, happiness.

remember

Creating the right conditions for productive collaboration means helping the business make sense of insights and unifying the functions to respond.

The Comic Postcard in English Life

BY THE SAME AUTHOR

View North: A Long Look at Northern England

'Social history is organic. It needs, to live, the moods, thoughts, flavours, significant incidents and memorable occasions, shifting perspectives which, once passed, can rarely be accurately recaptured.'

HARRY HOPKINS

"A "NUT" WITH A SMALL SCREW."

WHO TAKE'S WHO
AND FOR
WHAT?

I AM HAVING THE TIME OF
MY LIFE. — CHEERIO!

FREDERICK ALDERSON

The Comic Postcard in English Life

DAVID & CHARLES *Newton Abbot*

7153 4708 X

Printed in Great Britain by
A Wheaton & Company Exeter Devon
for David & Charles (Publishers) Limited
South Devon House Newton Abbot Devon

Contents

1	*Tradition*	10
2	*'Beside the Seaside'*	20
3	*'No Place Like Home'*	28
4	*'Smile, smile, smile'*	38
5	*'Daddy wouldn't buy me a bow-wow'*	49
6	*'I'm a genuine philanthropist'*	58
7	*'Where did you get that hat?'*	68
8	*'Ma, he's making eyes at me'*	79
9	*'We'll meet again'*	89
10	*Taboo*	99
	Acknowledgment	107
	Index	109

SCOUNDREL! VILLAIN!! BLACKGUARD!!!

"I visit this place every year."
"Are your stays long?"
"Sir! I thought you were a gentleman."

NOW LOOK HERE, GEORGE, IF THERE'S ANY MORE OF THAT SUBMARINE BUSINESS I'LL SMACK YOU IN THE PERISCOPE!

At the

We've been bothered with wind a lot since we arrived

Having a gay old time!—What would she say if she saw me now

"THE DAILY OBSERVER."

Reik jij de bekers uit. Ik zal de medailles wel vast spelden

I DON'T CARE A HANG WHAT PEOPLE THINK—
I'M DOING AS I PLEASE THIS WEEK!
ADMISSUN
TO 6D
SEE THE
BATTERED
OLD HULK

easide

IF I DON'T RETURN TO WORK YOU'LL
KNOW I'VE CLICKED WITH A MILLIONAIRE,
— OR BEEN LOCKED UP

PUTTING ALL OUR WORRIES BEHIND US—
THIS WEEK!
NO MUCKY POTS
NO BUS TO CATCH
NO ALARM CLOCK
NO WASHING
NO IRONIN
Taylor

1 *Tradition*

Sunday, October morrow: 'At the Vicarage I saw one of the first "Post Cards" that have been sent. It was from Lilian to Mrs Venables, very bright and cheery'.

Tuesday, 4 October: 'Today I sent my first postcards, to my Mother, Thersie, Emmie and Perch. They are capital things, simple, useful and handy. A happy invention'.

So the Rev Francis Kilvert writing his diary for 1870. He was as prompt in buying the new 'invention' as we are today in buying a new commemoration stamp. The General Post Office first issued cards, manufactured by De la Rue & Co and sold for the price of the halfpenny stamp printed on them, on 1 October 1870—the same year, as it happens, that James Bamforth of Holmfirth set up in a business which was to become one of the first, and eventually the world's biggest, for the production of 'bright and cheery' postcards—though not of the kind that Kilvert sent to his mother . . .

The two things that probably did most to keep families together, and relatives in touch during the age of large households and slow travel, were the 6d photograph and the 1d post, followed by the postcard. The photograph, replacing expensive painted portraiture, meant that girls out in service at home, and lads in the Services or living as emigrants overseas, could have likenesses of their family about them, and that their families could have likenesses of absent sons and daughters along with the rest, both old and young. The card made postal communication cheaper and easier just when literacy was becoming general and writing less formal.

From Rowland Hill's penny-prepaid postal reform, carried through in the face of 'obdurate Post Office obstruction' in 1840, to the issue of plain postcards seems a longish interval. The GPO's interest lay at first in pictorial envelopes, which could be used to diffuse a taste for fine art, 'very much wanted', and to convey in their symbolic design the benefits conferred on the world by British postage. In any case written communication was regarded as generally of a private nature. So although private postal cards were being sold to the public of Philadelphia from 1861 and their official issue was proposed at a German postal congress in 1865, while the Austrian Government sold one and a half million *Korrespondenz Karte* within a month of their coming into circulation in 1869, we took our time. It was no doubt in accordance with fiscal policy as, a century later, seems the virtual killing of the plain postcard, by requiring a 5d stamp for anything like prompt delivery, whilst telephone installation is being so assiduously promoted.

After 1870 the scope for both postcards and photography in private enterprise, however, makes a rich slice of social history and one that can be enjoyed, in unique mixture, from the story of one Yorkshire firm.

Holmfirth, last town on the Yorkshire side of the Pennines, is a dark stone chapel-cum-mill community, famous for its choirs, its fine worsteds, its anthem, and its great floods, snugged in between the slopes of two steep, narrow valleys. At the top of breath-taking Cliff Lane, in a stone cottage with its face to the rising sun, lives Harry Platt. He began working for Bamforths in 1888 and went on until 1946. When he goes downhill in summer for a game of bowls he generally drops in to see how business is going in the firm's premises near the lane foot and to 'keep in touch'. At ninety-three he's nearly as old as the business itself—a hardy, humorous, stoical kind of Yorkshireman. Starting under James Bamforth, the founder, he carried on under his sons and through the First and Second World Wars, until 'Mr Derek', grandson and present head of the firm, came back to resume control. As he says and as the writer found, there's nobody else now who knows about the early days.

James Bamforth, a mid-Victorian with a portrait appearance of handsome bearded Victorian dignity, was the son of a Holmfirth painter and decorator. His background, coupled with a certain artistic flair, an interest in photography, and skill in carpentry, made possible a departure from the family line. He saw the opportunity of producing lantern slides, as accompaniment to the songs, story recitals, and lectures of contemporary popular entertainment, and in 1870 launched out with that aim.

The magic lantern had already a longish history. Known to Samuel Pepys as 'a lanthorne with pictures in glasse to make strange things appear on a wall', it had developed by the mid-nineteenth century from rather a tricky scientific toy into the simpler and cheaper apparatus suitable for ordinary use. In the lecture hall, with a large screen and a 200 ft beam it could, in expert hands, produce as fine or even a finer picture than the colour-film cine-projectors of today. Photographic plates, instead of transparencies, made all the difference to the image obtainable, and producing those plates as slides exactly suited James Bamforth's abilities.

The secret of his early success lay in his employment of life models and realistic backgrounds—plus a Yorkshireman's business sense. Painting backcloths was James's forte. He could illustrate a scene from a song or story—backcloth ready and barely distinguishable from the real moss, bracken or boulders added in the foreground—within an hour. Later on he would demonstrate this skill before visitors when his 'studio' had been built, but at first the premises comprised a series of wooden 'pavilions' dotted up the precipitous 'cliff' slope. The 'life models' who acted and posed the events of the dramatic scenes (for which a preliminary sketch was carefully made), were usually found among his employees and their children, friends in the town or, if need be, from the tap-room of a local pub. For a railway episode, a bank raid, or a mining disaster, pictures were taken out of doors and local effects used. As a rule, with cameras so cumbersome and emulsion speeds slow it was better to use the controlled lighting indoors. The job of preparing the glass plates—for wet plate photography—washing them, coating with emulsion (or, when dry plates came in, dipping in a silver bath), and then developing and copying, was the responsibility of technical assistants like Harry Platt. James Bamforth himself undertook most of the photography, chiefly in summer. Other assistants, usually girls, coloured the black and white photographs, clamped them between protective sheets of glass and numbered them for reference.

The business of producing a lantern show was quite arduous. Bamforth's slides were in much demand for Temperance Society lectures, Sunday School occasions, Band of Hope meetings, Cocoa and Reading Room do's, and whilst the business existed to sell slides it was not uncommon to give a local charity show. Carrying two cylinders of oxygen and hydrogen up and down those Holmfirth hills to provide a mobile source of illumination seemed, to the technical assistant, no light task. On dark winter nights 'Lost in the Woods' might be the evening's theme, almost literally, and 'Slaves of Drink' an ironical comment on their thirsty labours. No doubt the audience, of sixty or seventy, enjoyed every minute of it, including the advertisement slides. For the operators, if there was a press of other work on, it could mean 'working through' from Friday 8 AM to Saturday midday.

James Bamforth first reached newspaper fame as 'King of the Lantern Slides'. He was originator and largest producer of the life model slides. One of his slide sequences for 'Billy's rose', a tear-jerking ballad by George R. Sims, the author of 'It is Christmas Day in the Workhouse', has some beautifully composed scenes. We see 'the garret's dismal gloom' with its drunken father and mother, the child's sunbeam vision of 'a land of shining gold' beyond their dismal alley, a Sunday school picnic by a stream in 'a green and lovely meadow', the same scene white with snow and Billy's sister kneeling in prayer, and, of course, finally the children's meeting in heaven surrounded by angels. Backed by this natural artistry, with sound effects and incidental music from the harmonium, no doubt even amateur reciters could produce a moving performance. The audience would overlook any hitch in the excitement of picking out children's faces they knew among the picnickers and angels. For the

At the Seaside

London Opinion.
"I wouldn't marry you if you were the last man on earth."
"Of course not - there would be no one to perform the ceremony."

BUY YOURSELF A COAT LIKE THIS:
NOW'S YOUR CHANCE, MY LAD!
IF YOU'VE NEVER BEEN A NUT BEFORE,
YOU'LL BE ONE THEN, BY GAD!

" BLIMEY ! — I WOULD BE WEARING A SHORTIE NIGHTIE ! "
QUICK JUMP!
A 'BAMFORTH' COMIC

'IT'S MY POP ART DRESS, DAD.'
'AH CAN SEE THAT, LASS — NAH GO UPSTAIRS AND POP BACK INTO IT !!'

Fashion

The Star, Rose and Dream

The Song the Angels sing

children reward was twofold: actually being a 'performer' and payment of 2d for a part in a crowd scene, or 4d if 'starring' in one of the photographs.

At the turn of the century Bamforths moved from the Illustrated Song Series of slides—for which by now the 'pavilions' hardly had enough production space—to a new venture which surprised even Holmfirth. A Bradford firm, Riley Brothers, had one of the new kinematograph cameras and a man who knew how to work it. This situation appeared to Bamforths, with their considerable experience of plot, costume, backgrounds, and amateur actors, a golden opportunity for the two firms to work together in the production of motion pictures. One of James's sons, Frank Bamforth, who was gradually taking over camera work, acted as director; 'Miss Janie', a daughter, was 'dresser-props-continuity girl'; the lantern slide models became 'junior leads' and 'stars'; and Edwin Bamforth, another son, took walking on parts. The first efforts were not very long sequences—screening time being five or ten minutes—but full of action, usually farcical. Snowball fights, involving Holmbridge schoolboys and a 'choleric squire', a tramp pursued by a policeman with a big dog as 'extra', two men trying to push each other out of a rowing boat on a nearby lake, formed the staple stuff. The more horseplay that could be crammed in the better.

In the event Bamforths may claim the distinction of being the first firm in Britain to make kinematographic films for public entertainment. (Robert Paul's 'Animatograph' was a near contemporary—with a difference.) Harry Bamforth (a third son) took these films to show in a public hall hired for the purpose, a phonograph with its huge tin horn providing the orchestra. Thus some of the first films presented to the public were made in Holmfirth and acted by Holmfirth people. During 'production', work stopped in the town and bystanders enjoyed the fun, while the main street suffered a barrage of custard pies or was drenched by fire hoses and buckets of whitewash amid the antics of 'cops' or suffragettes.

After this early start and the making of a number of short features which Harry Bamforth showed as far afield as Sheffield, Leeds, and Manchester, film-making was crowded out by the firm's main line of business until 1913. Bamforth's comedy production then recommenced on a much larger scale, with professional actors and dramas running to six or seven reels. Among the fifty or so pictures turned out for home and Continental showing the actress Miss Queenie Thomas made her film debut, starring in *Consider the Lilies*. Miss Lily Ward, Mr Syd Baker and Mr Reginald Switz also appeared. The latter, one of the well known early screen comedians, played an eccentric gentleman in a series known as *Winkey's Misadventures*. The most ambitious film was *Paula*, producer Mr Bertram Phillips. From 1913 until 1915, when war stopped everything, including fulfilment of an order for one hundred films for Russia, Bamforths were as far advanced as anyone in film technique. Two of their cameramen joined Pathé Gazette; some of their custard-pie comedies are stored in the vaults of the National Film Archive. At a showing in the Holmfirth cinema (of which, naturally, the present head of the firm is a director) of other Bamforth films which turned up a few years ago, the first class quality of the acting and photography evoked considerable surprise. But it would have taken vast capital investment and even vaster resources of labour to establish in the confines of the Holme valley full-size studios to develop full-scale modern film-making.

Meantime the slide business itself had expanded beyond the capacity of the old premises, and a new building—the present one—was erected in 1904. It contained ladies' and gentlemen's dressing rooms, make-up boxes, an extensive wardrobe, storage space for theatrical props—including the components of a railway signal box, a ship's quarter deck, a ballroom, a flaming gin palace, a prison cell, a church—and hundreds of backcloths, together with studio space of 5,000 sq ft, just over half the total floor space. In these conditions the boast that any song on the market could be illustrated in one hour was easier to maintain. Some gauge of the size of the lantern slide 'kingdom' can be taken from the output of this period—600 titles annually—and stock of some 2,000,000 slides not counting negatives. A catalogue for 1905 contains 336 quarto pages with a twenty-three page index. By this time the negatives made previously for slides were also being used to produce picture postcards.

Again a pioneer claim can be made. Edwin Bamforth, later to become managing director, was one of the first to recognise the possibility of postcards as a comic accompaniment to the seaside holiday.

It was the Paris Exhibition, 1889, that gave the habit of postcard sending, from the Continent, the fillip which turned it into a craze. One could buy a card with a lithograph of the Eiffel Tower, write it, and then post it from the Tower itself with the phrase that clinched the idea's success 'This is where I am just now'. The GPO followed up with a picture of Eddystone Lighthouse, to be posted from the top of a model at the Royal Naval Exhibition in 1890. When private printing of such cards became permissible in Britain four years later—long after its acceptance elsewhere—it was confined at the start to 'court' size. Even so Stewarts of Edinburgh and Corketts of Leicester both produced view cards of their cities. Between them rests the claim to be the first British firm to produce picture postcards.

Valentines of Dundee, who had already printed pictorial envelopes and sets of small lithographed picture cards that folded into booklet form—the writer possesses one of scenes from Victorian Harrogate—were producing view cards by 1895, using the new German collotype colour process. In 1899, as soon as the Continental size of card was allowed (5½in by 3½in instead of the 'court' maximum of 4½in by 3½in, minimum 3¼in by 2¼in) Raphael Tuck started up in full production. It was not until 1902, however, that the British Government sanctioned the use for correspondence of one half of the side reserved for the address, so making possible a picture completely covering the card. That year Bamforths and Hartmans both came in. The former's characteristic contribution then took the form of photographic postcards portraying life models in a variety of humorous situations.

Up to 1894 most of the small view-cards for sale in Britain had been printed in Germany, where there was no obstacle to private production of picture cards from the 70s onwards. After 1902 and licence in Britain to use half the address side for correspondence, such cards could not at first be sent abroad—until France, then in 1905 Germany, agreed to this revised practice. Nevertheless the view and picture-card sending habit at home boomed. From the start, as Bamforths realised, they were on to a 'good thing' with postcards.

Plain card collecting had already had its short-lived hobby magazine. The craze for collecting pictorial cards soon spread from the Continent and was in full swing before the turn of the century. Card-sending—sometimes by the senders to themselves, for the sake of the postmark, when

999
999
999

Sorry I shan't be home for tea.
I've got a sitter."

" WE WANT THIS PLACE TO BE RUN BY A PERSON WHO KNOWS WHAT THE TEENAGERS WANT TO DO—BUT OLD ENOUGH TO SEE THAT THEY DON'T DO IT ! "
OPENING OF
YOUTH
CLUB
ENTRE
A 'BAMFORTH' COMIC

FRED - COME AND SEE WHAT I'VE GOT !
Taylor

Hello ! Hello !
Who's your lady friend ?

Sex

abroad, or often to fellow enthusiasts at home—quickly reached huge proportions. 'In ten years Europe will be buried beneath picture postcards' was a newspaper editor's prophecy in 1903. The size and quality of one's collection was a status symbol, much as the style and number of Christmas cards one receives is today. In a competition launched by Raphael Tuck to stimulate the new industry the first-prize winner, collecting only Tuck's cards, amassed over 20,000. By 1908 no fewer than 860,000,000 cards a year were being sent in Great Britain, with their green halfpenny adhesive stamps; and in Germany about 1,500,000,000.

During this first peak period a London publisher estimated his production at 50,000 cards daily. The firm of Wrench and Ettlinger, starting from scratch, in two or three years built up a business with over 5,000 retail firms on its list. For a short time they were selling £4,000 worth of cards per month and had contracts with the railway companies.

In every family there is almost certain to be at least one of these early cards preserved, with its candid revelation of our pursuits and pastimes, our customs and costumes, our morals and manners. As likely as not the message on the back will read: 'My dear Edith, Thanks so much for the sweet pc. How will this suit? Is it as nice as yours?' or 'So glad you like my pcs. Am sending you one to match the other'.

Apart from their humorous series and use of lantern slide negatives for postcard production, with some ventures also in the field of advertising, Bamforths now began a new and soon extremely popular line of cards illustrating pantomime and other popular songs. Made up in sets of two or four, a different verse and picture on each card, these took up the 'hits' of the season and reproduced the atmosphere of stage and scene. An early favourite, going back to the South African war, was 'Good-bye Dolly Gray', originally sung by Leo Dryden. As soon as the public selected their favourite song millions of cards could be in production. 'Bluebell'—top of the pops for 1904—became a huge success, exceeding all sales to that date. Subjects were published at the rate of two dozen each month. The following year came 'Brighteyes', 'My Irish Molly! O', 'Rainbow' and 'A little Boy called Taps'. The scenery for 'Irish Molly' (sung originally by Lily Lassah)—a woodland glade, mountains and what might be the lake of Killarney, with a barefoot plaid-skirted colleen in the foreground—reveals all James Bamforth's expertise. The words like those of pop songs of any period remain *below* criticism:

> Molly, my Irish Molly, my sweet a-cushla dear,
> I'm fairly off my trolley, my Irish Molly, when you are near.
> Spring time you know is ring time. Come dear, don't be so slow,
> Change your name, go on, be game,
> Begorra and I'll do the same,
> My Irish Molly! O!

Local residents, staff, and family members of the firm continued to 'model' for cards as they had done for slides; but professional actors and actresses, 'borrowed' from the Huddersfield theatre or music-halls, played an increasing part. The Hymn cards—a natural corollary to the Pantomime Song Series—often have recognisable models. Among the prime favourites, such as 'Rock of Ages', 'Abide with Me', and 'Lead Kindly Light', could be identified people well known in the town. Hannah Hinchcliffe, for instance, who 'had an innocent, pure look and was often shown clasping a bible, looking demurely to Heaven', appeared on more of these pictures than anyone. That did not preclude her appearance also on the comic cards, in 'kissing scenes' with 'Mr Edwin'. Three members of the Bamforth family can be recognised in the picture for 'Ora pro Nobis'. Printed at first in black and white only, later in colour, on thick cards with a glossy surface, these subjects give a general impression of solid oak pews and stained glass windows. Both song and hymn cards are now collectors' items.

On the comic cards male characters were to the fore—a certain Fred 'Shiner' Beaumont, a french polisher who also 'starred' in the comedy films, and Alf Foy, in particular. His name has the authentic kinematographic ring! For the pantomime hits, with their stage characters,

The Song the Angels sing

Oft Times

'pros' would fit in four or five action poses during a morning at the studio and then perhaps provide one of the music-hall figures for the comic cards. The comics of this early period have the special quality, like music-hall itself, of *joie-de-vivre* which has marked out Bamforth cards ever since.

The firm—which by this time had agencies in all English-speaking countries, and offices in London and New York—became a limited company in June 1910. Before long the quantities of cards in various series became too many to cope with photographically and three-colour printing instead of hand-colouring had to be adopted to keep pace with demand. Life model subjects—which had been imitated by rivals such as Garners of Leicester and led to protection of copyright cases in America and in Plymouth—continued for some time during the war; but the next step, obviously, was to employ artists and print their figure sketches in the three-colour process.

With the artists, card production and Bamforth's trade name enters its most distinctive and, in some respects, most conspicuous phase. Two artists between them have covered the period from the beginning of King George V's reign, when a card sender from Southport wrote 'We have just been looking out for the flying machines', until this current year of the first moon-landing. Douglas Tempest joined the firm in 1911 and stayed over forty years. He overlaps with Arnold Taylor who has also spent over forty years in the artist's studio and has his own seasoned disciple-successor. The two have given a unique cachet to the modern seaside comic card, turning a quip as readily as the song cards jerked a tear.

Other artists, from Spurgeon and Fitton to Fitzpatrick, have contributed originality of style and viewpoint, but Tempest and Taylor can fairly be called the creators of the Bamforth hallmark. No less clear and characteristic than that which Donald McGill gave to the Pictorial Postcard Company, it is less confined to base metal and not set on such stereotyped ware. The counterpart of their best work can be found in the early comic series of Tuck and Valentine, and in Hendersons' reproduction on cards of Charles Dana Gibson designs.

The subsequent range and development of the comic postcard, through the Tempest-Taylor era, its lively reflection of social change and general manners, its part in the contemporary climate of opinion, its special topics and taboos, its expression of the 'common view', form the subject of the chapters that follow. These cards show us 'a microcosm of some once ordinary way of life, now become extraordinary by its mere distance from our times'. Bamforths continued and inaugurated other lines (including 'Photomatons'—an early type of seaside photographic booth) but, once started, the comic card business was to become a little empire of its own.

When Harry Platt, then well over forty, went to register during the First World War, he had hoped to join the RFC's photographic department at Farnborough. Instead he found that his job made him one of the 'Indispensables'—helping morale by the dissemination of humour. So he went on with his work at Holmfirth, adding to it slides for recruiting posters and, on occasion, copying X-ray slides for hospital instruction. After the war patriotism and sentiment died practically overnight, but the future of the comic card remained rosy. Timely grasp of this and concentration upon quality of design and of printing enabled Bamforths to build up their present unrivalled position in that field.

Some of their jokes seem to have perennial appeal. The public from Bournemouth to Blackpool have bought up to five or six million copies of one individual card which has constantly had to be reprinted throughout twenty years, in addition of course to the new inventions of the seasons. Nowadays it is a case of keeping pace with the demand, greater than ever in spite of an eightfold increase in postal rate since those halcyon Edwardian days. The artists 'dream up' some

The Buglar Boy

Just for tonight

hundreds of drawings and jokes each year, from which batches of three dozens are selected and marketed in January and June. The premises, unchanged externally, have had dressing rooms, prop stores, and studio converted to storage and packing rooms, whilst a new artists' annexe has been built in the grounds. The large old studio camera, cased in mahogany by a local carpenter, still finds use for copying. In the paternal role of managing director 'Mr Derek', from his residence high up by the woods, can look over Holme valley to a firm with a century's tradition and its founder's original company home and house. Only the problems, the techniques, the products are as new as the times.

Whilst their present output includes anniversary and view cards, coloured calendars and children's cards, it is for 'comics' that, throughout our own seaside resorts and overseas in Holland, Belgium, France, Portugal, Canada, Australia, South Africa, and the USA, the firm remains best known and prime favourite. Captionless jokes, speeded up to modern tempo, have recently swelled the overseas market. To those nearer home, however, the two names themselves, Bamforth and Holmfirth, provide a joke within a joke. Who could imagine that a small mid-Victorian decorator in a remote chapel-run textile town would have created around him the biggest modern production plant for cards that just-pass-the-censor? 'Capital'—but not perhaps for such as the Rev Kilvert!

2 *'Beside the Seaside'*

Caricaturists and comic artists have had a fondness for subjects in sight of the ocean ever since the fashion for sea-bathing took over from taking the waters at the spa. Rowlandson, with his gouty old men training their telescopes on the naked mermaids of Brighton or Margate, Cruikshank, 'Crowquill', Leech, du Maurier, French artists like Charles Henri and Albert Guillaume—all relished a scene where kicking over the traces and revealing usually hidden frailties go hand in hand. An album by Guillaume, in the writer's possession, is devoted solely to 'Etoiles de Mer' and the incidents of packing for, travelling to, parading at, and disporting in, a French plage of the 90s. The use of only three or four colours in the pictures make them eminently suitable for card reproduction. The captions set the coy, early tone. 'Rêverie' has a respectable flannel-suited petit bourgeois contemplating a plumped-out female costume that dries on the line. So it comes as no surprise that artists' cards began in France.

From the first, English comic postcards had another element. The institution of the statutory Bank Holiday in 1871 allowed a new class of holidaymaker to throw off the trammels, however briefly, and make for the sea and air. Trippers, the 'grey unnumbered multitude' of spinning operatives, weavers, twisters, warp-dressers, mechanics, asbestos hands, stokers, clerks, shopkeepers, could begin to enjoy some of the privileges of the middle class. Then, when 'Wakes' seasons closed whole industrial towns, they began to outnumber them at some resorts altogether.

Bamforth's cards, naturally, conceived at first with a northern slant, mirror the manners of both these classes. There is the genteel mode, with its self-conscious tilts at convention, its fashion-awareness and dashing airs of 'gaiety without Mrs Grundy'; and the more straightforward boisterous sense of release of the tripper class, heightened by undertones of anxiety about social pitfalls and all the scraping, the snags, and making-do of lodging house accommodation. As time goes on and seaside postcard senders become more and more identified with tripperdom, the pictures and jokes reflect their tastes, interests, and sentiment almost exclusively.

'Poor John in trouble again at the seaside. We are here enjoying ourselfs [*sic*] very much'. This card, written from Swanage has an obvious Mrs Grundy figure in action: 'Scoundrel! Villain! Blackguard!' she cries as she drives away with her umbrella the sidewhiskered male from the not very ravishing creature in red pantaloons. The publishers, Millar and Lang, were Bamforth's early rival in this field, along with Davidsons; both of these firms used artists' sketches—the latter, notably, employing the 'Punch' artist Tom Browne. Bamforth cards had the added piquancy of life models. A typical one of the latter kind, 'O! what would the congregation say?' shows a sturdy Holmfirthian (?) girl in shoulder-to-knee bathing costume confronting the vicar before a realistic backcloth of Flamborough Head. Another reads: 'I visit this place every year', 'Are your stays long?', 'Sir! I thought you were a gentleman', striking the period note of 'nut-tish' naughtiness. The shop-girl saying to the bather who has mistaken his machine, 'What can I have the pleasure of showing you, Sir?' makes clear how force of habit will reveal class even when clothes are off. 'Dear dad, Mother and me are having a good time here but I miss the donkeys. When are you coming down? I am your loving son, Freddy'. The message, printed in facsimile writing like those of Raphael Tuck's 'Amewsing Write Away' series, helps those who may need assistance when it comes to putting words together to join in the fashion of card sending.

These Edwardian cards richly combine period photographs with use of colour—achieved by a variety of processes 'all delightfully unnatural'. The characteristic Bamforth *joie-de-vivre* comes out in the sensitively posed figures and scenic realism. 'Oh, we do like to be beside the seaside!' sings the little girl in pink-ribboned hat and pink frock, which she is holding up to show a leg of white drawers in mockery of the straw-hatted 'nut' with his cane, mauve cummerbund, and white ducks on the Blackpool front. 'Accommodation seems scarce here' remarks another 'Johnnie', as he gazes after a fashionable, tightly hobble-skirted figure with pink parasol teetering along the cobbled tram-road to the Tower. 'Oh, John, did you see that gun go off?' asks a stern, caped and bonneted wife in ground-length skirts. Her husband's eye is on the ankle and flounce of petticoat revealed by the charmer crossing the rocks. We are still familiarly at home, in a sense; mother ever watchful, menfolk errant but intimidated. Only the seaside air has 'given us ideas' and emboldened us to let some of them loose. If that's too dangerous the cards will do it for us. Part of their tonic value is to make us feel naughtier than we are, and in our correspondents' eyes to be 'going it'.

With the artists, caricature takes the seaside scene and extends it, in whatever direction, slightly beyond reality—though still keeping close enough for us to recognise the form and impress of the times. The difference comes out in 'A nut with a small screw' with its accompanying drawing of flirtatious fashion-plates, compared with the 'nut' on the Blackpool front. Or in the cleric and the costumed figure at Flamborough, compared with 'Beautifully warm, here' and its 'goofy' parson looking in at the ladies' bathing station. The artist's advantage lies in the heightening of detail and colour and his ability to compose tell-tale situations. 'The Daily Observer' and 'We should like you to be with us' make good use of this. A card's success with the public, it is said, depends on a joke that 'jumps out and hits the prospective correspondent in something between five and fifteen seconds'. Bright colour is a main factor in first attracting the buyer's attention; so the line was obviously one to follow. It's a matter of taste whether one falls for the naturalism of the embracing couple shown on the shore in

And there's lots of girls beside
I should like to be beside

or the couple in exactly the same pose, coloured up, in 'Too busy to write'. One whispers, the other winks.

From the evidence of the cards of the first couple of decades of the twentieth century, the trippers' seaside holiday consisted of beer (in excess), bed-bugs (in superfluity), overcrowding

(in bed, boat, train), sea-sickness (spasmodic), and shortage of cash (chronic)—in spite of which they came home buoyant and bursting with energy. 'By gum! I'm enjoying myself and not 'arf' says Douglas Tempest's father-figure, blue-striped trousers rolled up, wide grin splitting his ruddy face, diminutive pail and spade in each hand. 'Come and have your annual—When father says bathe we all bathe' not only 'knocks' the habits of cleanliness attributed to the working class, but echoes one of Millar and Lang's most successful cards, 'When father says turn, we all turn', with its picture of seven in one lodging house bed. In the short-lived spending spree topers' noses turn to cochineal. 'If you're having champagne don't be asking for a pint pot and giving the show away'. 'I'm on the rocks', cries a fat figure surrounded by the waves; 'Be a sport and send me a fiver'. Another old girl, bulging in mauve, has nothing to come home on but a halfpenny stamp, 'So I look like having to stick it'. Plagued nightly with what they call 'jumpers' in bed (the wall plaque reads 'Seek and ye shall Find'), bothered daily with wind on the sea front, crammed to bursting into trip trains, they well know that only too soon they will be at bench, counter, or loom again. Then perhaps they'll be writing to others 'I hear you're swanking about but don't forget you've to come back to earth'.

The chance to swank about, to be taken for a duchess or more likely a film actress, is one of the fantasy situations that holidays permit and one that the cards both celebrate and correct. (Bamforth's had a song series actually called 'Wonderful Dreams'.) Desire to compensate for work-a-day drabness or class deprivation comes out in most of us. 'Perhaps they'll think you're a film star from Los Angeles' is the caption to one girl's overdressed progress between goggling bystanders down the pier; her turned-in toes and knobbly elbows remind us of the reality. Another red-striped generous figure with men around has 'Mary Pickford isn't in it with me'.

Romance comes in various guises. The girl with the good figure sees herself the cynosure of cameras in the bathing pool. But 'There are some pips lemonading about' tells us how not to overdo it. A hoity-toity girl, posing with her handbag and parasol, is shown, inset, with mop and pail in the same stance. The girl gazing into the eyes of the tall beach-Romeo can say 'I'm certainly looking up since I came here'. To console the also-rans, the bright-eyed scrawny creature in red, for instance, still on the beach, a card reads 'I ain't clicked yet but I'm living in hopes'. Sometimes we are warned of the fragility of such fantasies and romances. For man the hunted, not hunter, the girl with the devastating wink, in white fur and pink hat under a crescent moon (p oo), carries the verse :

Beware the pine-tree's withered branch,
But beware much more this awful glance,
It is your dear friend's best advice—
Excelsior.

But, for the most part, boy (ideal) meets girl (ideal).

Like the 'hidden persuaders' of certain forms of advertising seaside cards induce us to believe in the good time we may, or may not, be buying with our year's savings. Nearly everyone is given a taste of doing what he, or she, would like to do. Henpecked husbands find themselves with each arm round a pretty girl's waist. Housewives soak their corns in the briny, free to laugh and grow fat, away from sink and wash-tub. If the weather is not too good a case of stout brings them 'bottled sunshine' in the digs. Their daughters at the door of the bathing-hut are given peaches-and-cream complexions and charming décolletés on a card to send to absent friends, 'I wish you were going in with me'. The factory worker is simply stretched flat on his back on the warm sand, while an inset of smoking chimneys drifts remotely away like a cloud. At the end of his stay the wild waves will be saying 'Work next week work again next week!' Children score centuries at beach cricket or flash plump, bare bottoms in the breakers—with never a whine. Perhaps mum's good time is most often expressed from a bedroom window overlooking the sea—'Gee, it's nice to know you can turn over and have another ten minutes without the whistle going', or 'Am I enjoying my food? You bet I am when I haven't to get it ready'. The expressions of roseate bliss on all their faces are

By gum! I'm enjoying myself, and not 'arf
I dont want to come home, I know that.

When father says bathe we all bathe
Come and have your annual.

COME ON, BE A SPORT

London Opinion
The Sea-(in)-side smile.

Pleasure smacks!—I'd like to know where the pleasure comes in!

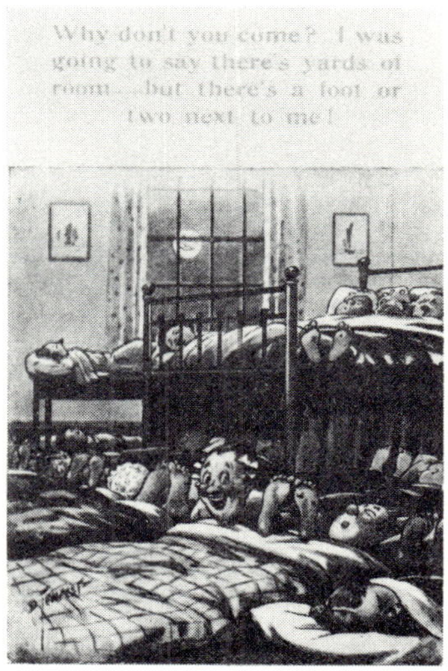
Why don't you come? I was going to say there's yards of room ... but there's a foot or two next to me!

You can tell how I'm enjoying myself if you squint through these!

Plenty moving pictures here and nowt to pay and no tax

the artist's 'hidden persuader'. Only dad, in a card dated 1922, surrounded by the placards advertising daily cruises, donkey rides, fishing trips, chara tours, remarks doubtfully 'Talk about PUT and TAKE!—they TAKE ALL every time here'.

One of the main differences between cards up to the end of the First World War and those of the inter-war period is that the earlier background of harassment, with kids beyond count, matrimonial bliss becoming a 'cross', and husbands defecting to the bottle, fades out. War itself makes little real difference to them: 'Now look here, George, if there's any more of that submarine business I'll smack you in the periscope!' An atmosphere of euphoria and *laisez aller* takes the place of harassment. The motor-coach replaces the char-à-banc, the accent is on having a good time and to H——L with appearances. Since the Boys Came Home flappers' skirts have risen, jazz has replaced ragtime, dance halls have opened, cinemas and cheap cafés have mushroomed, mixed bathing is in, undressing on the beach proceeds in defiance of the authorities, the sexes come together with more freedom than ever before. Everything that seemed so fixed, in convention and class, is seen to dissolve. Women, whose place was the home, have begun to apply to pleasure—seeking the liberation won in factory and office during wartime. They have even learned to go into pubs and pay for their own drinks!

The 'roaring twenties' and 'early thirties' show dad and mum, in their one-piece costumes doing beach gymnastics: their daughter, 'daring' in bra and briefs (1934), kicks up her legs to 'Bet you're giving the lads a treat'. The marriageable one is off on the pillion of a motor-cycle—'I expect you've got on all right but be careful where you get off'. Auntie, now with cigarette in holder, drink, chocolates, sweets, and novel to hand, leans happily back against the breakwater: 'Enjoy yourself lass! You'll have to do as the buzzer says next week'. If a husband casts an eye at the girls' legs on the prom, it is 'Don't be too hard on th'owd lad, it's only once a year'. The mood is permissive, the comparative luxury—'two of fish and three of chips: we are living like Lords', expressive of better conditions, 'fairer do's' all round. Bed-and-breakfast landladies still charged as little as 5s (25p) a night in some streets between the gasworks and the pier. 'Hope you're having a whirling time. Cheerio and the best of luck!' says the caption to the ballroom fox-trotters. Factory girls, who were really 'fast' and not just wanting to be thought so, adopted the crêpe de chine beach pyjama fashion of the Bright Young Things to wear, in cotton, with nothing underneath! All the cards say is 'I'll bet you blotted your copy-

book this summer—*I* couldn't imagine *anybody* clicking with you in those trousers'.

The earlier, sometimes malicious, cards of ugly spinsters, mean landladies, drunken husbands, reflected a harsher working-class world; in the newer world, though it may be no more permanent than a dream, everyone on the cards seems madly happy. Sun shines alike on the fat and thin, there's plenty of drink, for wives as well, but few drunks, and class doesn't count. The new seasiders have the confidence of numbers: the would-be better class avoid 'Wakes' when the big resorts are swamped with them, or else seek the 'select' satellites, Westcliff instead of Southend, St Anne's instead of Blackpool, St Leonard's for Hastings, Hove for Brighton, etc. While the satellites provide for recreation, the pleasure city resorts cater for conviviality. 'I care nothing for nobody here, they don't know me from Adam' or 'If they think I'm somebody, let 'em go on thinking' is the attitude of one in the crowd who are 'setting the pace'. As for the annual dip, all are now 'in the pink' without distinction, literally—matching costumes, no stripes and bowlers. 'Having the time of our lives and letting it rip' sums up the outlook. Only the aloof observer will note: 'There was a huge outing of violent girls, down (in Brighton) for the day from the "Lucky Tip" cigarette factory in London, shouting and sprawling over the town, permeating it with colour and affecting its quality much as a drop of permanganate of potash will affect a tumblerful of water' (*Hangover Square*, Patrick Hamilton).

Popular art tends to be vulgar. The common view is not the most refined or subtle reaction to a situation. Its expression requires bold outlines, strong colours, a certain crude acceptance of humanity in the mass. Bamforth's comic aim 'to portray everyday humour in every walk of life' resembles that of Dickens in *Sketches by Boz* with its sub-title 'Illustrative of Everyday Life and Everyday People' and its seaside exuberance with the Tuggs at Ramsgate. The aim is reinforced by the artists' style in obvious ways; their subtler effects are perhaps a response to more diffuse ideas.

Viewing in mass these seaside cards of the 30s, for example, one is struck by the aura of well-being, the images of health. There is a real glow in the physical exposure, a feeling of *dolce vita* in the sunbathing, the sand games, and dancing. The artists' tone is mellower, smoother, expressive of simple happiness; the actual figures are more lissom or, if fat, less grotesque. The levelling-up of holiday privileges has, by 1936, brought the service industries into line with production industries; so clerks, shop assistants, farm workers as well as spinners, weavers, miners, can look forward to a week's complete change, in

addition to six separate public holidays—and in more and more cases *with pay*. As the gap between the salaried and the wage-earning diminishes, the latter can at last afford the holiday he takes—and soon he will be getting two weeks with pay. There is now less need of fantasy in the situations; money is freer as well as behaviour. 'If I sent you a *tenner* I expect you'd just waltz through it like this . . . so I don't think I'll bother!' Hair can be let down without anxiety: 'People think we're daft: it doesn't matter so long as we have a good time'. Or, with satisfaction—no need to explain, 'I'm one of the crowd'. And in these sun-bathing 30s everybody, on the cards, seems to get brown, all over as far as possible; and all, fat or thin, join in the beach keep-fit class. Like hiking and holiday camps, it's one of the 'musts' of the era. Appropriately, Butlin's slogan of the 30s was 'Holiday with Pay—Holidays with play. A week's holiday for a week's wage'.

The post-Hitler War cards carry this 'corpore sano' frankness and freedom further—and in doing so gradually reveal a change of mood. Dads and mums are figure-conscious now, busily keeping down middle-age spread while still eating more than 'a little of what (they) fancy,' as the 'snoek' and food-restriction period peters out. The young male is modelled on the screen-type athlete, the bathing girl becomes a stylised beauty—in the image of each season's 'entirely NEW kind of girl'—and with woman's magazine perfection of hair and grooming. While the beach-Romeo adopts the class gambit of 'Give 'em the old school tie stuff' and the bar-lounger takes on the knowing airs of a 'spiv', the middle-aged so-called guardians of the young mutter, as they watch shameless displays of undressing on the shore 'WE'RE broadminded' (their behinds agree!).

Meanwhile the comic figures of the less handsome, semi-stereotypes, have a Disney cartoon look. Slickness and know-how are 'in'—over and above natural bounce and brashness. Soon the girls in bikinis will all be wearing 'KISS ME' bands on their American sailor hats or posing to say 'Look me over, boys'. Typists on holiday will no longer find the privilege of freedom enough, but need it underlined by the maid bringing tea to them in bed. Only dad will keep the new 'staggered holidays' and 'admass image' to the traditional lines—by his unsteady exit from the 'Red Lion'.

From the later 50s and into the 60s as spending power spreads, the 'show-biz' trends of holidays by the sea become prominent on the cards. The loud pedal seems to be on everywhere. Townee pleasures—bingo, all-in wrestling, TV stars—are the advertised lures of the big resorts, coupled with huge 'fun fairs' whose amplified 'pop numbers' drown out any whisper of what the wild waves may be saying. The 'digs' of course must have a TV lounge. 'Smashers' with 'vital statistics' flaunt their Lollobrigida bosoms everywhere; 'strip' dominates the side-shows. Beach undress is barely distinguishable from non-dress: the voyeurs can be shocked—or alerted—only by the 'topless'. 'NO HOLDS BARRED—not this week' is the caption to a clutching couple in the moonlight. The exhortation is to LIVE IT UP. The warning GIRLS WHO INDULGE BULGE is not really about food and drink.

'Sauce' is in—it was never out—but more often now it is sauce with a 'blue comedian's' leer. The seaside honeymoon hotel proves only one thing: 'So far so good' says the swain, 'Now let's get off home and find out if you can cook'. (In case such hotels should seem to be 'clip joints' their luggage is labelled 'Just married.') The puns and the jokes are post-Kinsey and post-Chatterley. 'HOW!' captions two rotund figures, male and female, their bellies touching. 'You think *you*'ve got problems' grimaces the youth clasping a mermaid. Beer is not enough: 'When Charlie's had a few pints he starts feeling rosy all over'—exit barmaid of that name.

The artists' style has the same hectic flush that Wolfenden noted about many young people of the time—'as if their metaphoric pulse-rate had to be high to keep pace with the speed of what was happening around them'—with today's image, today's sound, today's gimmick. 'Got this one lined up for you' requires a figure to out-Bardot Bardot with all its suggestion—though in essence no more revealed than the Edwardian charmers of 'Come on, be a Sport'. Only the children seem as wholesome as ever in this 'swinging age'—HAVING FUN DOWN BY THE SEA with the same heady mixture of donkeys and ice-cream, boating and bathing, sandcastles and 'fab' new friends. Or is it the seaside air that has changed?

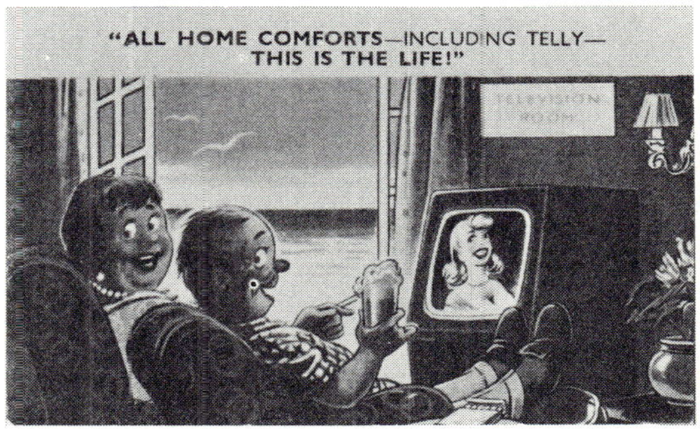

3 'No Place Like Home'

'Family life was the bedrock of society. People lived in much the same way as they had under Queen Victoria, even if many things were done in a less formal manner.' So Mr Macqueen Pope recalling good King Edward's golden days. Change 'bedrock' to 'padlock' and we have Mr Edwin Bamforth's comic record of wedded life a little lower down the social scale.

There was certainly no unfastening of the knot once tied. 'Pleasures of the honeymoon', with its picture of the husband tightening the bride's corset, might change to the card on which an irate 'respectable' wife belabours her spouse with an umbrella, but it reads 'Who said divorce!' As Mr Pope has it, 'Scandal was to be avoided at all costs. Divorce was social death for a woman and not much less for a man'. So friction and faction were confined within four walls. When the parson calls to see the master of the house, a working-class husband with black eye and poker in hand answers: 'Just wait a few minutes. Me and the old girl's in the middle of settling that question'. Only one thing was sure to bring peace to the house—according to this view. 'What is a jubilee, Nellie?' 'Well, twenty-five years is a silver wedding, fifty years is a golden wedding, and when the old man pegs out, that's a jubilee!'

A bill for burial in the Parish of Eccles, 1903, which the writer recently turned out, gives some idea of the Edwardian costs of life—and death. 'Making grave 8s, taking up and laying stone 1s 6d, muffled bell 1s, surplice dues 8s 8d, coffin and shroud £2 10s, car and two carriages £2 14s, two carriers and two coachmen 7s'—total £6 10s 2d (£6.51). This was roughly half a domestic servant's annual wages. 'Girl, 16, as General. 9 months' character: 5s weekly', also 'General, 3 years' character £12', are contemporary adverts. Coal, which the 'general' carried as one of her endless burdens, cost 19s 6d (98p) a ton. A new, six-room house with garden (no rates) could be rented at 8s 6d (42.5p) weekly, whisky was 3s 6d (17.5p) a bottle, cigarettes 3d for ten—at a time when a clerk could look to earn £2 per week. The cards of this period show both sides of 'doing things in a less formal manner', but still expecting 'to ring a bell and have it answered immediately'.

The servant has a lot to put up with. She also sees a lot that goes on, even in well-regulated households. 'Well, Mary, I hope you will like your new place; I don't think you will find me hard to please'. 'Oh, no, madam; I was sure of that when I saw the master.' He may be a nonentity in the house—or a nuisance. Some are bottom-pinchers, others secret drinkers. 'It's quite evident master didn't go to a temperance meeting last night' remarks the 'slavey' with dustpan and shovel, contemplating the hall's mess and disorder. Mistresses can be termagants—sometimes with cause. 'My word if I catch you bending' says one as the servant spies through the bathroom keyhole. Such girls need watching or they'll let one down. 'Where is the page, Mary?' 'He's helping me to clean up after the sweep, m'm'—sooty handmarks on her blouse and apron tell their own tale. The sweep and baker's man for housemaids, the milkman and the lodger for housewives, are seen as the conventional Don Juans of an essentially moral lower and lower middle class.

If one is a 'jew-'ell' of a servant, another breaks every other vase she dusts. They're so simple too, or else stupid on purpose. 'Are you sure your mistress is not in?' asks the vicar. 'I hope you don't doubt her word, sir.' Or, in the kitchen, 'Where's that chicken pie I told you to heat up for me?' 'Well, M'm, you told me to 'eat it and I 'ave.' As for cooks, they're always ready to take liberties—and 'followers' into the house. 'I've changed my mind, Mary; I shall stop at home, so you may go out this evening.' 'Thank you, mum, but I've changed my mind,

Pleasures of the Honeymoon.

Who said Divorce!

JACK TAKES TEN!

'WE CAN'T EXPECT THE LAMP OF LOVE TO BURN FIERCELY AT OUR AGE LASS!!'
'NO — BUT THERE SHOULD AT LEAST BE A GLOW FROM THE PILOT LIGHT!!'

"WHAT IS A JUBILEE, NELLIE?"
"WELL, TWENTY-FIVE YEARS IS A SILVER WEDDING, FIFTY YEARS IS A GOLDEN WEDDING, AND WHEN THE OLD MAN PEGS OUT, THAT'S A JUBILEE!"

It's quite evident Master didn't go to a temperance meeting last night.

WHERE IS THE PAGE, MARY?
HE'S HELPING ME TO CLEAN UP AFTER THE SWEEP, 'M.

too, and prefer to stay in' (on the policeman's knee).

To this comedy of the middle class, where appearances matter, the life models and carefully arranged backgrounds of Bamforth's cards add realities of dress and detail. The red plush drapes and lace curtains, the picture and panelling, the handsome carved organ of 'The HIM she likes best' vividly recall the tastes and subterfuges of another age.

With lower class subjects a rougher indication of actual conditions comes through. 'Owing to the increased cost of living we are having to economise': the room's bare floor, empty grate, peeling plaster, wooden chairs and candle in bottle frame a somewhat unconvincing couple. The comment, though, is apposite. Fear of rising costs was the main factor in the election of 1906, when Chamberlain and the Unionists proposed Tariff Reform. The industrial north then solidly and successfully backed the Liberal Free Trade opposition, whose slogan was 'Your Food Will Cost You More', and, incidentally, swept the Labour Party into Parliament for the first time. 'Everybody works but father', another apposite reference—to unemployment, which caused civil disturbances in Manchester during the summer of 1905—has a shirt-sleeved figure carrying mop, pail, three children, and a candlestick, whilst a bundle drops on the lino. In style it belongs to the tradition of music-hall sketch. As does the pawnbroker scene: 'Please muvver wants sixpence on this 'ere frying pan!' 'Hallo! It's hot!' 'Yes, muvver's just cooked the sossidges an' wants

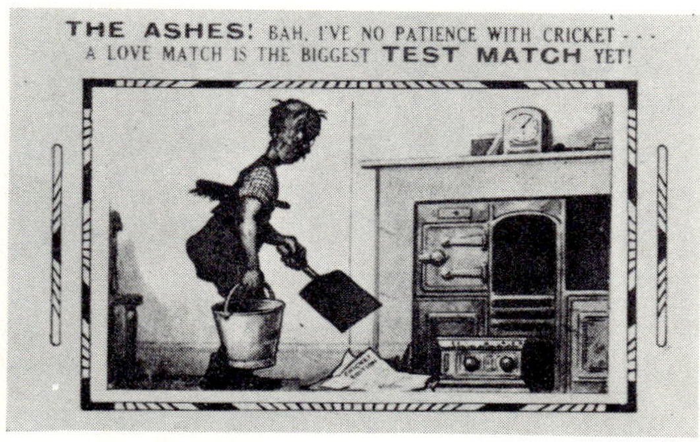

money for the beer.' More realistic are the boys sparring in a back street, with genuine background and street-urchin look. 'Wot's the good of fighting wiv you? If I gave you a black eye it wouldn't show on your dirty face.'

For realistic studies of mean streets one turns to the artists. 'An Englishman's Home', a card with a drawing by Harrison reproduced from 'London Opinion', strikes the note. It belongs to the same world as Phil May's sketches of costers and cabbies and tramps. The handcart 'flit' recalls another period piece:

> We had to move away
> 'Cos the rent we couldn't pay . . .
> Off went the cart with the home
> packed in it
> I walked behind with my old cock linnet

sung by Marie Lloyd.

So long as the lower and middle class myth about marriage remains that 'however much the man and wife may want to kick over the traces, when it comes to the point they stick it out as best they can', one of the card's aims is to offer some sort of condolence or fantasy relief. They embroider it with the wry humours of bringing up a family. In George Orwell's analysis, the comic conventions are that marriage only benefits woman, man being by nature a seducer, that

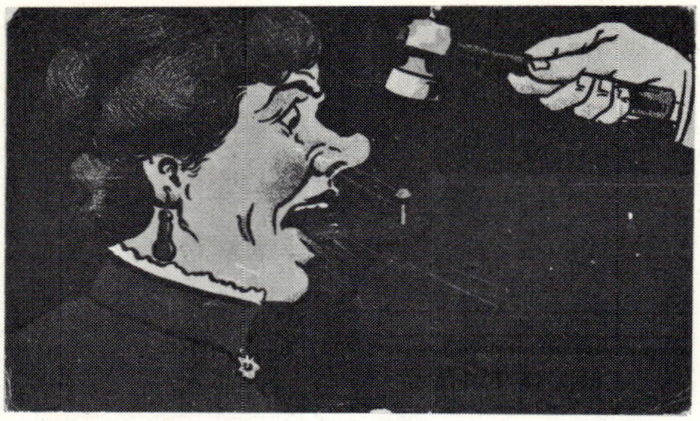

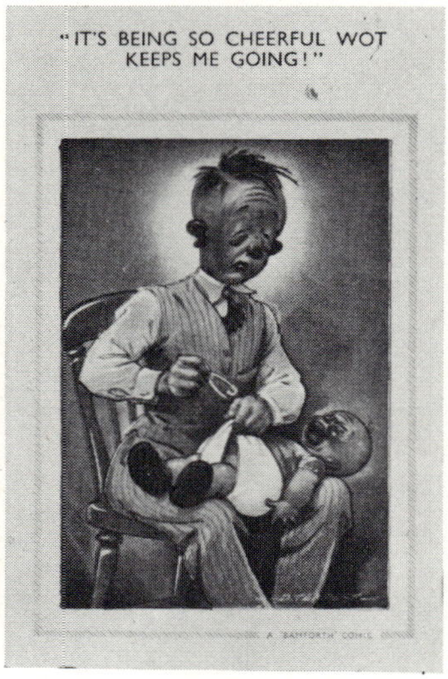

sex-appeal vanishes about the age of twenty-five, that there is no such thing as a happy marriage, and no man ever gets the better of a woman in argument. First it's a 'Sequence of Events'—girl, pursuing man, cupid, parson, nursemaid, and baby. Soon the vow 'Nothing shall ever come between us' will have a howling infant occupying the middle of the bed. The later philosophic 'We're pushing along very nicely' shows dad behind a double-twin pram and two more toddlers tagging on. As they grow up and the strain begins to tell, 'Say, father, why did you marry mamma?' has its riposte 'Oh, so you've begun to wonder, too, have you?' During wartime the broken-in family man, with his apron and brush, can grimly quip, 'Don't know what the single man's grumbling at—Compulsion's been my lot for years'. When a dog joins the family and husband ventures, 'You'll never get him to do as he's told', the wifely reply will come 'Certainly I will: you were just as awkward in the beginning'. It's the same for us all suggest the cards, it's part of *la condition humaine*. It could be worse: just look at this chap—'If you want a house you can have mine—if you'll take the missus with it'.

With Lloyd George as Chancellor (under the Liberal Government) old age pensions and the Labour Exchange system arrived in 1909; a contributory scheme of national insurance followed in 1911. They were the early landmarks of a new era in our social history and forerunners of the post-1945 welfare state with its comprehensive 'security'. As the cards show, these influences on the Englishman's home or his outlook from it, had their comic aspect too. Like various amenities they were not always applied in the spirit in which they were intended. Satiric artists, quick to seize on the misused amenity, the misinterpreted or misapplied 'welfare service', found a laugh line that is not yet exhausted. To some extent the slum-dweller replaced the 'swell' on the cards as a stock figure of fun—with a hint of malice as he battened on the benefits provided by the taxpayer, or gradually reached up to middle-class comforts.

In amenities, the obvious comes first: mod cons. 'I could do with these patent wash-basins but the water runs out before I've time to wash my face', complains the labourer come to town when confronted with a pedestal wc. Of the electric globe the same backwoods type grumbles, 'I could do with these new patent lights but they take too much blowing out!' Both were 'new-fangled' ideas to the many in the first decade of the century: signs of comfort, like the greater abundance of food, clothing, bedding, furniture available, that slowly filtered down the social scale as 'real wages' improved.

After the war such commodities were up in price again. 'It's got to happen sometime—things must come down' remarks the husband of 1921 shielding his wife's limbs and embarrassment with the *Daily Wail*. But it was in houses that universal need was felt. 'I think it's high time the Government got on with this house-building scheme' comes from a dog whose kennel has been 'taken over'. A roadman's hut appears in danger of being snapped up as a 'villa'. The traditional comic consolation is: 'Seeking a home? Well, take my advice, young feller, and don't bother. You're all right as you are' from a husband of long standing.

The same situation succeeds both wars. 'Doin' a bit of grandmothering, are you, Mrs Flint?' 'Aye! Just been taking him to have his name (*he* is six months old) put down for a council house.' Likewise with labour-saving devices. The contraptions alter, but not the attitudes of those newly involved with them. 'It's my new washing machine,' says the lady *in* the MARVO electric washer, 'it's a bit strange at first, but once you get used to it, THE SENSATION'S LOVELY.' And in spite of new appliances old methods persist. 'Could I borrow your carpet-beater, Mrs Clegg?' 'You could, but he hasn't come home yet.' Or, to come full circle in the mod con department, husband says to wife in their new

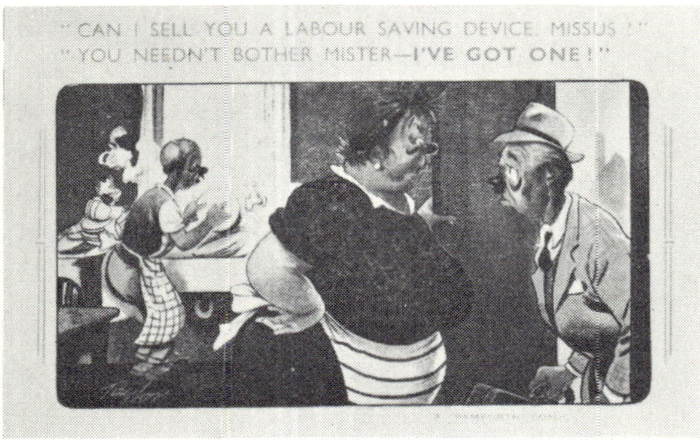

council flat: 'You've got everything you want here, luv!' 'Aye, lad—but when I pulled the lever on that washing machine the clothes all disappeared!' After the newly married couple have asked the furniture salesman to 'show us one of these new-fangled REPRODUCTION suites' the next stage of domestic progress, automation, appears to be already in the pipe-line. Confronted by a news poster 'AUTOMATION DOES THE WORK OF 20 MEN' the wife with nine or ten children in tow breaks out, 'Blimey, we can do without automation at our house, Fred.'

Not only the 'slowness' of the lower classes but the speed of admass science-in-the-home is being 'got at' in these jokes. With welfare, on the other hand, it is speed of adaptability to benefits, coupled with suspicion of bureaucratic methods, that raises the laughs.

From the outset National Insurance came in for quips. 'Your money'th quite thafe, Ikey, I have a leetle expectation from Lloyd George' says the young man about to buy a 30s (£1.5) ready made suit. 'Please, I want my thirty shillings' as the little girl holds her doll up to the GPO counter with its notice about 'Maternity Benefits'. The cheeky chappie receives *his* money order to the words of the 'hit' song 'Hold your hand out, naughty boy'. So in a later day the full flow of state services redoubles the flow of jokes about the beneficiaries. *Dentist*: 'Will you have gas, madam?' 'I'm having a light of some sort, mister: yer not messing about wi' me in't dark.' Or, when she is confronted by officialdom, the answer, like that of the old housemaid to her mistress, is provocative. 'How many children, madam? And what is your husband's employment?' 'Fourteen kids, an' my husband's an able seaman, Sir.' National Health presents its opportunities, no less than National Insurance. 'I tell you, you don't need any more spectacles!' 'OK Mister. Keep your shirt on. I'll GO GET SOME TEETH INSTEAD.' As does also the Ministry of Labour. 'Is your wife REDUNDANT?' 'I hope not, mister; we've got six already.' As to PLANNED FAMILIES, the little man supporting ten says to the Adviser: 'We've lost the ruddy plans!'

By this time the housewife is used to getting

what she doesn't want at counter and clinic. 'I was in a long queue last week, lass!' 'What did you get, rabbit or fish?' 'Neither, I got VACCINATED.' So at the mobile radiography unit one asks 'Are you going to be X-rayed, love?' of the young wife with the pram. 'Not flipping likely—I HAVEN'T GOT OVER WHAT THEY FOUND LAST TIME.' The old trick of malapropism plays its part in this confusion of new techniques and jargon. 'He's an absolute bounder' says one gossip to another. 'He OUGHT TO BE OSTRACISED.' 'Nay, Fanny, that's going a bit *too* far.'

'Over the backyard fence'—gossip shop of all housewives—offers boundless scope to observers of the domestic scene. The criticism, commiseration, curiosity, spite, and back-chat, of people living cheek by jowl and watchful of their neighbour's least move comes out here as nowhere else. United in their attitude to 'Them'—'The people who give you your dole, call you up, tell you to go to war, fine you, made you split the family in the 'thirties to avoid a reduction in the Means Test Allowance'—the lower classes are shown to be hyper-conscious about each other's doings and departures from the norm. Richard Hoggart has pinned this down as 'acting beyond the ideas of the group', 'acting posh', 'giving y'self airs', 'getting above y'self', 'being lah-de-dah', 'thinking y'self too good for other people', 'being stuck up', 'turning y'noses up at other people', 'acting like Lady Muck', or shocking by infringing the taboos implied in 'What will the neighbours say?'

The card artists, equally alert to northern inflections, have noted the pattern of both sympathies and antagonisms over the years.

The back-chat is crude and to the point: 'Oh, yes, I know what you're thinking.' 'Well, why don't you go then?'; or personal and obvious, from two bulging figures, 'Well, I'd rather have my bay-window than your back porch, missus'. The commiseration is in the look: 'My old man's a good'n, he makes the beds, washes the steps, and wipes the pots for me!' 'You're damned lucky, mine only wipes the floor with me.' Observation is accurate, visually and verbally: 'Aye, they've been drawing their divvy today' as one thin supports one stout woman home. Sensitivity is limited: 'You haven't walked through the streets with that (a china article) in your hand?' 'No, you fool, I came on the tram.' Comment usually has a double edge. 'Aye, we've shifted next door to the Labour Exchange, so me husband can be nearer his work.' Nothing, anti-posh, is missed. 'What's the dust-cart there for today?' 'Perhaps for fag-ends . . . Fellow next door has decided to get his wife a wrist-watch, wi' coupons.' Snubs to curiosity reveal all: 'I didn't know yer husband had gone away.' 'Yer not supposed to. He was dispatched to his destination in a plain van.' The norm is upheld: 'He's a lazy beggar: he even married a widow with five kids.' If things look like getting out of hand a husband may step in with: 'Give up shouting then! Have you forgotten what happened to the walls of Jericho?—and this is only a council house!'

On its own level this domestic humour could be regarded as coming somewhere between Rowlandson's image of humanity 'coarse, gross and vulgar' and the painter Lowry's image of it as 'sad, comic and largely futile'—an image from the Salford scene in the 20s. A regular theme is that ambiguous complaint, constipation. As a topic it crops up too regularly to pass over and is underlined in a variety of ways. 'Why's your little Willie sitting all day doing nothing, Mrs Briggs?' asked about the boy in the backyard, brings the pregnant reply: 'Nay, I don't know: I've been that way meself all week.' Or, Willie's answer to the biology teacher asking her class about the position of various organs, such as the bowels: 'I don't know where they are Miss: mam

moves 'em every Wednesday.' Then there is the apocryphal letter: 'Please TEACHER, Nellie hasn't come because she hasn't been, so I've given her summat, and when she's been she'll come. Yours truly Mrs Jubbs.' More recently, Mrs Briggs, asked what she is taking for her chronic complaint, is shown carrying a portable 'telly' which she says 'passes the time'. Jokes about Kruschen salts, Beecham's pills and 'Eat More Fruit' are almost as frequent.

It is not merely a case of mentioning the unmentionable, the sort of relief that vulgar jokes give to the ancient dualism of body and soul, the earthy and the pure in man. Two other examples will perhaps provide the key. In one, singing from 'down the yard' is explained as someone ensuring privacy while 'sitting', because the lock's broken. In the other, the husband, looking through a furnished house advertised as having all 'mod cons', peers in vain under the bed for a 'go'sunder'. Anxiety about bowel functions is part of the built-in inheritance of lower class life: nowadays, in the form of 'inner cleanliness', it is exploited among the middle classes also by such means as TV commercials for breakfast foods. But for those who have come from mean streets within memory, the shared wc at the end of the row, the waits and subterfuges, the lack of proper privacy, the use of 'articles' indoors instead, have all left their trauma. The 'hopper' earth-closet was invented in 1860 by a clergyman; more convenient wcs came considerably later into common use. Worry about performances of the function has not yet disappeared with better surroundings;—nor about the burdensome obligation of 'toilet training' children. Resistance to 'regularity' may in some degree be a sign of unwilling conformity with social habits, as well as an old anxiety symptom. Both are 'shown up' by new conditions; the jokes externalise and so help to neutralise the worry.

According to the planners a 'classless society' is to replace the older one of 'knowing one's place', 'not trying to get above oneself', and 'standing together with one's mates'. It will be a society where the occupations and incomes of the individuals may vary, but they will live in much the same environment, enjoy similar standards of health and education, find jobs open to all according to ability, intermarry freely with each other, and be immune from the more degrading forms of poverty. The outward signs of it are already appearing on the cards. They are largely negative signs—like the fading-out of the servant joke. The absence of indications of distinctive dress, furniture, food and, progressively, of manners and language, for the working class 'subjects' is significant now that this class is no longer to be thought of as segregated in vast industrial ghettoes. As button-pushers replace manual workers, semi-skilled machine attendants take over from labourers, and much of the dirt and sweat of work is succumbing to technology, higher pay packets, overtime and independent 'spare time' jobs follow. The resulting similarity between white-collar and blue-collar is translated into car-ownership (instead of proletarian push-bike) for all, new consumer 'durables' (on HP) in every house, and 'Woman's Magazine' ideas for every other housewife.

The cartoonist David Low saw in the 50s only 'lower-class workers', 'middle-class workers', and 'upper-class workers'—making up 'the endless middle' as it has been termed. The old 'face-to-face' living of the street is imperceptibly changing to the new 'window-to-window' living of the avenue. And there the old working class share most of the attributes of the now 'new poor' white-collar class, except its former competitive spirit, while the struggle of the old middle class to keep up appearances and differentials becomes ever more difficult.

This picture of social change is as yet truer of the south than of the north of England, where traditional strands in the pattern of society have been more durable; but from the card-view of life the joke can no longer be directed at a lower class from a superior middle. It is 'on' the middle. 'Come on Lil, you don't NEED an electric blanket' says the young workman/husband, but there is no doubt that he could buy her one. The young father washes, dries, and gets baby's wind up—in the newest automatic washer. 'Why don't you try to stop Dad saying MUCK instead of DIRT, mother?' 'Nay luv, it's taken me twenty years to get him to call it MUCK'—reveals a consciousness of the need to 'level up' in manners to match consumer standards. 'I wonder how we amused ourselves before we got Television?' said by a mother of eight, *implies* a new direction in family life.

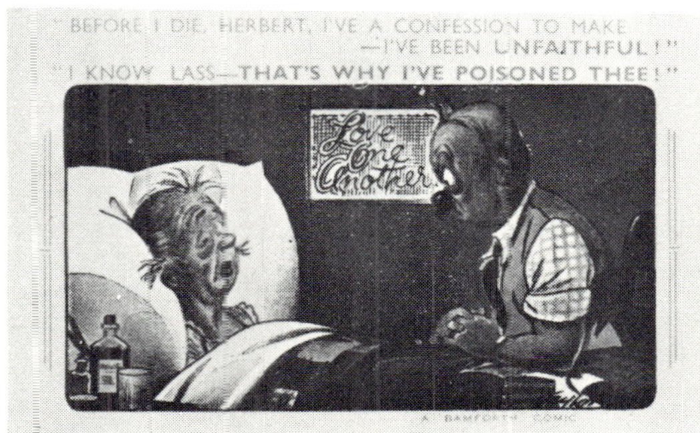

Two post-war jokes, at least, in the Bamforth 'padlock' tradition, preserve and remind these 'new lookers' of the old cutting edge and basic principles of domesticity. 'There's sixpence short in your wages this week. Are you KEEPING ANOTHER WOMAN?' And the macabre 'Before I die, Herbert, I've a confession to make. I've been unfaithful!' 'I know, lass—THAT'S WHY I'VE POISONED THEE!' The motto on the wall reads 'Love one another'.

4 *'Smile, smile, smile'*

Next to the pale buff Field Postcard sent from the front to those at home with the conventional understatement 'safe and well' the picture card sent from home to the troops was the most important single bond of morale in popular currency throughout the First World War.

Its use in war had a two-way ancestry. For Paris, under siege by the German army in 1870, there was no other contact with the outer world than by balloon. 'How odd, all the news and letters we get from Paris now coming by balloons and carrier pigeons,' notes Kilvert. Small, inexpensive balloons, able to carry four kilograms of mail were designed, and, weight being important, the Council of Defence encouraged civilian use of the newly invented postcard, first issued officially by the Austrian Government, 1869. It weighed only three grammes. The 'balloon cards' on sale at tobacconists and bookshops were usually decorated with the tricolour or a similar device. Large numbers of Breton troops also were out of touch with their families and had no easy way of sending news. It was the idea of a stationer near Le Mans, Léon Bernardeau, to design a picture card for their use. On it stacked weapons, drums, and banners formed a frame for the name and address of delivery. The idea caught on and the card with its caption, *Souvenir de la Défense Nationale—Famille, Honneur, Patrie, Liberté*, was reprinted in bulk for the whole French army.

From the first to the last days of the First World War picture cards to send to the front were widely bought; they reflect both the country's need and public mood. The cards issued by Bamforths fall into three classes.

Rallying to the Flag: and under this heading are included the later, less frank or friendly, persuasions to patriotic duty.

Remembering: of husband, sweetheart, son and by them of children, wife, mother, dad in messages ever more poignant as the 'sacrifice' went on.

Comic Relief: these cards, like Bairnsfather's cartoons, gave an air of assurance for the essential reply to the catchphrase 'Are we downhearted?'

There were cards also of the kind Bernardeau had designed for the Franco-German war, message cards from men in the field—though more likely to be used from the training depot. This type neither bulks so large nor registers the fluctuations of general mood and need.

> We've got the ships and the boys in blue,
> We've got the MAN to guide them too.

The card, one of the 'Patriot' series, shows Admiral 'Jackie' Fisher in full fig on his quarter-deck. He'd got *carte blanche* to order 612 new ships for the Navy! Another portrays the star-spangled scarlet tunic, sash and sword, the virile sweeping moustaches, whose owner made a clarion call to all Britons:

> Bravo, Kitchener! say what you want
> No one shall say you nay;
> And the world shall know where our bugles blow
> We've a MAN at the head today.

'The greatest recruiting sergeant England has ever known,' he was called.

They stand together, on a third card, in a frame of draped union jacks, with the white cliffs of Dover in the background and above their heads the words:

> Who mocks at the flag, the flag of the free,
> Dies like a dog, by land or by sea.

To show that what we said, though it sounded like something out of Henty, our allies also meant, another group with flags, fleur de lys, rose, and eagle shows President Poincaré, King

George V, and the Czar of Russia: 'One Heart, One Mind, One Aim: Vengeance! Victory! Untarnished Fame!'

It was the mood of war's beginning, fought as a 'war to end war', to make the world safe for democracy, to right the wrong done to Belgium, and sure to be over by Christmas. While Rupert Brooke in well turned sonnets was thanking God 'Who has matched us with His hour' for the bugles that brought Honour back 'as a King, to earth', the majority of the less long-haired boys were sending cards, already printed with a verse, 'TO MY PAL':

> Don't you just wish you were here, long with me?
> The drilling is fine and the life is free,
> The boys are all right and the fare's not bad,
> It's really A1 to be training, lad.

A devotional spirit was genuinely abroad at the beginning: instead of the anticipated 100,000 in six months the 'Kitchener Wants You' appeal brought 500,000 volunteers in the first month. With it went an overflow of sentiment, always associated afterwards with the 'Great War', and evident in such things as pocket editions for the trenches of *The Songs of a Sentimental Bloke* by the Australian C. J. Dennis which ran into thousands. Then, as the romantic, crusading conception of war turned out false, there was a strong strain of anti-sentiment. Both come out in the songs that soldiers sang: the sentiment on the postcard versions of revue and 'ragtime' favourites, the other strain in the battalion parodies of popular ballads. As the sentiment increased its pathos, while the 'war to end war' came to look as if *it* would never end, so the satire sharpened its bite. But it was *not* printed on postcards.

Up to May 1915, when recruits were all volunteers, the average age of second lieutenants or 'temporary gentlemen' was twenty-one and war weariness had not made itself felt. The local padre, seeing a draft off from the depot, could say 'And now God go with you. I will go with you as far as the station'—and get away with it. Trench life—the men getting soup in a ruined house in a ruined village, like Festubert, with the moon shining through matchwood skeleton rafters and dusky figures filing across the morasses and ditches and old earthworks—was of the Bairnsfather 'Old Bill' variety. It was borne more or less cheerfully as prelude to the BIG PUSH. 'Everywhere we go seems such a long way' was chief complaint of the infantryman. So far there had been Mons, with its supporting 'angels' and the Marne, in a war of movement; then Ypres, twice attacked, and the stagnation of the whole front—a strip of no-man's land at places only fifty yards wide, winding from the Channel coast to the French frontier with Switzerland. The large scale losses of Loos and Gallipoli's disaster, whose bones and billycans and bullet clips visiting 'Anzacs' still turn up on the beaches and in the gullies, were to come in the summer and autumn.

The songs on the postcards were in the well accented music-hall tradition, either of gusto or plangent emotion. They came in sets of two, three, or four, with one verse of song to each and life model figures to illustrate the action. 'Little Grey Home in the West', four verses, a favourite of early 1915, has an Ivor Novello-ish soldier leaning first on sandbags against a shell-torn landscape and lurid studio skies, then pipe-in-mouth against the wall of a honeysuckle covered cottage door. 'Tipperary', the 1914 top tune, is recalled again, to a background of shell-burst, in 'Somewhere in France, dear Mother':

> Out in a trench 'midst the Belgian and French,
> The Young Irish soldier lay down,
> In the midst of the fight took his first chance to write
> To his mother in Tipperary town.

'Somewhere', 'someday'—wistful, shadowy words—occur often in the lyrics of both world wars. 'Somewhere a Heart is waiting', 'Somewhere a Voice is calling', 'Somewhere in sunset land', 'In the misty land of Someday', 'Somewhere in France with you', are all on these cards. The later tunes include 'Somewhere I'll find you' or 'We'll meet again, don't know where, don't know when' which itself repeats the first war's 'Until we meet again'.

Towards the end of the war's second year 'The Long, Long Trail' took pride of place along with 'Keep the Home Fires Burning'. 'Home' and 'Homeland', 'Mother' and 'Motherland', were the song-writer's keynotes in all themes of devotion to duty and endurance. The 'Long Trail' card has a haloed inset of the girl in the land of the soldier's dream, the other a family circle in the glow of the hearth.

From the grim years of Verdun and the Big,

and barren, Push on the Somme with its 60,000 British casualties in the first day of fighting, 420,000 altogether, and from early 1917 when German submarines began sinking at sight and Vimy Ridge and Arras proved in vain, came some of the most stirring and haunting songs of the whole war. Military service was now compulsory. So Florrie Forde's 'Pack up your Troubles in your old Kit Bag' was the only remedy if 'Take me back to dear old Blighty' failed. George Robey and Violet Lorraine's revue song 'If you were the only girl in the world' with its unforgettable tune and 'God send you back to me' released the intense feelings of separation on both sides of the Channel. 'When you come home'—'you that I long for near and far, you that I follow like a star' expressed brave, yet diminishing hope:

> Day may be weary, weary and long,
> You will come home at evensong.

The singer shown on the card is already wearing black. 'Roses of Picardy'—how many roses there are in these pictures!—came in the same year:

> But there's one rose that dies not in Picardy:
> 'Tis the rose that I keep in my heart.

As the juggernaut of war ground on the mood had changed. From Brooke's glorification of the soldier to the hard actualities of Robert Service's 'Rhymes of a Red-Cross Man', questioning 'if war ever, ever can be right' (these verses were dedicated to the memory of his brother, killed in action with the Canadians, August 1916);

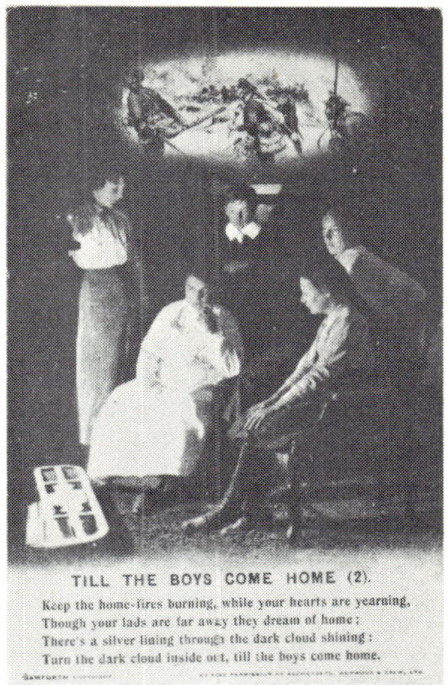

from Sassoon's outcry of horror at man's madness to Owen's and Rosenberg's agonised pathos. When the average life expectancy of subalterns on the Western Front was only three months it seemed as if the brave, helpless 'ragtime infantry' were simply fed into the slaughter by blundering obstinate generals. 'Lions, led by donkeys', said Ludendorff, a little hastily; but it is noticeable how popular pride in military heroes forsook the officer's mess for the barrack-room. There were no prayers or passing bells for those who died as cattle, no shrouds or candles: only

> The pallor of girls' brows shall be their pall,
> Their flowers the tenderness of patient minds
> And each slow dusk a drawing down of blinds.

In the cards death is shown as more decent, but no less frequent. Whether in the soldier pictured lying on his dying bed of 'Mother kissed

me in my dream'; or 'I hear you calling me' and 'on your grave the mossy grass is green'; or in the 'Soldier's Farewell', 'How can I bear to leave thee', with its attendant nurse and spectral form to whom he 'whispers soft while dying'—the note throughout is funereal. These are the real 'tear-jerkers', as some have called Bamforth's cards. Wives and sweethearts left behind, sorrowing parents and lonely graves, a little girl crying her eyes out, 'I want to kiss my soldier daddy', are their repeated themes. The emotional charge that they carry flows from the endless list of casualties, the communal grief of a nation. It ranges from 'Just before the Battle, Mother' and 'Let me die with my face to the foe':

> Farewell, Mother, you may never, you may never, Mother,
> Press me to your heart again;
> But oh, you'll not forget me, Mother, you will not forget me,
> If I'm numbered with the slain

to 'Just a Plain Silver Locket', 'the one thing on earth that is left me' that tells of a broken heart. Here the tears of the wife and inset of a wooden cross combine in a message surely too painful for solace. It was of this period that war artist Paul Nash complained that, officially, he wasn't allowed to put dead men in his pictures 'because they apparently don't exist!', and Robert Graves recorded that the only song his Welsh battalion sang about war was 'Oh, my, I don't want to die, I want to go home'.

The many cards invoking God or well loved hymns make clear that solace was not to be found on earth. 'In God's own keeping', 'Lord, let not my sacrifice be in vain', 'Come unto Me', 'Abide with Me', 'My God, my Father', 'O love that wilt not let me go', and 'Sun of my soul, thou Saviour dear' are just a few of them.

Fortunately for morale this vein was not the only one. Marching songs such as 'Way down in Tennessee', 'Dixieland', 'Down Texas Way' helped to take minds off the crippling mud and crucifying wire. Such images as 'dancing like a crazy loon' neath a harvest moon to a Southern tune made cards fresh and cheering. The songs hinted also that from where the tunes and the munitions were coming fresh forces of men would soon be arriving. In 1918 'Over There', from a London revue, told its hearers

> That the Yanks are coming, the Yanks are coming . . .
> We'll be over, we're coming over
> And we won't be back till it's over, over there.

The cards now offer pictorial versions of

America's Mighty Army. In the picture to verse three of 'Over There' a trio of Germany's boastful war lords, drinking good luck to the coming 'Day', *Der Tag*, are warned that their doom is fast approaching and 'now *they* stand at bay'.

The mood was premature. Haig's special Order of the Day, 11 April 1918, 'with our backs to the wall and believing in the justice of our cause each one of us must fight on until the end' hints at the gravity of the next to the last great German offensive. Passchendaele had been 'won' at bitter cost—300,000 casualties—in the previous year.

Haig's Chief-of-Staff, visiting the fighting zone for the first time after the three months' 'battle of the mud' was over, burst into tears: 'Good God, did we really send men to fight in that?' Now it was abandoned: but the Allied line in Flanders did not break. A last series of German assaults, which twice carried them to the Marne, was eventually held. The tide turned. Its new momentum began with a series of Allied attacks all along the front from Ypres to Verdun. By September British troops had advanced beyond the Hindenburg line. In November the Canadians re-entered Mons and the British army was back where it had started in 1914.

One of the last songs of the war has the crisp lilt of renewed confidence—'Give me a Blighty girl, a Blighty girl for me'. Soon after came 'The bells are ringing, For me and my girl, The birds are singing, For me and my girl'. War ended: but three-quarters of a million men failed to come back to Blighty to claim their girls, in what for want of a better word was called Peace.

Alongside the patriotic cards and the cards of sentiment—and glamour cards of the provocative Kirchner girls in lacy coloured lingerie that delighted those in 'dug-outs'—countless comic-relief subjects were sent. The other cards embodied the various emotions of a nation at war. These follow its course with echoes of all the poster slogans, regulations and stringencies,

the everyday hardships both in and out of uniform. Their wry humour may have helped to take the sting out of the real thing. Bamforth's 'witty series', cards drawn by artists instead of based on life models, reinforce propaganda, but with a lighter hand; at the same time they give vent to the feelings of the man in the street at being 'messed about'.

'WANTED'—an echo of Kitchener—'five minutes with the bloke who said "It's clothes that make the man" '. The caption comes above a Tommy blinkered by his hat and in a shambles of a uniform sizes too large for him. 'Are YOU in this?' might well be the slogan! Another, a means of recruiting subtler than the Government's poster 'Women of Britain say—GO!', shows a cheerful old sweat, kitbag tucked under his arm, hat cocked over the wink in his eye, and, inset, a typical nagging wife. 'On the Q.T. it's been a champion get-out for me.' Later an even more seasoned figure returns, clay pipe in mouth, arm in sling, sturdy legs in puttees, to be greeted by a music-hall type of wife: 'Never mind, as long as you've given the Germans a taste of what I've had for years—you've done your duty'.

In similar vein 'Somewhere in France' shows a smart young cavalryman with spurs, riding crop, leather gloves, and a smile on his ruddy face supporting the waist of a mademoiselle—far too classy for 'Armenteers'. Then, as measures for maintaining the supply of troops grew sterner, comic cards could take the edge off a little. 'I don't think you'll mind being called up by me' shows a delightful 'persuader' in furs and smart little hat at the telephone. Or, a tiny military figure with a large and cheery potato head says: 'I've summat to swank about; I'm going in the trenches and that's more than some of you are doing!' 'It's better to be a "good old has-been" than a "never was" ' runs the message above a terrier in service hat, one eye and one paw bandaged. It was better also, as persuasion, than the moral blackmail of 'What did YOU do in the Great War, Daddy?'

Details of the period abound. A khaki brassard with a red crown on it, issued to those attested but not yet serving, hangs on the bedpost of a civilian cowering under the sheets at home: the caption is 'I'm expecting being called up soon'. The Derby scheme of 'moral obligation' upset some people, but in the later deterioration of war-temper brutality takes its place. Nowhere was it clearer than in the patrio-sadistic reporting of the Press and the anti-German atrocity posters. When the plump conscientious objector is facing a Kitchener-moustached colonel, with 'tribunal rules' before him, the card reflects this attitude:

'What's your trade?'
'Pork butcher!'
'You don't mind killing pigs, then?'
'No!'
'Right! Just the man we want!'

As Sassoon noted, even mild old English ladies talked about German 'hell-hounds'.

After the entry of the USA—'300,000 a month, that's the stuff to give 'em' shows a Yankee trooper in close embrace with an English girl—the Tommy's image and his attitude to the enemy brightens. One with jaunty tin hat and grin is shown riding towards the clearing station on 'Fritz's' back: 'Gee up: I'll get you a job on the sands when the war's over'. Last of all the uniform jokes, on the recruit, is put right.

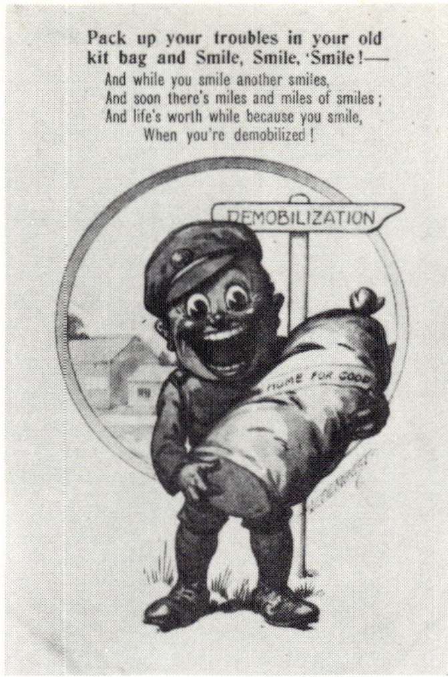

He appears now, half in cap, tunic, and polished leather belt, half in striped tie, stiff white collar, and smart suit: 'Glad to hear you've been promoted to Mister!' It's demob at last!

The Navy is featured less often than from its tradition and early send-off might have seemed likely. By comparison with the soldiers' battles, the sailors' war *looked* undramatic. Jutland, 1916, was the only occasion when the two grand fleets were engaged in European waters. A ready phrase when land campaigns were seen to go wrong was 'Thank Gawd, we've got a Navy'. But apart from a few cracks of the obvious sort—'I saw you having your bit of revenge the other day' (Girl in arms of sailor with *Revenge* on hat-band) or the tearful boy in sailor suit holding his middle and crying 'Wow-wow!—I've had some Turkish Delight and it's got into my Dardanelles', the Navy and its 'dreadnoughts' remain in the background. They come, of course, into the song cards featuring 'Land of Hope and Glory' etc.

Sailors had their own theme song, 'It's the Navy, it's the Navy that's Britannia's pride and joy', but their task seemed too remote or too much under 'sealed orders' for comic relief. The needs of 'security' and fears of admitting losses also had effect. In 'Day by Day' the sailor who was 'bidding his sweetheart good-bye, one sunny summer day', fails to return—picture of sinking frigate—but only because 'out on the bounding main a storm had struck the ship'. Very occasionally a light-hearted reference to other perils comes in. 'I'm not afraid of torpedoes, but I thought I saw *something*' says the small boy looking down below his middle in the bath. Almost the same picture comes on a Donald McGill card, where a Churchillian boy in bath-tub, one hand under water, the other holding aloft a Union Jack, is made to say 'What we have we hold!'

On the Home Front, stringency and security find plenty of wry, humorous relief. It is doubly valuable in war, when after truth, humour is always the next casualty. Stringencies included 'daylight saving'—almost the only lasting effect of World War I on British life—workers' holidays suspended, food shortages, 'starred trades', special 'home service', air raid precautions, and dearer beer and darker bread.

'Muvver says it's stummi-cake, I say it's war bread' complains the tearful infant, holding its tummy and winning our sympathy. Not so the beer-drinker: 'a tear stood in his bright blue eye, But, still, he answered with a sigh "I'll have another" '. Shortages and 'fiddles' led to scathing comment. 'Will you call for your joint later, mum?' 'No, you might just enclose it in an envelope and post it'. If shops were suspected of special favours, in spite of NO JAM, NO MATCHES, NO CURRANTS, NO SUGAR, signs, although counter attacks might cease in France, they took place here. 'Yer never have anythink so I'll give yer summat' says the old girl brandishing her umbrella over the grocer's head. More effective is the bull-necked corporal on leave, with his harassed wife at the counter: 'Have ye any bacon today, mister?—this is my husband!' Official rationing only began in 1918.

There are revealing contrasts. 'We are practising economy from A to Z—how are you going on?'—the little man in slippers warms his hands at a candle which serves also to boil the kettle. In other circles 'tightening belts' meant no bread on the table at dinner. 'People who want it must ask for it from the sideboard. If the whole of the well-to-do classes practised these disciplinary dodges the wheat problem would be trifling' (Arnold Bennett: *Diary*, May 1917).

Directed labour at home brought its laughs. 'What they sent you for?' asks the old farmer. 'Milking!' 'What job had you afore?' 'Tram conductor.' Exemptions caused acerbity, but humour helped. 'I reckon I ought to get exemp-

tion on this lot', says the wakeful father of eight. 'It's a one man business'. Two relatives of the writer, both of military age, were partners in the same business: the younger had to spend four years in the trenches, the elder made a small fortune at home—their wives were not on speaking terms for years. Even call-up, however, has its compensations, when the man with a khaki brassard sees one worn as a girl's garter. 'Bow-wow', is the 'wolf whistle' caption, 'I wonder what group she's in'.

For censorship the card artists show a hobble-skirted lady with a letter 'from the front' and the back of her dress gaping open: 'Opened by Censor—Well I never'. As for precautions, when the mysterious, unseen Zeppelins began to drop bombs on darkened streets and gas attacks were feared, people could buy respirators 'as used at the front'. 'She's going to buy one', says the winking husband: 'If it stops a bit of her gas it doesn't matter a hang about the other sort'.

So the jokes play down apprehension by harking back to stock themes and everyday situations. When the German submarine campaign was at its height and frying pans and rolling pins were of little or no use in the kitchen, a card showing them and a flat iron carried the thought: 'I wonder if the Kaiser's wife is throwing these at him yet? Or worse!!! WE HOPE SO'. There were many more in such comic-norm vein. And eventually, true to tradition, the hard-pressed housewife comes back into her own, even against the powers of war. Dominant, decisive with a poker-faced little girl holding on to her apron, she confronts a special constable: 'This 'ere *DORA has been boss long enough—now the war's over I'm the boss let me tell you'. Then we know Peace has broken out again.

When it did an era was over. Those cards, whose overloaded sentiment had accompanied times of tragedy and sorrow, were dead. Bamforths destroyed their stocks—some twenty million—and catching the mood of a new age, concentrated on 'comics'. 'We've got to the smiling part so smile — it smile'.

* DORA: Defence of the Realm Act: a multiplicity of regulations affecting everyone.

5 *'Daddy wouldn't buy me a bow-wow'*

One of the first subjects for British humorous postcards was a new invention which first took hold on the public at the opening of a new century—the motor car. J. H. Knight of Farnham produced the first British-built motor car propelled by internal combustion and exhibited it at the Crystal Palace Show, 1896. There were several other petrol pioneers, including F. W. Lanchester, but it was Daimler and Benz who really put the automobile onto a practical footing and into commercial production.

In the year of the Diamond Jubilee (1897) a Daimler car travelled at 12 mph—downhill. In 1900 there was a 1,000-mile trial run—from London to Edinburgh and back—which took the entrants over two weeks. It was organised by the first official body of motorists, the Automobile Club. In the following year a Daimler, built at Coventry, was fitted with the first pneumatic tyres. When Edward VII succeeded to the throne he pronounced his enthusiastic blessing on the new 'sport' and motoring was 'in', especially in the fashionable world.

Although perhaps 'Daddy didn't buy her a bow-wow' someone soon bought a stage idol, such as Isobel Jay, a sit-up-and-beg type of car. From the photograph Miss Jay appears to be in the driving seat of either a Hotchkiss or a Spyker. The Hotchkiss was a superb touring car which, mildly 'souped up', continued to be entered at Brooklands almost until the outbreak of war. The Spyker, produced by a Dutch firm, was of such excellent workmanship that the Bradford Motor Company contracted to take the entire output of 1903-6. Both models had the rounded radiators fashionable in this period and both gleamed with polished brass. The spirit of the new sport is evident in a contemporary *Windsor Magazine* cartoon:

> Lady passenger 'Can't you stop it?'
> 'No.'
> 'Where does this road lead to?'
> 'The sea.'
> 'Goodness! I wonder if mixed bathing is allowed?'

The motoring craze, like other crazes which follow, can be traced in some detail in Bamforth's cards, life-model as well as artist's variety. One of the former 'You won't go too far with me will you?' shows the driver in typical cloth cap and high-collared coat, his passenger in flowing blue cape and floppy hat (to be tied on

with veil), in the red button-upholstered seat of an early Sunbeam. Its bonnet is brass-bound and painted apple green; its radiator design and the card's date coincide in 1909.

Other cards show, only mildly in caricature, some of the special motoring clothing of early days—a goatskin coat for men worn with the fur outside—and hardships and perils of the new craze. 'You can come out now, it's geen o'er raining!' says a rustic to a driver in peaked cap and goggles, as he oilily emerges from 'underneath'. In a scene where a Sunbeam has just braked sharply in a cloud of dust the dialogue goes: *Man on hands and knees in road* 'What did you say?' *Man in car* 'I said, excuse me'. Lance Thackeray, a card-artist for Raphael Tuck, has drawn some devastating wrecks and crashes. Yet, whatever the suggestions of the life-model card, with its primrose yellow car and pedestrian lying underneath the wheels: 'While in . . . I ran across an old friend of yours', motorphobia was not as considerable in Britain as in some other places. After the abolition of the man-walking-in-front rule and the raising of the statutory speed limit from 12 to 20 mph (which obtained in theory until 1930), there was nothing for instance, like the Pennsylvania Anti-motoring Society. This stated: 'If the driver of an automobile sees a team of horses approaching, he is to stop, pulling over to his side of the road, and cover his machine with a blanket or dust cover which is painted or coloured to blend into the scenery, and thus render the machine less noticeable'. On the other hand, in the early 1900s, the British motoring press printed detailed maps showing the location of all known speed traps! Soon, however, all would be as phlegmatic as the delightfully costumed card of the lady, the Austin 15 hp landaulette (or Wolseley-Siddeley: the radiator is obscured), and the dust-coated driver: 'Are you engaged?' 'Bless yer dear heart, lady, I'm married and got three kids!' The motor cab had arrived in 1904 and within a year the motor bus followed.

Another craze, leading to a spate of cards, which, unlike early motoring, took hold not only of the wealthy, was 'rinkomania'. If 'daddy' could not run to a Hotchkiss or even a light car such as a De Dion Bouton, he could buy *her* a pair of roller skates and see her cutting a pretty and fashionable figure. Skating on special rinks, like the one at Holborn shown in the *Illustrated Sporting and Dramatic News*, 1876, enjoyed almost a generation of 'chic' and then a new wave of popularity around 1908-14. Along with other sporting activities—bicycling, golf, lawn tennis, cricket—it helped to create the 'new woman' and to shorten her skirts.

Bamforths got a whole series of cards, in photomontage with colour tinting, out of the less

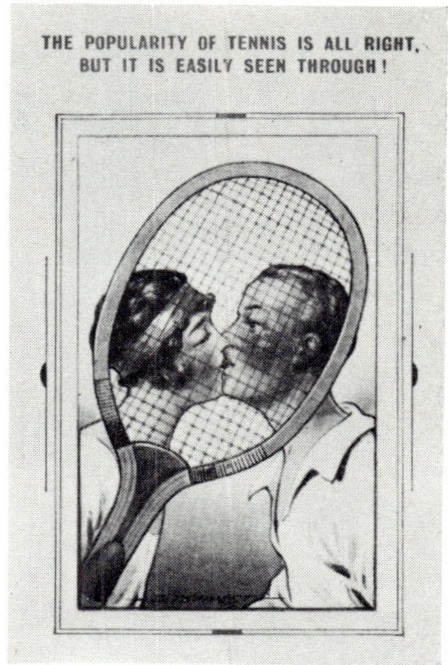

dignified situations that inevitably arise in 'rinkomania'. 'I'm making headway', for example, shows a young man in natty grey suit and short French beard coming into sharp contact with the ground in front of three girls who cling to another teetering male. A large panelled sign at the back of the rink reads: ALL SKATERS PLEASE OBSERVE THESE SIGNALS, and in the panel is the word REVERSE. 'Hold me tighter, Willie dear' notes a situation for closer association of the sexes; 'We met at the rink' gets its laugh with two frock-coated men in head-on collision. The rinks, with their festoons of bunting and flags, their refreshment bar and railed-in spectators' stand, are clearly a popular rendezvous. 'What ho! she bumps', shows how to do it in a flurry of petticoats, but *not* so gracefully. 'An awkward slip' has a girl in pink doing the 'splits' most professionally while others in the background skate in the safety of a 'threesome'—although the sign this time is SKATES OFF.

Lawn tennis also came into vogue in the 70s—when *Punch* suggested handicapping men by tying a scarf round their knees. The game figured in Du Maurier's *Society Pictures* (1891), then competed for the attention of the popular satirist later. Giving her a racket was another means of indulging a girl's fancy and of bringing young people together under the eyes of their elders, harmlessly. But card artists, like Tempest, saw the opportunities. 'Two Love!' says the girl, 'Is it darling?' smirks her partner. 'If you're going in for tennis don't make a fool of yourself by showing your ignorance' is the card's message. 'I've heard about your smashing serves'—in this one the rackets repose together, while the players kiss behind the net. 'What's your little game?' smiles a winsome maiden in pink, holding up her racket in a 'Sports Series' card, of another

firm. It was posted from Douglas, IOM, 4 June 1914—that long hot pre-war summer—and the writer's message reads: 'My holiday is coming to a close. You should see my face. Talk about a boiled lobster, worse than it was at Scarborough. Returning home on Saturday. Bye bye. Susan'.

After the war, in the Suzanne Lenglen era of Wimbledon, tennis had another fashionable run, conspicuously in the suburbs. 'Is it Lady Vere de Vere, or somebody from the next street going to the Park courts?' captions a Tempest sketch of a dressed-up tennis girl—with bandeau, of course—for August 1925. 'I can see you keep your end up' shows a female who has missed a return and keeled over the net. The secondary purpose of the game is still kept well to the fore: 'Is this what you call TENNIS COURT-ING?' shows a couple at LOVE-ALL. 'It's a good game played slowly'.

In the Albert Guillaume album the bicycle is obviously enjoying a vogue. 'Le Bienfaits du Tandem' shows a French couple in beach costume spinning away across the sands. Although essentially a manly sport at first, bicycling became fashionable for women by the 90s, ceased to be 'chic' about 1896, then filtered down through the middle to the lower classes. German cards just before the turn of the century show ladies in costume of gaiters and knickerbockers on a mixed cycling excursion. On the popularity of this sport were blamed the decline in church-going, in chaperonage, and in parental control!

By the time British postcards came to reflect the common view bicycling had passed into an accepted convenience. It was the motor-cycle that drew attention. 'I've spotted a nice girl' says the speedster in goggles, reversed cap and leggings (1910) who has splashed the hobble-skirt of a passer-by. Another 'hobbled' girl perched on a pillion smiles: 'I've got a good spark, so I'm all right'. A card of 1914, 'We are coming to see you' has pillion seat and a giant side-car with all six of the family plus the cat and dog aboard. In this version of 'motoring' the artist usually gets in some quip at the slight indignity that it involves. 'When father says go we're off' shows dad steering, mum sitting behind, a child pick-a-back, and two more perched

by the handlebars of a new lightweight—the poor man's 'chariot' of 1920. 'Anybody can see father's in front and mother's behind' reads another card, where the lady sits side-saddle.

But youth takes to it in the manner born. 'My word. They're alright. Fits him like a glove, doesn't she!' says one housewife to another as a flapper, astride, clings round the waist of the driver. Those who stick to the side-saddle habit run the risk of taking off altogether—or else giving a lingerie exhibition to all and sundry. 'Talk about pillion-riding—it's strange how little you really notice as they fly by': on this card machine and riders have been rendered almost invisible except for the girl's legs. Anyhow, in spite of the old dears' comment: 'Ugh, they are fast things! Not at all lady-like'—it's better to be 'a tart on a tray than a stale bun on the shelf'. For some the cheap and somewhat skimpy 'cycle-car'—such as the 'Swift', a make in which the writer was given a very early drive—provided the next step to pukka motoring.

Just after the war it looked as if the light aeroplane might oust the light car as the fashionable means of transport. 'Flying's all right' says a 'popsie' in a strut-and-spar open-cockpit biplane, 'but if you're not used to it you do get the "WIND UP" coming down'. Pleasure trips were letting civilians taste some of the adventurous rôles of the RFC. 'Hold tight behind there for the second loop!' shouts the pilot in a biplane with service roundels—but only an umbrella remains in the seat. Even family models were envisaged: 'We shall very likely come home like this, so get somewhere ready for us to land': the picture on

IS IT LADY VERE DE VERE, OR SOMEBODY
FROM THE NEXT STREET GOING TO THE
PARK COURTS?

"I've spotted a nice girl."

I'D LOVE TO FLY WITH YOU.

I've got a good spark, so I'm all right.

HOLD TIGHT BEHIND THERE,
FOR THE SECOND LOOP!

I'M HAVING A FLY TIME HERE.

WE'RE GOING TO ASK "MARS" CONSENT.

the card shows buckets, spade, shrimping net, and trunk aboard. 'No, there's nowt like flying—you can see all that's going off!' But, of course, you might come down in a tree or the sea, according to Tempest's fancy. So perhaps a 'run-about' on terra firma was better after all.

'If you haven't one of these, you might as well GET OFF THE EARTH or GET UNDER!' The car shown appears to be one of the immortal 'bull-nose' Morris-Cowley, vintage 1926,* a mass production type that was to bring motoring within reach of the multitude. 'Father, what's a pedestrian?' asked the schoolboy in the two-seater, a Vauxhall perhaps with its then fashionable boat-deck style of body: 'I'll show you, my boy . . . we might run across one soon'.

Motoring manners, especially of the emancipated girl in her 'run-about', come in for the usual satirical notice. 'Didn't you see me put my hand up, Miss?' 'No, officer—a man with a dainty hand like yours shouldn't be on point duty!' One flapper is shown striding over into the driving seat of her blue 'run-about' and, of course, displaying a blue garter. *Some* cars had no door on the driver's side—including the 1926 Morris. 'How do you like the style?' 'Splendid! and blue suits you!' Another in a red two-seater, with red devil mascot, pleads: 'I wish you would use both hands, Dick. I should enjoy it much better!' 'Yes, I know, dear . . . but the jolly old thing won't steer itself!' A typical period look is that of the languid lady at the wheel in chamois gloves, fur cape, and close-fitting hat: 'If only life was one limousine after another'.

With the depression many of the potential customers for drop-head coupés, with or without dickey seats, boat-style sports models, and bull-nose saloons, were reduced to the 'baby car'. Everywhere one saw Austin sevens. 'It *is* the day of the small car. Just so . . . it always has been!' declares a card of 1931 with inset of pram. Or, from the man in blue: 'Now then, young feller, keep off that causeway . . . I don't want you to get trod on!'

The gambits and styles of the motoring fraternity continue to flit across these cards with topical reference. As the woman driver crashes into a lamp-standard and flies through the air: 'Are yer trying that Amy Johnson stunt, missis?' That year is 1930 when the Yorkshire girl-in-the-flying-machine soloed to Darwin. Then comes a quip at the new traffic lights—a car fitted out as a travelling bed: 'Comfort while waiting for Robots to change to green. Third party insurance under the pillow, etc, etc.' The backseat

* Veteran = cars up to the end of 1904. Edwardian = cars from 1905 to Nov 1916. Vintage = cars from Nov 1918 to end of 1930.

driver, of course, is always with us: 'Don't hold your hand so high, Herbert, he (policeman on point duty) might think you want to get out'. Speed and risk increase in more ways than one: 'No, Aunt, it doesn't need castor oil to move this bus!', said of a supercharged Mercedes type. A poster astonishes the country couple: 'Babies run at 100 mph at Brooklands'. We meet the salesman's approach: 'Of course, I know all the parts of a car: why?' *She* 'Well then, stop mistaking my knee for the gear-lever!'

Most of the crazes and mechanical luxuries of the century, as they make their initial impact, feature on Bamforth's cards. No sooner have regular seats at the cinema been reserved 'for me and my gal' than the next craze seems to come along. 'Are you going in for wireless, or is it your wife who is doing all the LISTENING IN?' It is summer 1922, the year that Mr J. C. W. Reith joined the board of the British Broadcasting Company as managing director. People really went to town about it then. 'A couple like you ought to have a wireless set. You could

CANOODLE between items without an audience looking on!' And 'Oh, isn't it spendiferous' bleats the girl in the earphones. Even six years later a lyrical advertisement in *Pall Mall*, which has ironic overtones for anyone reading it today, declares how pleasant it is to idle through a sunny afternoon in peace 'only the Langham Portable, with its mellow music, breaking the rustic silence . . . It will work perfectly anywhere, and has a full loud-speaker range of over 1000 miles' [*sic*].

In those days married men sat up late 'waiting for America' and got china instead—from their spouses. Trust the 'comics' to bring highfalutin' notions down to earth. 'It isn't everybody who needs a wireless set—they can intercept waves quite well without': the gay 'spark' is 'tuned in' to the passing bright young things. And at night for some there's another wireless signal—'2LO calling' as the twins bawl their heads off.

Among the younger generation cycling made a comeback in the 30s and 40s. Adding to the inducement to discover picturesque England—while there was still time—was the chance to enjoy the cheap week-ends away from home newly provided by the Youth Hostels. The Association was formed in 1931. So again, buying her a bicycle was the thing to do—but this time a sports or racing model.

The adventurous spirits of the 20s—the anti-DORA era—tango-ed, Charleston-ed, one-stepped, black-bottomed to the music of the Savoy Orpheans, Jack Hylton, Jack Payne, Henry Hall, or Paul Whiteman, and sang 'Bye, Bye, Blackbird', 'Valencia', 'Chinese moon', 'Moonlight and Roses', 'Don't bring Lulu', and other foolish carefree, merry tunes like 'Barney Google', 'Horsey, keep your tail up', 'Yes, we have no Bananas', 'Does your mother know you're out, Cecilia?', in the mood of 'The more we are together'. Those of the depression era ('Buddy can you spare a dime?') sought wide open spaces and the unrestricted freedom of the roads and beaches. The cards, naturally, made game of them. 'I'm glad we bought a bike, Bill!—We *shall* get sunburnt', says the large girl on the rear seat of tandem. 'Sez you, lass! . . . I didn't even know the blooming sun was shining'. Arnold Taylor sketches a representative pair, both in shorts and short-sleeved shirts, with deep tan and drop-handlebars, who set the normal style. 'Keep a look out for us: we'll be coming your way!' When two cycles rest together beside a hedge the gamekeeper pointing to the sign 'DAMAGE TO YOUNG TREES—Prosecuted', disturbs a 'touring' couple: 'Who the heck's touching your trees?' comes the retort. The freedom of the road seems to give all the advantages of the ballroom for half the upkeep. Though, if it's scenery you're after the back seat of a tandem isn't always the best place for a view.

So one might go on, discovering from the cards how the first transistor wave washed up the streets and shores of Great Britain, how the first

TV signals hit the receptive gaze of the GBP, how, as one MP put it in the 50s, 'a noisy exhaust became a modern mating call'. And, of course, how, after Jive, Bingo infected everyone with its delirious patter and disseminated still further the gambling mania of the Pools, today's great indulgence. 'A BINGO bride enters the church with EYES DOWN, after a while CLICKETY CLICK and she's under DOCTOR'S ORDERS and then BINGO, she's got a FULL HOUSE'. Bingo or Ten Pin Bowling, take your choice and choose your card. For those who like this sort of thing this is just the sort of thing they'll like.

6 *'I'm a genuine philanthropist'*

'In old English democracy is a thing so alien to our traditions and rooted sentiment that the line of its progress seems hitherto a mere track of ruin.' Writing in 1903 George Gissing puts forward the view that the Englishman is aristocratic in his sympathies. He is willing to pay free proud homage to blue blood in return for the patrician's generous instincts and gallant championship, but haunted with misgiving when his master is the Plebs and his champion someone selected from among the grey-coated multitude. In their ways Gissing and Gilbert share the same belief. The bureaucratic monster is suspect, like the Plebs 'born more likely than not for all manner of baseness', however philanthropic its declarations. See *Princess Ida*:

> If you give me your attention, I will tell you what I am:
> I'm a genuine philanthropist—all other kinds are sham,
> Each little fault of temper and each social defect
> In my erring fellow creatures, I endeavour to correct . . .
> I know everybody's income and what everybody earns,
> And I carefully compare it with the income tax returns;
> But to benefit humanity however much I plan
> Yet everybody says I'm such a disagreeable man!
>
> And I can't think why!

The cards tell why. By visual and by verbal response to the various intrusive attempts to correct 'social defects' they express the 'common view' of the Englishman's new master—many-headed democracy.

Postcards which presented some of the problems troubling the first decade of the twentieth century on a completely serious plane were then described as 'a significant sign of our times'. When factories were being closed and social unrest was rife in the industrial regions, a series of cards designed by Ralph Rutley graphically portrayed the general anxiety. One showed an unemployed man, alone in a grimy cobbled street, appealing for sympathy against a background of idle factories. Bamforths themselves

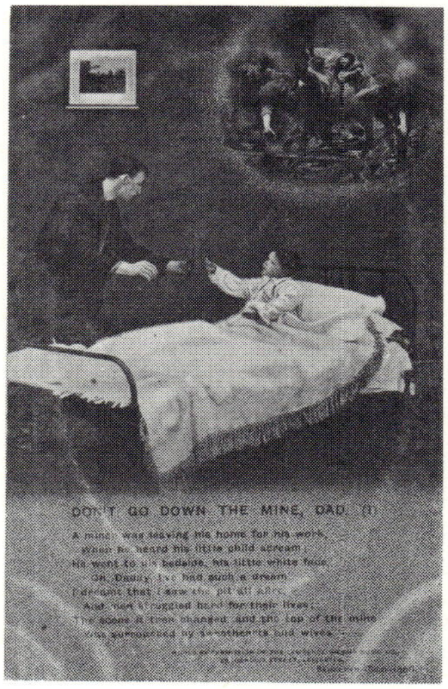

published a series of cards, revealing sympathy with the hard lot of the working man, at the time of a Cumberland mine disaster. Their designs were based on actual photographs taken at the mine-head. The song set 'Don't go down the mine, Dad' evokes conditions of peril, if not of toil underground, with its inset pictures of rescue workers, smoke-blinded men and swirling flames:

> I dreamt that I saw the pit all afire
> And men struggled hard for their lives:
> The scene it then changed, and the top of the mine
> Was surrounded by sweethearts and wives.

Ere the day was ended the pit *was* afire, a score of brave men lost their lives . . . but one miner was safe at home.

These cards provide the background. On the whole the topic of industrial trouble is aired through ironic or satirical comment. 'FACTORY CLOSED ON ACCOUNT OF STRIKE' reads a placard. The man in dungarees, scratching his head, says: 'Which proves conclusively I'm right when I say, if there was no work there'd be no strike'. Another notice: 'SALEM CHAPEL: SALE of WORK to be opened by J. Smith Esq., August 16 1908' calls forth the comment, 'Say, Bill, work's that scare now they're selling it!' Disputes and strikes among miners, railwaymen, dockers, and cotton-workers were specially prevalent from 1908 to 1911, the 'three-shift' system provoking considerable reaction in the mining areas.

But there are two sides to the working man's problem. One is his own attitude. *Out-of-work man to navvy*: 'What time do you commence work here?' 'I dunno. They are allus at it when I come here in the morning!' Sympathy is not

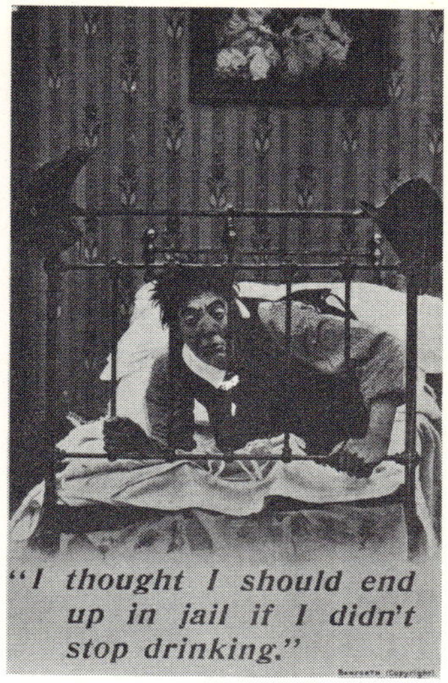

necessarily lacking, but the criticism is realistic: 'Wot are you chaps on strike for?' 'Shorter hours'. 'Ah! I've allus said that sixty minutes is too long!'

A more cynical view, from a later card, is expressed with northern bite: 'Nay lad, if thi' hours gets much less tha'll be meeting thi'sen coming home every time tha' sets out for work!' When Balfour's Licensing Act had reduced sale-of-liquor hours, a bystander remarks to the bill-poster who is putting up on the hoarding a placard reading 'Would you rob the working man of his BEER?' 'This is the fust time I've seen you work since I've known ye'. 'You're right, Bill, it's the first job I've ever been able to put my heart into'.

When it comes to interference with individual liberties—whether in the name of correcting social defects or of benefiting humanity by bureaucratic means—the cards are less ambiguous. There is no question that DRINK was a social evil, 'from the top to the bottom of society when Queen Victoria died' (G. M. Trevelyan). It was regarded as the chief cause of family ruin both by social and religious crusaders. Promoters of the pledge of abstinence turned to postcards, with the idea of sending such subjects as 'Death in the Bottle' or 'The Drunkard's Doom' to anyone known to be addicted. The idea took hold on the Continent, where it caused several recipients to bring actions for slander, but in this country it received very neutral support. A series which was called 'Drinkers, ancient and modern' appeared to encourage rather than deter. The cards published by Bamforths, while showing the consequences of drunken helplessness, often turned it to comic instead of serious effect. 'Won't you come home, Bill Bailey?' is a serious card (1904) of some pathos. But a typical reversion of the missionary role is seen in a later card with a lecturer for the 'Teetotal League' addressing a cochineal-nosed audience. 'Gentlemen! reconstruction means no BITTER feeling, STOUT hearts, plenty of SPIRIT, and your sup-PORT in every way!' Another message—'If your nose is red don't worry, keep on drinking and it will soon turn blue!' could hardly be considered blue-ribbon propaganda!

Even a life-model card 'I thought I should end up in Jail if I didn't stop drinking' shows the bleary-eyed addict, with his boot on one knob and bowler hat on the other, safely in bed looking through the iron rails! As for early closing hours, when war brings its restrictions, the only concern shown is to 'get round in time', with a man frantically rushing to the Red Lion carrying a quart jug. And so it goes on, for fifty years: two posters, set side by side, DRINK IS YOUR ENEMY: LOVE YOUR ENEMY, are still on the cards.

The image of authority comes in for similar sniping. Prior to the Labour Exchange the Workhouse system, with its built-in need to make conditions there less attractive than in field or factory—in fact 'maximum of deterrent with minimum of subsistence'—provided an obvious target. 'The Order of the Bath' shows a petty tyrant in uniform applying workhouse regulations. Uniform of any kind, except that of HM Armed Forces, usually tempts the card artist to caricature or deflation. It may be the wartime 'special'—So that's what you've joined, is

THE ORDER OF THE BATH.

London Opinion
"Now then,-Are you coming quietly?"
"I dunno: what do you call it?"

For tampering with His Majesty's Males

Not ______ likely

"WHAT ARE THE WILD WIVES
SAYING?"

BEARDED LADY
DANCER
SUFFRAGETTE: "HOW DID YOU MANAGE IT?"

Votes for Women
WE DEMAND
THE VOTE.

it? Who are you that you should think you can keep law and order?'—or the copper on the beat, shown with red nose and walrus moustaches, taking away a Cyprian 'for tampering with his Majesty's Males'—or the intrusive cleric, 'You seem to know all the ins and outs of this place, my man'. 'Aye, I know all the inns, but I know nowt about outs'. The would-be corrector comes off worse. Sympathy is reserved for the victim of official processes, even if it's a house-breaker: 'Now, then—Are you coming quietly?' 'I dunno; what do *you* call it?' grunts the man with two heavyweight coppers on top of him and a thumb in his teeth.

Movements to acquire power are treated in much the same way. Woman, who had got into the club, the colleges, sports circles, and some of the professions, and now wanted a way into Parliament, earns more sarcasm than support. 'WOMEN SUFFRAGE MEETING in TOWN HALL tonight' silhouettes furiously conflicting figures, with banners, umbrellas, shoes, pokers raised to strike, to a mere man's comment 'What are the wild wives saying?' 'How did you manage it?' has a suffragette with long cane, long nose, and collar and tie peering at the 'bearded lady' in a show window. A drawing by Alfred Leete, reproduced for Bamforths from *London Opinion*, has a militant suffragette being marched away by three policemen and a beggar holding out his hat with a grin, 'Can you spare a copper, lady?' 'My wife's joined the suffrage movement, I've suffered ever since' represents the 'little man's' attitude at home. In the Houses of Parliament one of Bamforth's 'Mouse series' shows a Report of the Suffragettes lying on the table and prophesies:

> The militant captain said 'Close up',
> Soon they'll wish she'd said Close down'.

One of the gambits common in cardology is to diminish the reference of a debate or legislation. If it's a question of whether or not to keep the gallows, take it on shopkeeper level: 'Have these hares been well hung?' and you get the reply: 'Lor! No Mum! The boss don't believe in capital punishment'. If the debate is for or against Free Trade, show a small girl pushing a book

VOICE: "WILL THEY CURE UNEMPLOYMENT?"
QUACK: "THEY WILL, SIR! BUY THIS BOX, TAKE SIX PILLS TO-NIGHT, AND YOU'LL BE FULLY EMPLOYED IN THE MORNING!"
CURE
EVERYTHIN
PILLS

Please make muvver and father see the error of their ways, and remember the League of Nations!

OUR HOME RULER!

WHATEVER SORT OF GOVERNMENT WE HAVE, SOME OF US WILL ALWAYS FAVOUR PROTECTION!

THIS COAL QUESTION IS A PROBLEM---SOMEBODY OUGHT TO PUT THEIR FOOT DOWN!

I'VE JUST HAD TO SPOIL A CHAP'S BEAUTY FOR TALKING ROT ABOUT ASQUITH—WHAT DO YOU THINK ABOUT ASQUITH?

How to Kill Pain down the seat of her knickers with the remark 'Whatever sort of Government we have some of us will always favour protection!' Or if there is a promised panacea for the out-of-work, give the topic an airing thus:

Voice: 'Will they cure unemployment?'
Quack: 'They will, Sir! Buy this box, take six pills tonight, and you'll be fully employed in the morning!'

This method of *reductio ad absurdum* rubs off on the major issue. It makes it somewhat less world-shaking and the protagonists not so much larger than ordinary life. Even Irish troubles may be reduced in this way. 'Our Home Ruler' shows a father on hands and knees with scrubbing brush and pail, a four-year-old upstart in pinafore giving him orders. A Tempest card applies the method to international affairs. With the small boy and girl saying their prayers goes an inset picture of their being caned: 'Please make muvver and father see the error of their ways, and remember the League of Nations!'

A few political personalities are featured comparatively unscathed. Before the 1903 election Ettlingers produced a card 'Cock of the Walk' portraying Joseph Chamberlain, and, by pressing it, one could make the figure squeak! Lloyd George, in the first flush of social security measures, when people's expectations were being rewarded is treated less ambiguously. A card with his portrait and the National Health Stamp reads: 'The Stamp that wants a lot of licking and the Man'. His leader is defended in another: 'I've just had to spoil a chap's beauty for talking rot about Asquith', says the burly navvy to the top-hatted business man in the tram—'what do you think about Asquith?' Churchill gained nothing but healthy respect a generation later and no doubt, if Beveridge featured, he also would emerge unscathed. In Macmillan's heyday there is an oblique 'scratching': 'We've never had it so good, Fido', remark the dogs apropos of their choice between lamp-posts, crossing beacons, speed-limit signs, parking meters, one-way signs, and other such pavement impedimenta. The common view of politicians can be summed up in one comment. *Orator*: 'At this moment our MPs are sitting'. *Voice*: 'So are our hens, mister, and we don't get any results either'.

Cards seldom resort to the savaging of individuals or even types—as, for instance, Max Beerbohm's satire did. The drawings in his *Survey*, 1921, provide several examples. 'Urgent Conclave of Doctrinaire Socialists to decide on some means of inducing the Lower Orders to regard them once more as visionaries merely' is filled with recognisable figures. The cruel 'When Labour Rules' or 'What M. Cambon frightfully foresees' shows an aristocratic French foreign minister meeting a proletarian British one—with a prophetic *physical* resemblance to Bevin. Equally damaging is the caricature called 'The Patron', in which a gross-featured future Minister of Education interviews a poet seeking 'outdoor relief'. In another the ogreish figure of a Captain of Industry declares to a recognisable Dean that 'the desire of the manual workers to be paid exorbitant wages for doing the least possible amount of work is a sure sign that they have lost faith in a future life'.

The approach of the card artist is different. He provides a stereotype of the 'faceless official' at a lower level, one or more of whom is known to and can easily be 'filled in' by the common reader from experience. So the Ministry 'nark', the Assistance Board official, the National Health examiner, the means tester, the union official, even the driving tester and other tools of democracy, are the targets and their self-importance is subject to comic erosion.

They are tempting targets. In the welfare

state, the 'planned society' set in motion with direction of labour, productivity drives, and pep talks, who has not at some time longed to take the organisers down a peg or two? 'Genuine philanthropists' or not, they are still 'them', as opposed to 'us', ordering our lives when it touches them, in an unnecessarily complicated way, getting to 'know everybody's income and what everybody earns' so that they can 'carefully compare it with the income tax returns'. The cards may be seen as part of the 'little man's' struggle to remain an individual in spite of being regarded as a citizen in a democracy, where workers' equality seems to have been bought at the price of workers' liberty.

So if awkward questions are asked the citizen may give an awkward answer. A Ministry Survey official at the factory entrance confronts a bosomy employee: 'Age?' 'Twenty-two'. 'Colour of eyes?' 'Blue'. 'Sex?' 'Occasionally!' Get round the system by hook or crook as you would round 'benefits'. 'Doesn't your husband ever work?' 'No, he's joined six unions so he's bound to be on strike'. In fairness to the 'faceless men' the joke is sometimes played the other way. 'You'll have to help me, Sir, I've no visible means of support!' from another bosomy girl in strapless summer dress at the National Assistance Board. 'Blimey, Lady, you're telling me'.

Usually the retorts are of the crude 'beer-bottom-lavatory' joke order. *Employment Bureau official*: 'If you go hawking Beecham's Pills you can't draw the dole, my good man'. 'No, Sir, but I can get RELIEF any time I like'. The faceless ones in the lower grades of uniformed and pensioned jobs are really only separated from the working class by their function as agents of 'Them'. They are attuned to the same stock responses.

'Society in exchange for protecting him, requires man to obey certain rules, many of which conflict sensationally with his natural inclinations . . . During sleep, with the force of the social censor diminished, these drives and conflicts burst forth in the form of dreams. Mostly the dream itself is then subject to further repression—forgetting almost immediately'. So declares Dr Christopher Evans, experimental psychologist. The comic cards, it could be maintained, represent waking dreams in which the social censor is temporarily over-ridden and the ordinary man's natural inclinations expressed. Everyone has felt the dynamic urge to hand out to authority the devastating comeback just at the crucial moment—even if only on the shop floor. Machinist to foreman, who ticks her off: 'How long have you been a foreman?' Foreman: 'Twenty years lass!' 'Blimey, that's a long time to be idle isn't it?' The presentation of spivs—all of whom have one thing in common, no visible

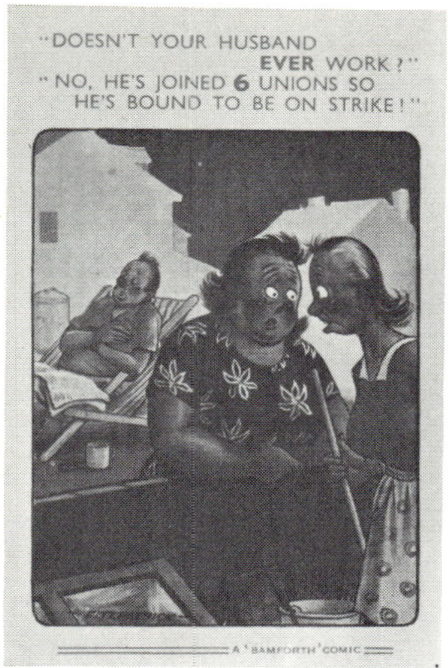

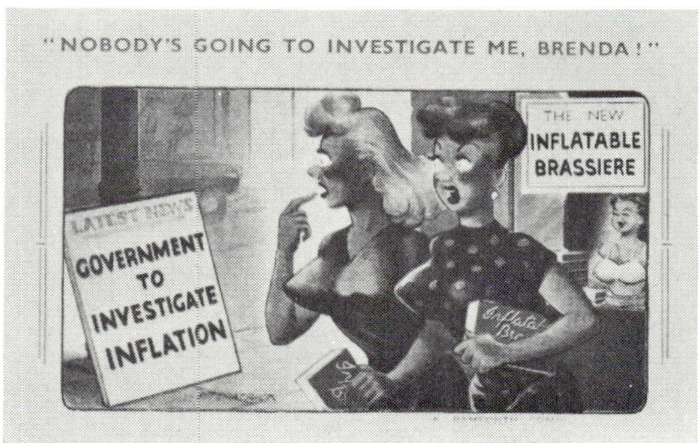

means of support—with a wry tolerance suggests the card-audience reaction to such social rules as 'WORK OR WANT'.

The fact that there are fewer digs these days at the 'disagreeable men' of democracy need not cause surprise. Labour in office has now become the Establishment. Max Beerbohm remarked in dedicating his *Survey* to Britannia, 'a satirist instinctively goes for what is very strong: the weaker things he derides with less gusto if not at all . . . he looks out for the weak points that all strength has and rudely points them out'. But the card artist cannot wholeheartedly represent the common view now as anti-establishment. Instead he tends to fall back on the old 'antis': 'WORK is the curse of the working-class! BEER helps me to forget it—Come and help me lose my memory, old cock!'

7 *'Where did you get that Hat?'*

Mrs Browne: 'I wonder what kind of bonnets will be worn this Spring?' *Browne*: 'Last year's my dear'. The joke, captioned 'After the Slump', comes from the *Windsor Magazine* 1906—a vintage year for anyone with an interest in 'Spy' cartoons, which the magazine was then reprinting in their original colours with all the various celebrities of sport, stage, society, science, the services.

It is a joke that might well have been 'on the cards'. A constant reflection, in their slightly distorting mirror of the manners and modes of the times, is of contemporary fashion. 'What the Ladies see': 'What the Gents see' (on a Bamforth card of 1908') shrewdly depicts the double appeal of such reflection. An Empire 'promenader' of the period in sweeping skirt, feather boa, and plumed hat appears in one half, with her face and hair dimmed out. In the other face, feet and ankles are emphasised while the gown is dimmed out to a transparency that reveals her limbs. To let the generations see themselves 'as others see' is in any case a 'revelation' and bound to have comic results—for both men and women.

In order to put mere man in his place—and get him out of the way—it should be noted that 'Where did you get that hat?', catch-phrase from a music-hall song, was attributed there to Edward, Prince of Wales. He, it was, who set the fashion of the Homburg, in green velour, instead of the man-about-town's summer straw hat, and winter bowler. In the song he took objection to an 'old-fashioned tile'.

The soft felt hat was often called a trilby—the link being with Du Maurier's novel and successful play which caught the manufacturer's fancy. It took on and has remained *the* hat of the twentieth century. So when shoes, instead of brown or cloth-topped boots, had come in about 1910, the 'knut' of the period might be expected to declare himself by two things: his hat and his sock display. We see both in the card 'Oh, Horace! you are a dear!'—a green velour, bright green-striped socks, and green bow tie. The high stiff collar was still *de rigueur*. Leonard Woolf remarks in his autobiography of the sensation he had caused, a few years earlier, by daring to wear a green flannel instead of a starched white one! Another card 'A "nut" with a small screw' has a display of red and white socks, red-striped blazer, extra high collar, and spotted bow. In the more discreet *London Opinion* drawing the dark lounge suit and stiff collar are relieved by a soft felt hat. (The lounge suit itself—a coat with long skirts and back-slit, trousers turned up and narrow—gave later 'Teddy' boys their basic style.) The fashion-conscious Edwardian male is satirised in another drawing: 'By Jove, Percy—there's the very thing for your new suit: a nice quiet check, not too showy!' says one bowler-hatted male to another as the tartan-trousered Guards officer goes by. But on the whole, men's dress keeps its tendency to be stereotyped over long periods.

Women naturally claim more attention. They intend to do. Their various compromises between modesty and exhibitionism express the spirit of the age. What they plainly show commands men's attention. What they don't show seldom fails to fascinate by some kind of decorative emphasis.

'Come along, John! I can show you something better at home!' Her husband gazes into the window of a lingerie shop at a lady's corset, 1904 model, designed to 'throw all the fullness upward into the stomach and chest'. His wife, chokered to the throat, holds her skirt hem off the ground, revealing two lace-trimmed petticoats, which no doubt 'swished' as she walked. A side-window in the shop has a one-piece pink woollen combination garment. John might have said, in self-defence, 'Without an understanding

Oh, Horace! you are a dear!

"Say, dear boy, the Germans are arskin' for it."
"By jove! there'll be twouble if we go."

CHESSNUTS

"By Jove, Percy,- there's the very thing for your new suit: a nice quiet check, not too showy!"

"COME ALONG, JOHN! I CAN SHOW YOU SOMETHING BETTER AT HOME!"

IT'S LEAP YEAR, AND IF YOUR KING AND COUNTRY DON'T GET YOU—I WILL

of the foundation on which the dress is based there can be no real comprehension of the dress itself'. The age of tight lacing and trimmed underskirts was a generally prosperous one. Attention was fitly divided in dress between the seductive swishing of silk and the opulence of the bosom. Both the age and the social climate were matched in the 'fine woman', tall and statuesque, of mature form and rounded contour. And if the right specifications did not exist by nature then the foundations for the modes of the period created them.

as the "embongpong" got lower . . .' As to carrying a fresh bouquet through the evening 'a well-developed girl should experience no difficulty in concealing a bottle of the size generally known as "split soda", to hold two or three rosebuds in rain-water in the centre of the bosom beneath the corset'. Then as the night proceeds and 'the water in the dainty improvised hothouse becomes tropical, the buds go off one by one with a surprised little "pop" ' and they unfold into glorious and exquisitely fresh roses. But, says Pitcher, 'be careful that the bottle does not become re-

The dignity and the absurdities of this opulent early Edwardian style provide rich material for contemporary columnists and magazine artists. In 1901, according to a *Vogue* editress, the 'upper half of the (woman's) figure seems set six inches in front of the lower half'. A smoking-room writer, 'Pitcher' of the Pink 'Un, has amusement a-propos one Grace Romer. She is 'out after' an exceedingly 'oofy' widower and having the misfortune to be physically without 'form and void' is advised to try one of the 'patent Parisian self-heaving busts'. On the way to the races with the widower 'the bust left its moorings and began to descend inside her upper undergarments' and 'the widower began to cast unpleasant glances

versed'. This send-up ends, 'Hats, dear, are to be larger than ever, whilst the best-cut skirts are tighter round the top and much fuller round the bottom—which may sound like a paradox to a mere man, but which *you* will understand quite perfectly, I feel sure'.

Apart from making game of them the cards show some delightful toilettes. The full skirt, rich velvet bodice, white fox furs and osprey-plumed hat of the later Edwardian lady in Bamforth's zoo-joke card present the 'tall and statuesque' figure at its best. Another lady is in walking costume—ostrich-plumed hat, a 'must' of 1907, full wine-red coat, the fashionable colour after mourning for the Queen had ended, with a muff and pet dog. Her escort is dressed equally smartly—to match their conversation. *He*: 'In Turkey a bride never sees her husband before the wedding day'. *She*: 'How odd! We never see our husbands after'. Their most life-like replicas can be found in Doris Langley Moore's costume museum at the Assembly Rooms, Bath.

Fur muffs were an important accessory of the decade, often with hats to match. The hand-coloured Max Ettlinger cards show delightfully natural fur-hatted models. These cards and the glamorous studies of Gaiety Girls and actresses—

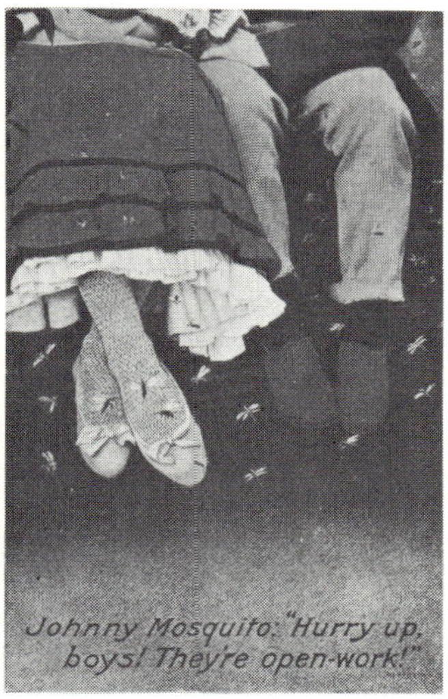

with well known names like Mrs Patrick Campbell, Lilly Langtry, Maxine Elliott, Ethel Barrymore, Billie Burke, Marie Studholme, Edna May, Amelia Bingham, Isabel Jay, and evocative, if less well known ones, such as Fritzi Schiff, Trixie Friganza, Lulu Glaser, Bonnie Maginn—play upon the more extravagant details of the fur, ostrich feather, and swathed gown era. The above charmers all came from Bamforth's stable, but many other firms featured 'pin-up' celebrities, the rage of early postcard collectors. Rotary Photo Company had more than one hundred different 'views' of Marie Studholme alone.

Just before the First World War the use of synthetic dyes made it possible for cheaper furs—cony, marmot, musquash—to be made up to represent dearer. Fur with everything was the rage—especially fur and velvet. We see the result in the card of the three graces, from a drawing by Oscar Wilson—ermine stoles, fur ties and collars, fur muffs, velvet jackets, and long gloves. In 'I wish I were single again' another trend is noticed—ankle-flattering striped stockings, successors to the 'Cinnamon-brown lace lisle-thread hose' that 'Pitcher' had noticed on all the smartest girls at Brighton. His comment about hat-size is borne out in the Bamforth life-model card where one large hat 'covers a multitude': a couple concealed by it embrace in the public park.

It would not be difficult to follow the ebb and flow of women's fashions in full detail, card by card, but save for the specialist, tedious. It has been remarked that women generally see in fashion's changes an ever progressing evolution towards something more sensible in the way of dress, regarding yesterday's fashions as ridiculous and today's as both beautiful and practical. Whereas, in fact, fashions are largely based on display: the display consisting of exposure of or emphasis upon various portions of the female body taken in series. According to James Laver there are 'sterilised zones', those exposed by the fashion which is just going out, and an 'erogenous zone'—always shifting—the point of interest for the fashion just coming in. So from bust and ankle to calf and back, to knee, buttock and thigh and back again to bust—the course is obvious. In the modern mass-reproduction period, the pace of fashion-change speeds up as more are able to chase it. Even so the highlights deserve notice. In them from time to time the larger image of the age can be recognised.

The narrow tailor-made skirt and matching coat put an end to the era of voluminous petticoats. Their volume was made up for by an even larger hat, a potent social symbol. 'The latest fashion at Southport'—with a hat actually made of cloth pasted on—shows the style well. 'How do you like this? I thought it would just suit you' writes the sender in January 1911. When a whole dress was made of one material, trimmings of numerous buttons were used to offset its plainness. A sketch with a husband on his knees fastening them—'Why the deuce didn't I marry a dwarf?'—shows three dozen down one seam. Moving about in these 'hobble' skirts was difficult as the card 'Accommodation seems scarce here' has already shown. Within the next few years ways of 'catching up' some portion of the skirt eased the situation and gave the wearer added appeal, as can be judged from the card 'No wonder Adam fell'.

By 1914 tunics with narrow skirts under them had predominated and the so-called 'lampshade' tunic came in for comic attention. 'Are you never taken for a man, Clara?' says one eye-glassed, nonplussed dude to a wearer of what appear to be trousers. 'No: are you?' retorts cigarette-smoking Clara. Even more startling was the decline of the choker, high-necked bodice, or blouse, in favour of V-necks, which came in about the same year. These two changes, the open throat and the end of the trailing bell-shaped skirt, marked a new freedom and one which women would not lightly give up. The cards of the same period, 1910-15, are full of references to another movement for women's freedom and equality. As the mother seeing her small daughter break a cheval-glass says: 'Oh, the darling! the little pet is going to be a Suffragette!'

From cards covering the First World War, fashion-spotters could trace two general trends—gradual raising of hemlines and progressive lowering of necklines. 'Isn't it funny, dear, that skirts are going up while blouses are coming down' is still a valid observation for two young things looking into a sales window in 1919. The change came by degrees; its result was a recognisably modern style.

When women were taking up such jobs as tram conductress, post-woman, chauffeuse, the long narrow skirt previously worn under a tunic proved impractical. It was discarded, the over-tunic being lengthened to mid-calf and forming a flared skirt. The card 'There'll be lots of things left undone when all the married men have gone' with its three-tiered dress, unbuttoned at the back, the woman in GPO uniform and the

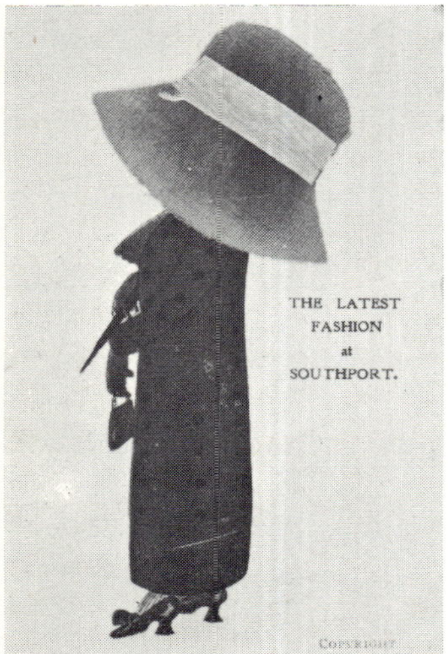

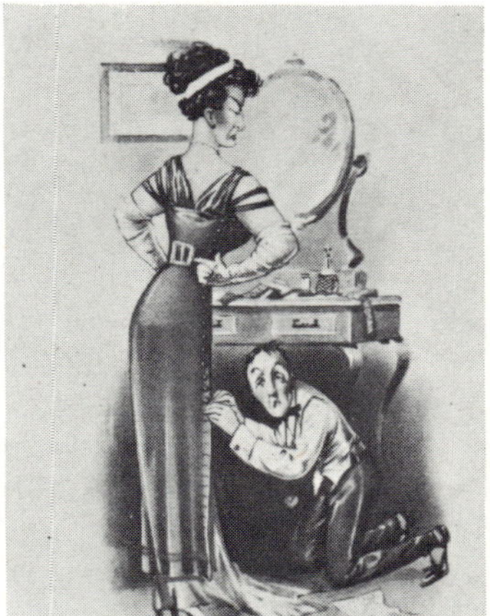

tram conductress costume, indicate the stages. 'Girls are doing all the fellows' jobs now!' shows the mid-war style with the addition of high-laced boots—a military touch. By the end of the war, emancipated woman, given the vote in 1918 as a reward for services, would be ready to show her sense of freedom in clothes. Women had earned their own living on a massive scale, for the first time, tasting man's work and the economic freedom that went with it.

The first freedom was from boned corsets. Waists, after a slight struggle, went out—or down to the hips. The straight-up-and-down, mannish look, accentuated by long blouses and jumpers, put busts at a disadvantage. Angular lines prevailed: to be thin was to be fashionable. To complete the transformation of woman in man's image, buns were reduced to 'bobs' (1923) and then, via the 'shingle' with its tight-fitting cloche hat, to the schoolboy shortness of the Eton crop (1927). In contrast to the mature statuesque figure favoured of Edwardians it was

the fashion era of the boy-girl 'flapper'.

The card artists were alert to these trends and the new frankness of spirit that went with them. The passing shock to older standards they turned off into humour, whilst satirising excesses. 'I'd just stripped for gym when I got your wire to meet you.' A snatch of conversation, overheard between two fashionably attired misses, one wearing a bow tie to her blouse, sets the tone. 'Jim! good heavens, the brazen hussie' mutters the old lady. 'By jove! but I bet you are making the lads stare' comments a card of summer 1924 apropos the girl obviously without corset in slinky jumper and skirt. Now that busts were out, backs came in and even at this time might be bared in a wide, deep V. 'Hullo, I see your daughter's back!' The remark from a surprised old gent invites her mother's sternest look. As legs revealed themselves, stocking jokes started. 'It's a silly place to keep money, also . . . it's encouraging robbery.' The warning, that same summer, is to the girl tucking pound notes into her hose top and displaying her knees. On the cropped look the comment goes 'I admit it's ladylike through the mirror, but you do look a lad from behind'. Another, viewed this time from behind, earns the quip: 'Why don't you wear trousers and do it right?'

While women seemed to be modelling themselves on men, men's styles took over feminine fulness. The old sporting costume of Norfolk jacket and tight knickerbockers turned, perhaps under the influence of some of the baggy riding-breeches of wartime, into plus-four suits. And the plus-fours came near, at times, to plus-eights. 'Where've you got them things?' says a critical spouse. 'Never you mind. I got them at a man's shop. So let that do!' 'Getting quite common: they'll be wearing skirts next', say two old dears contemplating their husbands' extensive rear view. The advent of 'Oxford bags' in 1925, so wide that they resembled split skirts, with 'sports' jackets bold in cut and colour, reinforced this sartorial extravagance and display. 'Bah' says an unwilling wearer, 'if some of these fellers had to wear my father's cut-downs they wouldn't be so potty about 'em.'

In general, though, men are still shown in

trilby and single-breasted lounge suit, a little shorter in coat skirt and without slit, but essentially the same as pre-war. In the late 20s a double-breasted waistcoat goes with it.

The accent on legs and their trimmings fascinated the card artists—and the male public—for years. A man seemed to see them wherever he looked, in flesh-coloured silk stockings from 1926 onward, often with a garter worn below the knee. In winter some women added 'Russian boots'—a wartime derivative. On the promenade, where it was sometimes hard to tell mutton from lamb, in tram and bus, where to sit opposite a girl with legs crossed was 'worth every cent of the fare', getting out of cars, bending over prams, dancing, playing golf—female legs couldn't be overlooked. 'Women will powder their faces: it seems funny because nobody looks at their faces today.' The year when skirts were at their shortest provoked a retrospective card '1897-1927' with man's gaze riveted first on ankles, then on thighs and in the third panel, the gazer has been blindfolded against future revelations. A card, captioned simply '1930', comes nearest of all to mini-skirt standards. It adds piquancy with the bare back, cloche hat, and fur tie of the period.

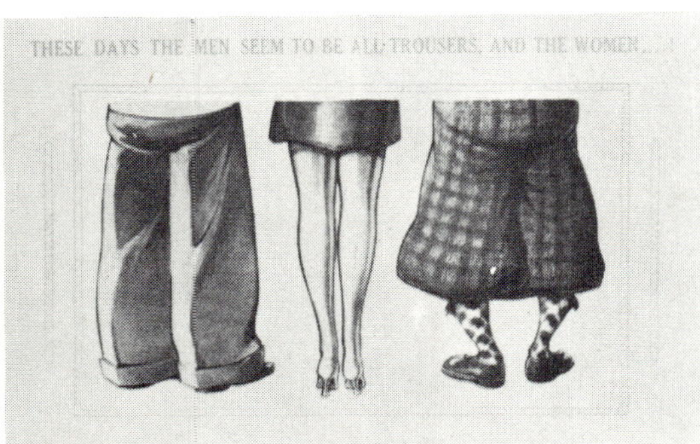

For about five years women's appearance stayed almost uniform—small hat, straight-lined dress with low waist, short skirt and long stockings, low shoes. The next zone of interest, legs having occupied attention as far and perhaps as long as they could, was to be the back and hips. Still mannish, not motherly, figures confronted the 30s in longer skirts and shorter jumpers, with tightly covered posteriors and hips made to look narrower by wide shoulders. It was the decade of the Ruhr, the 'Blood-Purge' Abyssinia, Kipling's and the King's deaths, the Abdication, the burning of the Reichstag and the Crystal Palace, a decade of diminishing illusion which evolved a less flippant style. This Greta Garbo mode gave the postcard artists much less of a field day. There are fewer overt comments on fashion.

Arnold Taylor's girl in 'Conductor, I want to get off!' 'Well, now's yer chance lad, make the best of it while the tram's empty!', shows the degree of difference from the twentyish modes. Hair is being grown again, by degrees. One card refers to the 'long bob', an intermediate stage with curls on the nape of the neck. Mid-calf is the accepted length of two-piece costumes. The back alone now hypnotises attention. As in bathing suits, so in dance frocks, its area of exposure extended gradually from deep Vs to half bare, then three-quarters bare until eventually only gowns backless to the waist made the male head turn. As one seaside minx parading before eye-popping men says: 'If I don't return to work you'll know I've clicked with a millionaire—or been locked up'. Another card 'How am I doing?' discloses the real origin and purpose of the style. A sun-bathing girl discloses her back beautifully brown to the waist.

When war comes, women in uniform appear chiefly as either sylph-like and seductive in spite of it; or else even more Junoesque and overpowering because of it. The artists take advantage of air-raid warnings to show girls caught in their undies—the familiar matching frilled bra and briefs—but even they have gone 'utility'. Interest revives only after the war when another new look comes in, a reaction to the continued austerity. This time it is the real New Look, Paris-inspired; a return to femininity with full

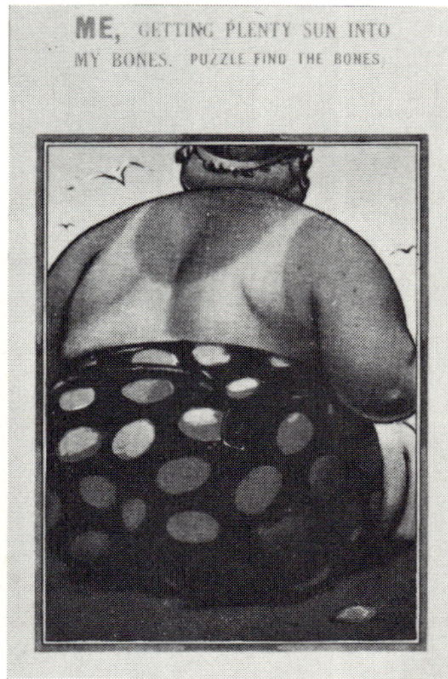

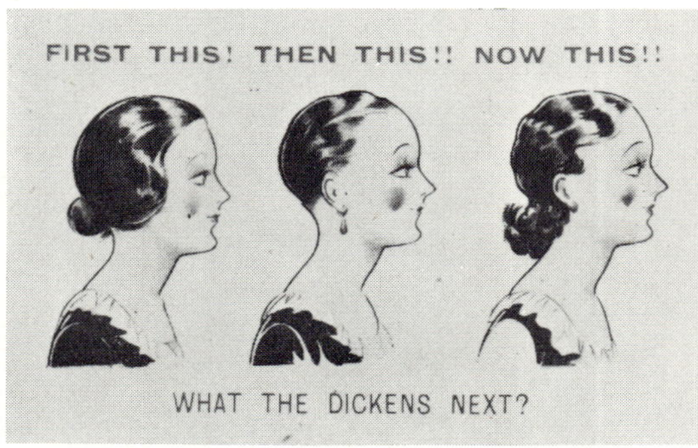

skirts, accentuated hips, and wasp waist—minimised by a 'cincher'. The mood is signified by a card: 'They're rather expensive aren't they, darling?' 'Well, what if they are—I've been going without these things long enough.' But, of course, she is buying a pair of 'frillies'. Lowered necklines—the 'plunge' as it later becomes—start to catch the eye and a new area, 'development area' the jokes call it, has arrived for humorous observation.

equivalent to the old school tie of privileged circles—was the Teddy Boy outfit and hairdo, costing as much as £100. Unlike its immediate predecessor, the 'drape' suit with wide satin, painted tie, and its successor, the short boxed jacket with narrow lapel and narrow tie, the Teddy suit had an English origin—even to its green velvet collar. Comic postcards being what they are, its excesses were less noticed than those of the teenage girl. One youth, however, with

The major change in post-war fashion, however, was neither in 'plunge' nor 'uplift', 'self-supporting' dress nor 'swagger' coat, backless for evening nor bikini for bathing, but in the age group on which fashion centred. Before the 1950s were out the 'real' earnings of the under-twenties had risen by fifty per cent from their pre-war levels, and the margin for free spending was biggest among semi-skilled workers. To them, therefore, the 'admass' high-powered selling methods were directed—with ever fresh 'images' of style drawn from the new young stars of the entertainment world.

So instead of descending from the socialite Bright Young Things, as they did in the 20s, fashion trends now ascended from the wage-earning teenagers. Youth's 'gang uniform'—an

Marcelle-waved hair, seen heading towards adjoining doors labelled 'Ladies' and 'Gents' got the caption: 'This should settle the argument once and for all, Albert'. The fun really begins with the 'admass' miss. At a time when the foundation garment industry was directing its appeal to twelve-year-olds, according to the *Financial Times*, the jokes began at schoolgirl level. 'Please, miss, have you anything to fit beginners?' says one sprat in gym tunic and plaits to the brassière-counter assistant. If she hadn't, the next step was obvious—'falsies'. These, on the cards, become another pitfall for the bridegroom-to-be, as are 'inflatables' for the flag-sellers!

Looks changed so quickly, from gamine à la Audrey Hepburn to sultry-squalid à la Juliette

Greco or waif-in-mackintosh à la Bardot, with hairdos from 'poodle-cut' to 'haystack', 'beehive' to 'ratstails', 'gold lights' and 'silver streak' to pink rinse or piebald, that only a whole catalogue of cards could illustrate them all. One dress style, for example, 'The Sack' (1957) reappears as trapeze-line, H-line, tulip-line, and twenty-ish chemise with dizzying speed. The artists stuck to the essentials. 'It's my Pop Art dress, dad', says a bouncing girl of bountiful bosom. 'Ah can see that lass—nah go upstairs and Pop back into it'. Of 'shortie nighties' and 'mini-skirts': 'Some say created by the devil, but whatever your views they're still four inches below SEE LEVEL'.

The distorting mirror of the cards had no lack of comic images up to the 60s. From the girl 'right on the beat here' in tight, slipping jeans, bare midriff and separate top, to the long-golden-haired couple of ambiguous sex at the altar—'Who takes Who and for What?' asks the vicar—and the newer 'Unisex' fashions, 'birds in boys' gear', as designed by Cerruti. Like the songs of the decade, 'Rock Around the Clock', 'Livin' Doll', 'Itsy Bitsy Teeny Weeny Yellow Polka Dot Bikini', 'Only Sixteen', 'Singing, High, High, High', 'Bless Your Beautiful Hide', the styles of youth were 'way out'.

Bamforth's cards are not so grotesque as some—such as 'Fair Shares for All' a design for Kardorama Ltd which sends up the 'beat' type. They annotate not only the show pieces but the less conspicuous, more significant, norm. The lady in black strapless evening gown, with escort in frilled shirt front and new/old cummerbund, who puts her hands up at gun-point and reveals all, is the *reductio ad absurdum* of this particular style; but most of the mature subjects offer more modest disclosures. Over the back fence, at the shop, in pub or works, or in winter undies, there are to be seen no dowdy, out-of-date women now. The Marks and Spencer type of development of the dress trade in the 50s, the mass-producing and distributing of quality goods as decently for docker's wife as for doctor's, has altered all that. By 1960 the British woman of limited income is the best dressed in the world—and the cards can't deny it. Everybody now has a chance to make the best of themselves. Even old Joe's wife, Alice, the stout party in the back room by the gasworks, wants a new image and reads *Ideal Woman*.

8 'Ma, he's making eyes at me'

One of the fallacies of everyday thought, or thoughtless acceptance, is that men chase girls. Sometimes they appear to do; in stag-party circles they boastfully claim to, and certainly it flatters the male ego to maintain the belief that they do; but in fact . . . ? The comic cards, holding their mirror up to everyday manners, may slightly distort the facts, but they neither camouflage nor conceal them. And the cards show conclusively that almost the reverse is true: if girls don't actually chase men, they engineer men's illusion of chase and often make the running for them. How they manage to do this within the terms of licence between the sexes, varying from chaperonage at one extreme to casual 'intimacy' at the other, is a subject that postcard humorists have explored with some fascination.

'Won't people be jealous when they see you squeezing me?' 'But I'm not squeezing you.' 'I know—but I thought you were just going to.' The basic situation lies between this oncoming wile of the enfranchised girl and the comment to a card with a similarly static pair: 'It isn't what a woman does that attracts a man, it's what she won't do!' In short, judicious management of the rein and the curb creates the illusion of chase.

Of course, men also *like* to think that they are being encouraged. A wish-fulfilment image that will remove doubt or timidity such as 'Oh, I do feel spooney! Come and stir me up' helps to apply the spur. One assumption remains constant: whatever the nature of the amorous adventures illustrated by Rowlandson in Regency times, or by continental contemporaries like the artists of *La Vie Parisienne*, these postcards of

the post-Victorian era do *not* imply a background of promiscuity and philandering, but of support for the moral code and matrimony. That is why women, rather than men, have a major stake in the chase.

Some of Bamforth's early life-model cards show the chaperonage conventions and the accompanying dodges with an ingenious charm. Just as the Edwardian miss knew all about using her wiles—a glance under the brim of a hat, over a fan at a dance, across the top of a lifted muff or from beside a bicycle, apparently in trouble—to attract a male without losing modesty, so she was ready for ruses in the cause of encouragement. She is shown sitting in the park with her father, whose eye has a bandage, deliberately on the blind side to give her 'follower' a chance of a kiss or squeeze. At home, while parents stay in one room with its door open she and a young man are trusted at the piano in another. But it is clear that two hands can keep up a duet whilst the other two engage elsewhere. Occasionally ruses backfire. A girl with her schoolboy brother as watch and ward sits on a garden seat; her suitor's arm and hand steal round her back to reach her hand—but he closes on the boy's.

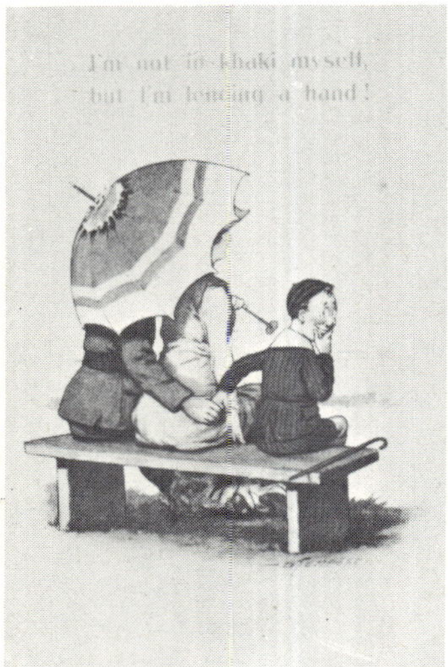

One convention is always upheld by the artist. It might be called the 'safety gap'. No embracing couples are shown with their figures completely met together in front—to avoid misconstruction. So a variety of devices occur—couples leaning over seats, stiles, walls, tree trunks, chairs, to kiss. The marble columns of public monuments even serve the purpose, as in a card with the verse:

Two lovers bold are seen embracing,
Hearts through lips are interlacing,
For when kindred souls are missing,
You'll find them—somewhere—somehow—kissing.

It's almost a case of the inanimate chaperon!

A delightful near-surrealist card—'I've got you bottled now'—with its young man-about-town in eye-glass and white tie contemplating a girl's head coming out of the champagne bottle, puts the man one up. But although 'opportunity knocks at every man's door'—pictured with a 'masher' catching the eye of a glamorous promenader in hobble skirt and feather boa—it is the girl who takes the tricks. 'Isn't it lovely to be engaged?' shows one, with finger on lip and calculating eye. Another card has a girl in low-cut mauve velvet, surrounded by a gold hoop with five diamonds, triumphantly telephoning 'I've accepted the ring'. Finally, in 'How it feels to mere man' the picture of bride and bridegroom kneeling at the altar has the latter diminished to half size. That's the penalty for chasing, as you thought, 'hot stuff' and catching eyes behind fans!

The reputation of the Edwardian age as 'fast' depends on comparisons and well publicised instances. The Empire promenade, the Gaiety

I've ACCEPTED THE RING.

OPPORTUNITY KNOCKS AT EVERY MAN'S DOOR.

ISN'T IT LOVELY TO BE ENGAGED?

theatre, the 'modern Babylon' aspect of London, the King's conquests, Monte Carlo, Maxim's, the Jersey Lily, the Smart Set's doings, etc, make a total impression greater than the sum of the parts would warrant. For people in ordinary walks of life the age was expansive, pleasure conscious—a watershed of ideas which would eventually liberate people from Victorian stuffiness and censoriousness—but no more unconventional than your, or my, family-group photographs of the period suggest. 'There was an almost imperceptible slackening of discipline and a little more looseness of speech. But not much. Women began to go about more freely and even to smoke, sometimes in public—but never in the

"How it feels to mere Man."

street' (W. Macqueen Pope). That is as far as the 'fast' age went for most. It took a war to break the continuity of normal life before any real difference in the 'Ma, he's-making-eyes-at-me' behaviour pattern earns comment among popular humorists.

'I knew I should get off—I wonder if it's an officer.' The girl on the promenade seat feels what she thinks to be a bottom-pinch. It is actually a dig from the stick under an old man's arm as he sits with his back to her. This is obvious expectation, however, of a bolder approach and readiness to respond.

In war 'both love and fashion are stimulated: men in uniform always stir feminine emotions—and women in love want to look their loveliest'. This opinion of a former editress of *Vogue* is supported by songwriters and artists. 'All the girls love a sailor' . . . 'It's the khaki what does it every time, you know . . .'—the small boy in service cap is 'clicking' with the small girl. And the girls don't play so hard to get—there may not be 'another time'—nor stick for long to slow starters.

I saw you with your soldier boy last night
Yet can it be my memory plays a game?
For I could swear he was a different height
And really didn't look a *bit* the same.

And, as the card shows, she was dressed to 'look her loveliest' or most fetching.

There are risks, as well as opportunities, in wartime speeding up of courtship's preliminaries. 'Beware' reads the caption to the sketch of a girl with 'bobby-dazzler' feathered hat, tight green velvet jacket, pink umbrella and hip-clinging skirt, with her eye on two Tommies:

Beware! some boys are green, some larky,
Yet both look just the same in khaki.

And then there are 'manoeuvres' of various sorts: 'I hear you're moving—trust the night will be a fine one'. The trooper with his arms round two charmers winks knowingly. (A day's 'manoeuvres' in the Second World War will bring him back to billet wearing a pink 'issue' bra under his battle-dress!)

Risk of another kind, on a card which might have run into censorship troubles just prior to the Wolfenden Report days, is due to kilts. 'Well, I'll be . . .! I've followed for two miles and then it turns out to be a Jock! One never knows, does one?' But of the 'come-hither' appeal of kilts in the right context there is no doubt whatever. 'I'm Scotch, and neat at that! How'd you like me—with or without?' The lassie on the bench has bare knees, a glad eye, and red tam o' shanter.

As well as bringing down barriers in the mutual approach of the sexes, conditions of short leave and long separation brought sexual relations more clearly into the open. 'Oh dear! he's been gone that long now that I've nearly forgotten what *men* are like' says the woebegone wife going upstairs to bed with her candle. As if to tantalise the deprived, or titillate the doubtful, another card shows a small nude boy clasping a book to his middle, with the words 'How to . . .' visible. 'I shan't show it to you—it's FOR ME AND MY GAL'.

There is no question now, as man-shortage mounts, that women are in chase. '300,000 more men wanted' (*Daily Wail*) calls forth from the all dressed-up girl 'Hi—it's *us* that wants 'em'. Leap Year (1916: Battle of the Somme) accentuates the point. 'Come on girls! there's an eligible.' 'I never did like these' (enlarged flea) 'but they're harmless compared with these' (predatory female) 'in Leap Year'. From the burglar, trapped under the spinster's bed and wishing he'd never come, to the 'reserved occupation' gent, hooked by a large determined matron, men show anxiety only to escape. This clear statement of the role of chased and chaser extends beyond 'leaps'. A man on the park seat with a wasp attacking his rear, turns to the female beside him: 'Good Heavens, madam, stop it!'

Frankness is conspicuous in the drawings also. The girl on a soldier's knee, reciprocating a close embrace, has come quite a long way from the Edwardian 'safety gap' convention. But then, as an equally intimate piece remarks: 'It's wonderful how general service brings people together'—inset, Tommy with housemaid. No doubt night shifts for munition girls, air raids, and darkened

With the 20s when 'girls went as near naked as women have been at any time in Europe since the Directoire', came the jazz, cocktail, night-club, silk-stocking, sun-bathing, Valentino age. At the level where the cards reflect it, intercourse between the sexes comes off quite mildly. Women certainly have begun to enjoy new freedom vis-à-vis men. 'Two small ports and I feel quite saucy' declares one in a low neck and high flush, to male stares. 'It's a nice wicked place this, but I don't want to leave' says another. 'THE MUSTARD CLUB AGAIN' reads a caption: 'You were out with him last night—what's he like?' 'Oh, he's a hot member.' There is plenty of 'black bottom' and 'tango', sea-side 'clicking' and pillion-riding, and leg-show. The girl with her hose-tops showing—'Haven't had a bite yet, but the bait's all right . . . they're nibbling'—knows what she's doing. The one who declares

> I've had a couple of cocktails
> With a man that's rather nice,
> If I risk another,
> Bang goes mother's good advice.

admits the danger. But the general drift is 'so far and no further'.

As the artist of swift romance for two has it: 'Mind you don't mucky your ticket'. (Romance only stopped being 'romantic' when they all started calling it sex.) As for the men who say 'When I've had one over the eight I'm a regular devil with the girls—didn't you know?' they tend to seek safety in numbers when it comes to the point. Manners are obviously freer. Morals are governed by 'Safety first: go slow' and 'If you can't be good be careful'. But the signs of the brakes coming off are there. Freedom to get away from them all, to roam beyond the range of surveillance, beyond neighbourhood codes of respectability, chances even of recognition, *and* to have a mobile courting covert into the bargain has come—with the cheap car.

The 'robot flapper of the future' was a card fiction of the 30s. It shows a girl with road signs—'STOP, CAUTION, GO'—on her back, catching the eye of two sporting types. The real problem was getting them to obey the STOP signal when a girl *was* out in a sports car. Of course it was on the cards that she might set the pace: 'Is it nearly time for the car to break down, George?'

Or, in film slang from the kerb, 'How about taking me for a ride, Big Boy?' the retort being 'O.K. I'll risk it . . . I've got a fire extinguisher'. At the parking place, with luck, a patrol might intervene: 'Come on, you've been there long enough'. More likely she'd be driven out into the backwoods, and if the pace wasn't hot enough, have a long walk home. 'You lose, big boy' says one damsel: 'I brought my hiking shoes just in case'. In 'Another motorist has his licence endorsed' the intended victim leaves Romeo with a black eye.

Variations of the gambit become a favourite theme of this decade. Promiscuity is now a recognised possibility—and in more ways than one. The car's the thing to make the catch—especially if it's 'on the firm':

> In Birmingham she was Bessie,
> She was Margaret in Perth,
> In Bradford she was Jessie
> And the sweetest girl on earth!
> In London she was Florence
> And the dearest of the bunch . . .
> But they're down in his expenses
> As PETROL, OIL and LUNCH.

Sex has come out into the open. Hollywood has helped to see to that. 'Look, mummy! I'll bet they're film stars!', says the little girl, pointing to a couple in a clinch in the park. The skit on sex situations is likely as a rule to be some way behind the pace-setters of the times. Although revue and music-hall comedians get away with much risqué material, the gap between what could be said and what could be printed was still, in the England of this period, 'rather exceptionally wide' (George Orwell)—even on comic postcards, except those of the lowest order. So what offended, if spotted by the censor, in entertainer's patter, had presumably passed the barrier from offence to acceptance by the time it featured on these cards. When the 'fast worker' in the snap-brim felt and Errol Flynn moustache says: 'I love seeing experienced girls home!' 'But I'm not experienced',

'You will be by the time you get home, my dear!', he is certainly not at odds with the assumptions of his day. Nor is the chap in natty double-breasted blue and 'art' tie at the perfume counter: 'This is a nice perfume for 30s, Sir. It's called "Perhaps"'. 'It's no good to me, Miss—for thirty bob I want CERTAIN.' Things moved quickly. By the 1940s 'Ma's' function is quite obsolete: 'Now you're getting married, if there's anything you want to know go to your mother'. 'Nay Pop, for years now she's been coming to me!'

To bring into sharper focus the rapid development of sexual mores in mid-twentieth century, jump a short generation and sample the cards of the 60s. 'Smile please, you're on CANDID CAMERA!' sets the tone. It is addressed to a just-married pair, nude, in bed. 'We've nothing to worry about, love, we haven't been drinking' says young-man-with-girl-in-car (her bra and slip hang over the window) as the constable shines his torch. In the bachelor flat it is all quite simple and explicit: 'Say when, darling!' 'After the drinks, darling!' Or in the bridal suite: 'Am I the first man to sleep with you, darling?' 'Blimey', replies the up-to-date bride, 'You will be if you doze off.' Even on the sofa, in front of TV we meet the knowing leer: 'And which lucky couple is going to hit the jack-pot tonight?' (*her* bra and slip are off too). The 'pint' was now no longer the badge of manhood, remarks a social critic: it was 'having sex'.

A wordless female, standing puzzled before a hospital sign '←MATERNITY ACCIDENT→' sums up the permissive decade. She is in the same predicament as the girl at the doctor's. 'You're either going to have a baby or you have a bad cold, Miss.' 'That's funny, doctor, I can't think who could have given me a cold.' And so on. Few girls object now: 'You say you only want my heart, but you're looking for it in some damned funny places'. In the woods it is more likely to be: 'Fred, come and see what I've got',

with blouse cut low almost to non-existence and skirt held high to show—her bunches of flowers! 'What do you think about UNO, Miss?' The response falls pat 'I never think of anything else, mister!'

How did everything become so explicit and so, seemingly, un-wicked? The climate of opinion with regard to sex has been through several types of forcing house in the last quarter of a century. War again and the GI invasion; the Kinsey Report with its remorseless statistics and Sunday paper follow-ups on petting, orgasm, and pre-marital intercourse. Continental films and transatlantic war novels (eg *The Naked and the Dead*—a British bestseller), reinforced by strip-tease and ubiquitous 'pin-up' publications. Then the Wolfenden Report and its recommendation about 'consenting adults'; 'call girls' and 'models' instead of 'prostitutes' and 'street walkers'; the publicity attending the Profumo case from 'the most prostituted press in the world'. Following that the freeing of *Lady Chatterley* and the four-letter word ('I know now what I'm going to be when I grow up, mum', says the boy in short pants caught reading it), and the *Fanny Hill* testimony on 'How the woman feels'. Hip-rolling pop singers and 'blue' records. The magazine medical advisers and guilt-therapists ('Frigidity and how to avert it'), the 'intellectual' peddlers of the erotic and the 'public school' of dramatists. To clinch matters, the Lambeth Conference, with bishops' recognition of intercourse for purposes 'other than procreation', and, after slot-machine contraceptives in colleges, 'the pill'. All these, with cumulative pressure, helped finally to crack the old insular English-Puritan crust. Society, whilst it called for teenage continence, was seen to revolve commercially round continuous exploitation of sex. The unmentionable became mentionable. 'The illustrations (to *An ABZ of Love*) are a delight. One especially, of a couple enjoying cunnilinctus has a purity . . .' (*Observer Review*, February 1969). Any mirror held up to humanity in this mass-communication world was sure to reflect, writ larger and clearer than ever before, and whatever their 'kinky' nature—THE FACTS OF LIFE. The show *Oh, Calcutta* even demonstrated them.

Tradition dies hard. 'Woman was born after man', reads a card of the 20s: 'She's been after him ever since'. Underneath, perhaps, it's still the same. In a subtler version, of the 60s, women still show, or show that they know, the way. One of Bamforth's latest cards has a bouncing redhead, one who obviously 'knows what it's for', waiting impatiently in bed. It is her anxious-looking husband, clutching her waist with one hand, who needs to hold in the other a book entitled *Sex Instruction*.

9 *'We'll meet again'*

'Bravo, the Air Force!' The picture on the card, of course, shows a 'popsie' having trouble with her skirt over a hot-air grating. This Bamforth issue hits, spot on, the opening difference between the two wars. A 'gamey' instead of a high devotional spirit: and almost total dependence on a 'game'—and gamey—small body of airmen based in England, instead of on the 'Old Contemptibles' and the vast build-up of infantry in Flanders. This most junior and most technological of the Services sets the tone, as it originated the characteristic slang and humour, of World War II.

'Hey, mister, what do you think about Hitler?' 'Dunno, I've never seen him play.' The new terror of Europe is cut down to size even before the Battle of Britain begins. 'I hear your husband's joined up, Mrs Binns?' 'Yeah! the war won't last long, now, he never keeps any job more than a few weeks!', brings echoes from October 1916. But as to 'Peace by Negotiation'—a move which Hitler thought could hardly be resisted after the BEF's evacuation from Dunkirk, and one which would ensure him a free hand against eastern Europe with no second front—a card with that title shows the unmistakable spirit of the defenders. On a small boy handing up a note the tall, severe, tight-faced teacher bends a withering look and holds her cane at the ready.

As to restrictions, 'rationing'—an early starter

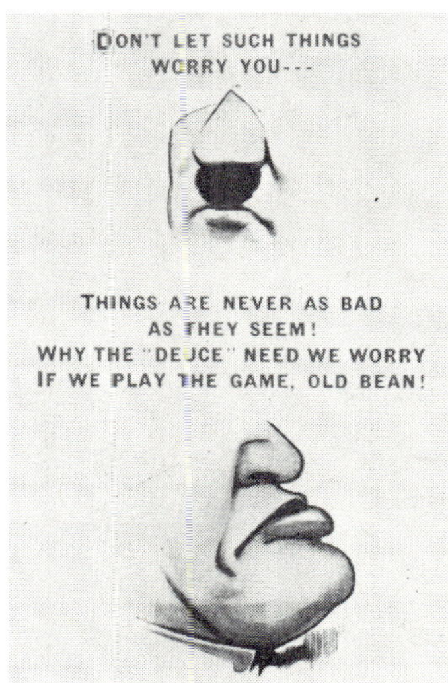

HEY, MISSUS! YER GOING DOWN THE
WRONG A.R.P. SHELTER!!
GENTLEMEN

WHEN THE AIR RAID WARNINGS SHRIEK OUT LOUD
WHAT FUNNY SIGHTS THERE'LL BE,
PEOPLE DASHING OUT DISTRESSED,
SOME IN NIGHTIES, SOME UNDRESSED!
OH, DAMN THE BLACK-OUT--IT'S TOO DARK TO SEE!
Taylor

OH, SO THAT'S FER ME, IS IT? WELL, YER'D BETTER GO
BACK AND BRING ONE WI' A SHOE HORN!
Taylor

THEY SEEM TO BE ALL NICELY ASLEEP NOW---LET'S BEGIN!

I'M TELLING YOU!
N.B.G.
COMMERCIAL
TRAVELLER
IF HITLER WANTS ANY
MORE TERRITORY
HE CAN HAVE MINE!

NOW THEN, LOVE, STOP IT! CAN'T YOU SEE THE SYMBOL OF PEACE!

this time—is met in the mood of 'we've seen it through before' and with another echo from the first time.

Put your little bit of sugar
In your old cup of tea and
STIR, STIR, STIR

sung to the well remembered tune. The threat of air raids and ARP provide opportunities for the perennial comic artist's vision of fat females caught in the bath: 'By gum, shouldn't I look daft if we had an air raid now', or of charmers half-dressed—in bra, panties, and slung civilian respirator—the serious point. We are in the little man's usual world of missed chances.

When the air raid warnings shriek out loud
What funny sights there'll be . . .
Oh, damn the black out—IT'S TOO DARK TO SEE!

With apprehension deflected to the trivial embarrassment and contretemps our nerves are made all the steadier. 'Hey, missus! yer going down the wrong ARP shelter!'—the rotund lady disappears down the GENTS. Then there is a humorous contempt for the official idea of 'specifications' in the system of precautions. 'Oh, so that's fer me is it?' says the overweight lady to the men who've brought the Anderson shelter: 'Well yer'd better go back and bring one wi' a shoe horn!' This is normality reasserted. In the street, when the all clear has sounded, two cats confer: 'They seem to be all nicely asleep now—Let's begin!'

Refusal to be rattled, a cynical 'we've heard it' both to threats and promises, a steady, angry determination to prick the balloon of 'that man'—these are the popular attitudes. The mood was sparked off after Munich—with disillusion and distrust in the wake of Chamberlain's 'Peace in our Time' bargaining. The cards have it. 'Now then, love, stop it!' says the half-seas-over husband to his red-jowled Teutonesque wife with rolling pin at 2 AM. 'Can't you see the SYMBOL OF PEACE!' and he brandishes his umbrella. We all knew the answer to that one. So if Hitler wanted any more territory 'He can have mine'

says the pot-bellied little man with NBG Commercial Traveller on his case. Defiance was focused. 'It's all because of Hitler, The cost of mild and bitter, but remember this my friend,

When at night you grope about,
Adolf's going to pay for this
HIS LIGHTS WILL BE PUT OUT.

The personal note stemmed from Churchill—'I will *not* be beaten by "that man"'. 'It was the

A LITTLE PRESENT TO THE BOYS WHO
ARE DOING THEIR BIT!
TAKE YOUR PICK, LADS!

KEEPING UP THE
GOOD WORK
WITH A CHEERY SMILE,
THAT'S THE SPIRIT, GIRLIE,
YOU'LL FIND IT'S
WELL WORTH WHILE!

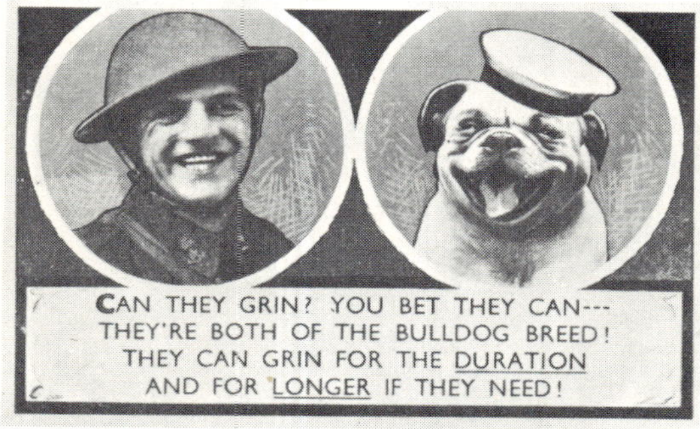
CAN THEY GRIN? YOU BET THEY CAN---
THEY'RE BOTH OF THE BULLDOG BREED!
THEY CAN GRIN FOR THE DURATION
AND FOR LONGER IF THEY NEED!

WE'VE GOT THE PLANES,
AND THE PILOTS, TOO---
BRAVO, AIR FORCE!
YOU'RE THE GOODS!
WE'RE REALLY
PROUD OF YOU!

There'll Always Be An England
HER SONS ARE
BRAVE AND FREE,
THEY FIGHT A
RIGHTEOUS CAUSE
O'ER SKY, O'ER LAND
AND SEA!

PILOT: "ONLY JUST MANAGED TO PULL OUT OF THAT DIVE.
WE MIGHT HAVE HAD AN ACCIDENT!"
OBSERVER: "MIGHT!---I'VE HAD ONE!!"
15

nation that had the lion's heart. I had the luck to be called upon to give the roar'. (W.S.C.)

Those few sentimental cards that mark this war's send-off have shed both roses and tears, hymns and grey-haired mothers. They are crisper, more confident, cheerful. They also include women in uniform, which made quite a difference to the men working beside them. 'KEEP SMILING', 'Keep up the Good Work', 'Happy Landings', 'Here's Hoping' (to see him or her on leave), 'You're not forgotten' (to the Ack-Ack and searchlight crews). 'That's the spirit, Girlie', 'Take your pick, Lads!' (with a picture of four smiling girls outside a hangar), and 'We've got the PLANES and the PILOTS too'. All services seem to have remarkably photogenic personnel.

The farewells are brief. 'Good-bye, Daddy: God bless' or 'I'll think of you without a doubt'. The groups of soldiers or sailors are really in service, not just studio takes. Emotion, when present, is realistic too: 'I do miss my hubby', says the young wife sitting up in bed, 'No cup of tea. NO NOTHING'.

Perhaps the most typical card of this kind has a tin-hatted soldier and a sailor-hatted dog, seen as if through binoculars:

> Can they grin? You bet they can,
> They're both of the bull-dog breed!
> They can grin for the duration
> And for longer if they need.

Hitler's War Directive no 16—invasion plan—had these words: 'As England in spite of her hopeless military position has so far shown herself unwilling to come to any compromise . . .' At the same point Churchill's Chief of Staff gave him this advice: 'The real test is whether the morale of our fighting personnel and civil population will counter-balance the numerical and material advantages which Germany enjoys. We believe it will'. The song card—one of few in a period of forces' broadcast songsters—reinforces this belief: 'There'll always be an England'.

The cards, not so abundant this time, reveal some of the quirks and catchphrases of Britain's unbroken morale. No shooting a line for aircrew, however intrepid or suicidal their actions. *Pilot*: 'Only just managed to pull out of that dive. We might have had an accident'. *Observer*: 'Might! I'VE HAD ONE!' The sentiment—and the savagery—could safely be left to poets, just as the nervous presentiments were left to the dramatists.

'Gosh, I wish I'd one of them Dictators here—just for two minutes!' The heartfelt cry, on a card, comes from the householder digging a slit-trench in his front garden. 'If this were Hitler'—a bending, brown-uniformed figure—'what would

YOU do, Chums?' Searchlights, raids, invasion scares call out the usual crude jokes, the ordinary grumbles.

'When the daylight Alert has sounded, calling us to what? not fear but application . . .' wrote Edith Scovell. The cards deal less with the application than with minimising the fear. 'Who wants blinking searchlights tonight?' grumbles a soldier with a girl on his knee in the park. 'Look quick and come to bed, Alfred,' reads ANOTHER BLACKOUT TRAGEDY: 'Heck. Where am I? They don't call me Alfred'. In this would-be normal comic world the obvious reference has to be made. 'If there's an air raid in the night, don't be in a hurry or you might put your foot in it when you jump out shouting JERRY.' Even the crucial task of the AFS, as London becomes the chief battle area, gets its quip and implied understatement: 'Do you like playing with fire, Mr Smith?' the frisky blonde is saying to the officer at readiness. And as billeting becomes the order of the day, the stock joke of the man-hungry old maid comes, not unkindly, into its own: 'I'm going to have six children', says one of them to the other.

The mood—stoic, anti-sentimental, almost mock-heroic—was born out of a time when all were, or tomorrow could be, in the front line. The old question 'What did YOU do in the war, daddy, How did you help us to win?' was turned off lightly with 'Circuits and bumps and turns, laddie, And how to get out of a spin'. At a deeper level, perhaps the feeling was 'After the first death there is no other', as Dylan Thomas was to write in 'A Refusal to Mourn the Death, by Fire, of a Child in London'.

As in the Kaiser's war, the minutiae of restrictions and regulations came in for mock derisive comment. 'Talking about food rationing do

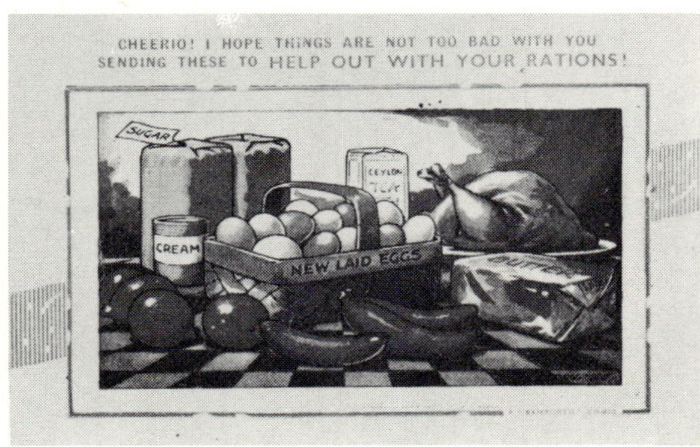

you know what they're selling for bacon at Woolworth's' 'No. What?' 'Frying pans.' As always there are the tantalising visions—fresh eggs, butter, bacon, sirloin, sugar—and the hints of 'under the counter' supplies. 'Don't know how you're getting on, that's why I'm sending you this.' The picture is loaded with rationed goods. 'Even if you've got enough a bit extra will not come amiss. PS, DON'T TELL THE GESTAPO.' As time went on the Ministry itself went one better:

> Those who have the will to win
> Cook potatoes in their skin,
> Knowing that the sight of peelings
> Deeply hurts Lord Woolton's feelings.

At a time when the official slogan was BE ABOUT IT?' Careless talk cost lives: but bath water, as well as talk had to have limits. The typical maid with her eye to the keyhole nudges our memory: 'The *cheek* of that officer. I told him there were no baths this morning'.

Other restrictions are wide open for refitting some of the ageless jokes. The window cleaner, seeing nude girl in bathroom lighting a cigarette, exclaims: 'Gosh, a full twenty Players!' And the girl with only handbag and pink undies walking down the road: 'If you haven't any coupons, WHAT CAN YOU DO?' Only the lady at the hardware counter shows a trace of vindictiveness, after knitting so many balaclava helmets and pullovers for the troops. 'Hey, mister! Give me a bale of barbed wire: I'm going to knit a singlet for Hitler!'

'God Bless' in wartime was on most people's

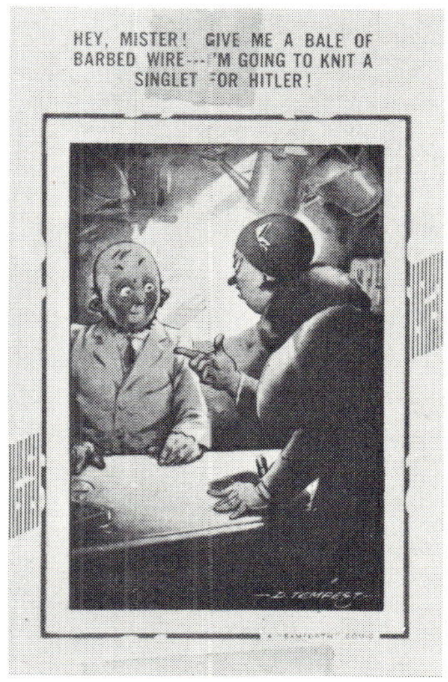

LIKE DAD, KEEP MUM the cards supplied their own twist. The sailor whispering in the girl's ear carries the comment: 'You can bet he's not telling her anything of national importance'. The reminder, alongside the artist's version of Hitler's drooping lock and glaring eyes is: 'BEWARE, you are warned not to talk, but that doesn't mean you can't write! So WHAT lips, civilians' especially. But while prayers to and invocations of Him in the First World War were constant subjects, in the second, in line with the less prominent role of public religion, they occur far less often. A wife at home may 'pray with might and main, Until the bells of peace ring out, And you come home again'. And one of the hit songs sung by Vera Lynn, the 'Forces' sweet-

heart, was 'I Pray for You'. But, as a general rule this wife now is in the forces, on the farm or in the factory helping to ensure that her man *does* come home. The usual invocation is simply for 'Good luck' to help along 'British pluck' to bring the men safely through 'these stirring times'. Rarely does a card make the direct appeal 'Have Faith', with head of Christ and verse in the old tradition :

The world is dark with suffering,
Evil runs its wayward way,
But brave men fight for what is right,
And right SHALL have its day!

The high proportion of cards wishing luck indicates, just the same, need for a feeling of providential support when fighting in a cause that is just.

Luck in carrying on the war if necessary alone, as Churchill promised after Dunkirk, was certainly necessary. And luckily it was forthcoming. A 1943 magazine Quiz question 'Do you know your WAR?' asked 'In what year immediately after the Battle of France did Churchill say we should be ready to take the offensive? Was he or will he be right?' The answer was '1942 : we took the offensive in North Africa in 1942'. The luck which made it possible was that Hitler, having called off 'Sealion', the proposed invasion plan of Britain, launched 'Barbarossa', his attack against Russia, 22 June 1941. The blessing in disguise, additional to the luck, was, paradoxically, the *defeat* and rescue of Dunkirk, whereby a trained army had providentially been saved from another long war of attrition in Flanders.

Until 'Barbarossa' Britons 'took it' alone. 'Tools for the job' were coming from across the Atlantic, at great hazard and loss of merchant shipping. Action upon the declaration 'America will see to it that Britain wins the war' came considerably later. There are no 'Yanks are coming' cards this time. The references to them are oblique : beginning with 'John Bull for Great Britain, and what for America?' 'Uncle spam, teacher' and going on to 'You will come to our American tea, won't you Mrs Meakin?' from the vicar to the housewife : 'O.K. Big Boy'. The implications are well on target. As the war in the Pacific unfolds a native girl at a South Sea trading post greets a sailor with four piccaninnies : 'But I thought we'd only been to this island three times, Joe'.

Meanwhile the personalities of Nazidom came in for verbal sharpshooting, more so than their predecessors. Deflation before retaliation. 'Lord Haw-Haw', 'the donkey that's braying from Hamburg', is turned into a music-hall dude. Hitler is pictured as a cloth-capped workman

pushing a pram-wheeled barrow inscribed 'Mr Schicklgruber Painter and Decorator'. Another, not unflattering representation of the Fuhrer, with arm raised in Nazi salute, carries the caption: 'This chap's always wanting to leave the room! Why the heck doesn't he want to leave Europe and please everybody?' The punch was to come later. Goebbels or his understudy is shown at the microphone: 'The Luftwaffe shot down ten RAF bombers!—one of our towns is missing!'

As for the enemy's secret weapons the seaside quip comes in handy: 'Gosh! You gave me a scare missus', says the little man contemplating a huge red-costumed bottom breaking surface; 'I thought it was a MAGNETIC MINE!' Finally, by way of retort to our own indignities in air-raid shelters, Hitler is shown raising the lid of a swastika-marked dustbin, from within.

He looks anxiously across to Goering, whose large bemedalled rear projects from his bin: 'Have those naughty bombers gone, Herman?' The Reichsmarschall's resemblance to a porker is *perhaps* unpremeditated.

In a war that started 'total' and became as wide as the seven seas, keeping up with its phases on postcards was neither possible nor politic. Other media for encouraging the troops' morale overseas proliferated—from ENSA and

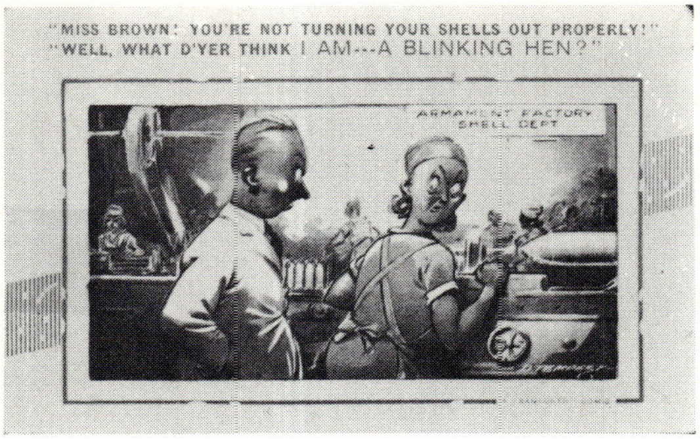

ITMA and 'Jane' to army newsheets, *Reveille* and P/O Prune. Britain under Churchill could take the big threats, it seemed. 'Sunk without warning, Constable—you'd better report it to Winshton', as the drunk submerges in the fire-precautionary bathful of water, reveals the war-leader's buttressing position. It was the little things that irked. And the little things were those which helped most to maintain one's individuality during a vast conflict whose very nature demanded some suspension of personal identity.

For this individuality the cards could provide some sort of safety valve. Make-up, for instance—blow the official view!

> Let them have their lipstick, bless their little hearts:
> Surely they have proved themselves girls of many parts.

Or about the shortage of silk stockings, especially fully fashioned: 'What happened to the girl who wore cotton ones! Why NOTHING I've heard them say'—so *do* something! The regulation amount of bath water might have personal compensations: 'Wonder what she'll look like in 5 in of water' winks the window-cleaner. 'You've had it, Chum' mocks the man trying to pour Scotch from an empty bottle. But '*They* haven't rationed REAL food yet. You can get it every day' smiles the other chap with the tankard of beer. If you can't drive a car about as you'd like, laugh it off. 'Will exchange for 5s and a petrol lighter' reads the notice against the family saloon. And if MAKE DO AND MEND has to be the motto—'Before this lot's over' says the once-comic northern housewife with patched bloomers on

the line, 'I'll bet Hitler's pants are worse than ours—so why worry?'

In total war literary activity, like any other, is compelled more or less to serve the interest of the community. Whilst we lived with

> A throbbing cello-drone of planes
> Entombed beneath this caving liberty
> (Day Lewis)

fringe literary activities such as jokes on cards expressed an attitude, a way of self-assertion sometimes, that played its part in seeing things through. Through from 'Torch', the North African offensive, 1942, to 'Roundup' later renamed 'Overlord' (cross-channel invasion), through from D-day to VE-day. 'Not how to avoid defeat but how to inflict it', it goes without saying was our purpose. Even by those who 'saw through that guff' and listened to no 'laboured Augustan speeches' the unforced sangfroid of these war humours could be felt to underly it. MORE NAVAL MANOEUVRES—but the sailor and his girl are heading 'To the Woods';

At one stage *Life* magazine had thought that Hitler might bore the British public into making peace, but hastened to correct this view. 'The Britisher has the qualities which above all others may help him to win: he can laugh at his own troubles.'

10 *Taboo*

Nothing, it seems, is more serious than a joke. 'Since our individual childhood and, similarly, since the childhood of human civilisation, hostile impulses against our fellow men have been subject to the same restrictions, the same progressive repression, as our sexual urges.' Freud sees in the civilised joke against a person a means of satisfying deep-down hatred and hostility against him. In the civilised dirty joke he sees a means of satisfying repressed sexual urges. Put another way, codes of law, morals, and religious systems are the enemy of 'natural' man, the one whose 'tastes lie toward safety, soft beds, no work, pots of beer and women with voluptuous figures'. His problem is to subordinate or reconcile his instincts to the rules of society. So the joke acts as a token of hostility and defiance, cocking a snook at the Puritan 'to whom all things are impure', and satisfying his urges *without* breaking down civilised standards. Many jokes—in some series of cards the proportion is incontestably high—revolve round obscenity, precisely because society, in its public Christian guise, has insisted on a lofty sexual morality. The straight sex joke probably accounts for a good half of Bamforth's later cards.

Backsides, 'jerries', knickers, belly buttons, breasts or now 'falsies',—these are seen by Richard Hoggart as, in the dirty postcard view, the 'circumscribed possible situations for humour'. To which might be added, until recently, nudity.

One need not look far for reasons. The polite attitude towards such items has in the not-so-remote past appeared to combine the pathological sensitivity of Swift with the mingled false delicacy and prurience of the Victorians. Take only Chloe, until her wedding night, in Strephon's view:

> No humours gross, or frowzy steams
> No noisome Whiffs, or sweaty streams
> Before, behind, above, below,
> Could from her taintless body flow.
> (She) would so discreetly Things dispose
> None ever saw her pluck a Rose.
> Her dearest comrades never caught her
> Squat on her hams, to make Maid's Water.

But thereafter:

Strephon who heard the fuming Rill
As from a mossy Cliff distill,
Cry'd out, ye Gods, what sound is this?
Can Chloe, heavenly Chloe—? . . . and worse.

With the Victorians 'bosom' instead of breasts, 'limbs' for legs, 'lower back' for bottom, 'nether garments' for breeches, 'unmentionables' for pantaloons, marked the extent of their susceptibility and its concealment. Even tables and pianos required leg coverings, and beds 'valances' in case a certain 'article' (jerry) might come into view. So long as these human appurtenances were capable of causing shock and their mention in genteel circles regarded as taboo, their place in the comic postcard repertoire was assured. The joke brought the problem into the open again. It relieved the inhibition, gave animal-man a look in, and assured us that it was Swift not ourselves who was abnormal.

The more obstinate the attempt to conceal some feature, such as the 'jerry' or a man's nervous tendency to 'micturate' at awkward times, the more persistent the joke theme. None of us care to be reminded, in *some* circumstances, of the indignities or gross forms of our bodies. For our general sanity, it is a good thing not to turn knowledge inward, as did the writer of 'Strephon and Chloe', but to laugh it out of the system. If your bottom is like a Hottentot's, lady, admit it and look at an even bigger one. And the cards, where everything becomes larger than life, will ensure that you can!

Persistence of this 'beer-bottom-lavatory' humour, as Hoggart calls it, and the 'extraordinary changelessness' of seaside postcards, is both to be expected—a truism of observation, in fact—and only a partial truth. The subjects of taboo may change, in some circles slowly. How slowly the many bannings by 'Jix'—Sir Wm Joynson-Hicks, Home Secretary in the 20s—would show. But they have changed and continue to change, today perceptibly.

Keeping up, ie abreast of them, and keeping also within the rules of what may be printed, whatever current freedom of speech suggests, is one of the comic artist's problems. Pure/impure satirists, like Gerald Scarfe, can of course get away with a great deal more. The problem is not unlike that of the 'advanced' fashion designers, who find themselves striving to maintain interest by shifting the 'erogenous zones' of display, when nearly all available ones have become the 'sterilised zones' of fashions just going out. 'Attention is riveted on the bust line . . . For evening, necklines dip to the nipple level, just . . . though Courrèges caters for most tastes with target-shaped crutch concealers, tightly-stretched trousers and unexpected cut-outs in a variety of places' (*Observer,* Feb 1969). Where does one go from there?

No one would dispute the vulgarity of most comic cards. In the nature of the 'comic', as already exposed, vulgarity not only pays, but is to an accepted extent its *raison d'être*. These cards are not, however, obscene or indecent—within the context of current taboos. Card designs have always been submitted to a Censorship Committee—at Cleethorpes, Great Yarmouth, Folkestone, or currently, at Blackpool—whose rejections do not reach print. But the fluctuating nature of taboo will no doubt have become clear from the chapters on fashion and sex relations, with their advancing exposures and admissions. Its recent developments hardly surprise in this age of permissiveness, 'the sexy sixties'. For in view of our stage 'happenings' it seems like the pot calling the kettle black when a theatre is said to base its posters on seaside postcards so as to 'capture the comic vulgarity of the theme' (*Dutch Uncle* at the Aldwych), whilst another West End billing is for *Vagina Rex*!' The Lord Chamberlain's censorship of the stage ceased in 1968.

For an example of taboo fluctuation consider comic treatment of the female bust over the last few years. In line with what could appear in popular weekly papers such as *Parade*, as opposed to 'pin-up' magazines of the kind *London Magazine* calls 'Wink, Kink, Spank, Wank and Co', the bust on cards before 1965 was presented covered and regarded as 'untouchable'. Except in representations of paintings, or possibly in steamy bathroom mirrors, something was left to the imagination. It was certainly out of bounds to male hands. Since that year, when

in *Parade* even vestigial cover was left off, cards also have come by degrees to reveal the whole bust.

First it was by implication; as in the card 'Sorry couldn't find you an uncensored card' showing a girl clad in black stockings only, with a CENSORED sign just obscuring her navel and nipples. Then in jokes with statuary. 'Help' cries the sculptor hanging by one hand from the obvious protuberance of a huge marble breast. Or else in jokes about nudist camps or coloured girls in their own country. 'Blimey, I thought you said this was an undeveloped country!' says the man in the bush-hat staring at the shapes of a shapely pair of beauties. Later comes touching-in-error. 'Those aren't the marshmallows, Fred!' objects the girl in the cinema with reveal-all blouse, as her escort misses his aim for the bag of sweets. Or, again, by transference. A sharply defined bust, touching his back at the bus stop, makes the man with the bag of cash put up his hands.

In a characteristic suggestive card two US astronauts contemplate two 'space' girls with well developed breasts instead of shoulder blades. 'I'm not too keen on their faces, but I bet they're fun to dance with!' reads the caption. Finally the joke is actually focused on nipples: 'Fancy any-

thing for afters?' one fish says to another below a girl swimming in the nude. The 'disapproved' version—July 1966—of this read: 'I'm tired of the same old diet—I fancy a few tit bits'. A captionless joke, of an optician testing a girl with a squint, dressed only in her briefs, makes the obvious point—with more humorous impact.

One suspects here that wit tends to mitigate possible offence. A 'disapproved' joke of the same season, showing a stout lady with bare but nipple-less breasts in a large cooking-pot, has one black warrior saying to another: 'Blimey—just one is a meal in itself'. But perhaps the real offence was to the susceptibilities of coloured people. Stop press comment, in this titillating series, is reserved for a girl lying on the beach, a narrow, near-transparent strip round her breasts and a folded newspaper across her middle. Its headline—'TODAY'S SPORT'.

Much the same kind of special attention has been devoted, with progressive blatancy, to other formerly 'defended zones': the buttocks (female; shapely, not gross), the crutch (male, risible: female, tantalising). What is there left? Although 'briefs' falling off ballet, trapeze, or skating stars with results obviously in public view get by, it appears that some direct physical references are still taboo—at any rate in cards which aim to avoid prosecution.

'Blackpool Tower isn't as big as I thought it would be either,' says just-married bride in transparent shortie-nightie looking out of hotel window, in one Bamforth artist's sketch. (Disapproved: Nov 1968—male apprehension, perhaps?). 'Blimey—what size shoes do YOU take?'—man-to-man comment in the stalls of a urinal. (Disapproved: 1968—homosexual overtones?). This subject with its size, has been an *idée fixe* of popular pornographic thought since, and no doubt prior to, Cleland's *Fanny Hill.* Freud quotes a parallel example in discussing mistakes of speech and their intimate mechanisms. A lady in society says: 'Yes, a woman must be pretty if she is to please the men. A man is much better off. As long as he has five straight limbs he needs no more'. She is confusing under the assumed pressure of secret emotions 'four straight limbs' and 'all five senses'

and in doing so breaking through the barrier of taboo. The nearest thing to this in early cards is disingenuous. With a rolling-pin concealed under her apron—'A married woman soon gets to know what things are for'.

'Have you ever been picked up by the FUZZ?' (American slang for police). 'No, but I bet it's damn painful.' (Disapproved: 1968.) But all right now on stage—vide *Beard* and *Hair*, where remarks such as 'How good are your orgasms?' come across the footlights—though not from one Beat-girl to another on postcards in print. Here the Censorship Committees dig their toes in. 'That's Cynthia Brown', one youth remarks to another about a busty girl, 'I used to pinch her bull's eyes at school'. (Disapproved: ah! July 1964—would probably pass now.) 'Until I took this job I thought these 'ere feelings had died within me': a charlady with feather duster contemplates fig-leaved male statue. (Disapproved: September 1953—sure to pass now.) In the nude finale to the first act of *Hair* a reviewer noted both men and women 'riveting their gaze on the undressed men' and expressed surprise that this taboo should take so long to be defied. By computation based on the above taboos and their relaxation, how long will it take for this particular male bastion to fall—ten years, five, two—on the open-sale cards?

In the physical field one joke, where female sensitivity is at stake, has recently changed its direction. It was long since a commonplace of cards, Bamforth's or McGill's and others, to refer to pregnancy: 'Now, which of you is going to be mother?' as the waitress brings a pot of tea to two heavily paunched men, or 'Is your old man going to have one?' said by stout woman to equally stout woman in pub about pot-bellied husband outside. But the figure referred to was always mature or middle-aged. It was not done to 'knock' the image, maintained in all these cards, of youth as goodlooking and of sex-appeal as unalloyed in women of under, say, twenty-five. Nor, of course, until after the First World War, was anyone beyond that age expected to retain their good looks. Wives all became either gross and shapeless or else angular and grim-visaged. So the recent joke-card showing an ex-glamour puss heavily pregnant on a balcony, with a caption: 'Romeo, Romeo, wherefore art thou, Romeo?' breaks through a minor taboo as well as giving a new look to an old predicament.

Various bans are imposed by Censorship Committees—one or another may clamp down on any sketch that has, a bed, a nun, a 'pro', a reference to drugs, to angels, or to *lèse majesté* (the Union Jack sewn on knickers)—on grounds that are sometimes far from clear. Quite apart from these some subjects are treated as taboo by the joke artists themselves. So whilst the goofy curate or pompous vicar have seldom been spared, the Salvation Army is always respected—as indeed, in the common view, it deserves. So also with the Jew. Often a joke topic for his ways or looks or speech pre-war; never since the Nazi camps. So with Royalty, which has been and still is often pilloried by caricaturists—whatever may be inferred about politicians. So, too, with our coloured citizens no liberties are taken—apart from the chestnut about 'where I've been albums are black'. Certain topics may be spared, such as homosexuality, or have been spared whilst persecution was rife, out of the normal man's sympathy for the less normal. Though oddly enough, suicide is not spared, nor cremation.

Other topics which do fall foul of the censor, one suspects are kept in cold storage until the taboo is lifted. For how many jokes that appear today could not have been printed five years ago?

When the taboo is lifted on some of the 'further-out' sexual themes most of us will have ceased to be shockable on such topics. The 'dirty card's' role may then turn into one not of cocking a snook at codes of morality, but of keeping up the illusion that we are shockable, as an eventual escape route back to modesty. Meanwhile, it is open to argument that future social historians will find in the 'comics' of the 50s and 60s evidence of a freer, happier and more wholesome era than that in which cover-up was the rule, when to admit enjoying Bamforth's jokes one had to be oneself a bit of a card.

The Male is late!

"Many a battle has been fought under this grand old flag!"

BINGO
FULL
HOUSE

"[redacted] FEEL LIKE A RUDDY BARMAID FRED!"
"I DO LAD — BUT WHERE CAN WE GET ONE AT THIS TIME OF NIGHT?"

FROM TH' OWD LASS,
WITH ALL HER LUV!

FINISH

"THE EXPERIMENT HAS BEEN A COMPLETE SUCCESS PROFESSOR!"
LABORATORY

Acknowledgment

The author wishes to acknowledge his indebtedness to Bamforth & Company Limited for their courteous and unfailing assistance throughout the preparation of this book.

Acknowledgment is also made to Messrs Raphael Tuck for permission to reproduce 'The Subscription Ball', which appears on page 84.

Apologies are tendered for any inadvertent omissions in acknowledgment or failure to trace copyright holders.

Its a well known fact
that
TWO BLACKS DONT
MAKE A WHITE!

"I WISH I WERE SINGLE AGAIN."

'WATCHING STRIP TEASE AT THE CLUB EVERY NIGHT —
YOU CAN SEE ME STRIPPING CAN'T YOU ?'
'YES LOVE — BUT THE TEASE BIT SEEMS TO
BE MISSING !'

LORD, LET NOT MY SACRIFICE BE IN VAIN.

'BUT WHY DID YOU HIT ME? —
I DON'T GET IT'
'YOU'RE DEAD RIGHT BOY — YOU DON'T!'

Index

Abyssinia, 76
Ack-Ack, 93
ARP, 91
An ABZ of Love, 88
Anderson shelter, 91
Animatograph, 14
Anti-motoring Society, 50
Anzacs, 40
Arras, 40
Asquith, Herbert, 65
Austria, 38
Automobile Club, 49
AFS, 94

Baker, Syd, 14
Bamforth, Derek, 10, 19
  Edwin, 14, 15, 17
  Frank, 14
  Harry, 14
  James, 10, 11, 14, 17
  'Janie', 14
Bamforth & Co Ltd, 18
Band of Hope, 11
Bank Holiday, 20
'Barbarossa', 96
Bardot, Brigitte, 27, 78
Bath, 71
Beach-Romeo, 22
Beard, 103
Beaumont, Fred 'Shiner', 17
Beecham's Pills, 36
Beerbohm, Max, 65, 67
Belgium, 39
Bennett, Arnold, 47, 84
Bernadeau, Leon, 38
Beveridge, Lord, 65
Bevin, Ernest, 65
Bicycling, 52, 56, 80
Bingo, 57
Biplane, 52
Blackpool, 19, 21, 25, 100
Blackpool Tower, 21, 102
Bournemouth, 19
Bradford, 14, 49, 86
Bright Young Things, 24, 77
BBC, 55
BEF, 89
Brooke, Rupert, 39, 40
Brooklands, 49
Butlins Holiday Camp, 26

Canadians, 40
Capital punishment, 63
Censorship, 48
Censorship Committee, 100, 103, 104
Cerruti, 78
Chamberlain, Joseph, 30, 65
Chamberlain, Neville, 91
Chaperone, 80
Christmas cards, 17
Church-going, 52
Churchill, Winston, 65, 91, 93, 96, 98
Cleland, John, 102
Cocoa and reading rooms, 11
Comic artists:
  Bairnsfather, Bruce, 38, 39
  'Crowquill', 20
  Cruikshank, George, 20
  Du Maurier, George, 20, 51
  Guillaume, Albert, 20, 52
  Henri, Charles, 20
  Leech, John, 20
  Low, David, 37
  May, Phil, 31
  Rowlandson, Thomas, 20, 79
  Scarfe, Gerald, 100
  'Spy', 68
Copyright cases, 18
Courrèges, 100
Coventry, 49
Crystal Palace Show, 49
Cumberland, 59
Cycle-car, 52

Dancing, 24, 56, 75
Dardanelles, 46
Darwin (Australia), 54
Day Lewis, Cecil, 99
D-day, 99
DORA, 48, 56
De la Rue, 10
Dennis, C. J., 39
Derby, Earl of, 44
Diamond Jubilee, 49
Dickens, Charles, 25
Directoire, 85

Disney, Walt, 26
Divorce, 28
Domestic servant, 28
Don Juan, 28
Douglas (IoM), 52
Dover, 38
Drink, 60, 87, 98
Dryden, Leo, 17
Dunkirk, 96
'Dutch Uncle', 100

Eccles, 28
Eddystone Lighthouse, 15
Edward VII, 49
Edward, Prince of Wales, 68
Eiffel Tower, 15
Empire Theatre, 68, 81
ENSA, 97
Envelope, pictorial, 10
'Etoiles de Mer', 20
Eton crop, 73
Evans, Dr Christopher, 66

Fanny Hill, 88, 102
Films, 14, 15, 55, 86, 88
Fisher, Admiral 'Jackie', 38
Financial Times, 77
The Comic Postcard/2/74830/L.S.
Flanders, 89, 96
Flynn, Errol, 86
Folkestone, 100
Forde, Florrie, 40
Foy, Alf, 17
France, 20
Free Trade, 30, 63

Gaiety Girls, 71
Gaiety Theatre, 81
Gallipoli, 40
Garbo, Greta, 76
General Post Office, 10, 72
George V, 18, 39, 76
Germany, 15, 17, 93
Gestapo, 95
Gilbert, W. S., 58
Gissing, George, 58
Goebbels, Joseph, 97
Goering, Hermann, 97
Graves, Robert, 42
Great Yarmouth, 100
Greco, Juliet, 77
'Grundy, Mrs', 20

Haig, FM Douglas, 43
Hair, 103
Hall, Henry, 56
Hamburg, 96
Hamilton, Patrick, 25
Hangover Square, 25
Harrogate, 15
Hastings, 25
Haw-haw, Lord, 96
H-line, 78
Henty, G. A., 38
Hepburn, Audrey, 77
Hiking, 26, 86
Hill, Rowland, 10
Hinchcliffe, Hannah, 17
Hindenburg Line, 43
Hire purchase, 37
Hitler, Adolf, 26, 89, 91, 93, 95, 96, 97, 99
Hoggart, Richard, 35, 99, 100
Hollywood, 86
Holmbridge, 14
Holmfirth, 10, 11, 14, 15, 19
Homosexuality, 102
Hottentot, 100
Hylton, Jack, 56

Ideal Woman, 78
Illustrated Sporting and Dramatic News, 50
Irish Home Rule, 65
ITMA, 98

'Jane', 98
Jay, Isobel, 49
Jazz, 24, 85
'Jersey Lily, The', 81
Jews, 104
Jive, 57
'Jix', 100
Johnson, Amy, 54
Jutland, 46

Kilvert, Rev. Francis, 10, 19, 38
Kinematograph, 14, 17
Kinsey Report, 27, 88
Kipling, Rudyard, 76
Kitchener, FM Lord, 38, 39, 44
Knight, J. H., 49
Kruschen salts, 36

Labour Exchange, 32, 36, 61
Lady Chatterley's Lover, 27, 88
Lambeth Conference, 88
Lanchester, F. W., 49
Lantern, magic, 11
Lantern slides, 11
Lassah, Lily, 17
La Vie Parisienne, 79
Laver, James, 71
League of Nations, 65
Leap Year, 82
Lenglen, Suzanne, 52
Licensing Act, 60
Life magazine, 99
Lithograph, 15

Oh dear! he's been gone that long now that I've nearly forgotten what men are like!

Do you think there's any chance of us meeting?

HOT STUFF

I saw you having your bit of revenge the other day!

Beware! some boys are green, some larky,
Yet both look just the same in khaki.

BEWARE THE PINE-TREE'S WITHERED BRANCH,
BUT BEWARE MUCH MORE THIS AWFUL GLANCE.
IT IS YOUR DEAR FRIEND'S BEST ADVICE—
EXCELSIOR!

streets helped. 'Oh no! Count Zeppelin ain't no friend o' mine' says the little girl in nothing but a vest rising above her middle. (Sub-pornographic cards of children with bare, smacked bottoms or in a bath together—'If she's that scared o' torpedoes she'll have to clear out that's all!'—always focus attention on adults' forbidden areas.) Of two girls in a specially warm embrace the caption reads: 'This is another job the men will want back when they come home'.

'You've carried on with me, Sir, all through the War—surely you won't dispense with me now!' What the 'comics' said teasingly of office affaires Arnold Bennett noted seriously: 'The sensual appeal is now very marked everywhere, in both speech and action, on the stage. Adultery everywhere pictured as desirable, and copulation generally ditto' (*Diary*, October 1918). And a little later: 'There was a bonfire in Piccadilly Circus on Tuesday night (Nov 12): girls are still very prominent in the 'doings': the staidest girl suddenly put on a soldier's hat and overcoat and went promenading in it . . . The feature of last night was girls with bunches of streamers which they flicked in your face as you passed'. From excess of death, in fact, to life urge in excess. A Bamforth card balances the account. 'There's a vacancy here—won't you come?' The girl on a park bench embraces a figure in white shadowy outline—one of the men missing, and missed by thousands of women.

Lloyd George, D., 32, 34, 65
Lloyd, Marie, 31
Lollobrigida, Gina, 27
London, 18, 49, 86
London Magazine, 100
London Opinion, 31, 63, 68
Loos, 40
Lord Chamberlain, 100
Lorraine, Violet, 40
Los Angeles, 22
Lowry, L. S., 36
Ludendorff, General, 41
Luftwaffe, 97
Lynn, Vera, 95

Macmillan, Harold, 65
Manchester, 14
Margate, 20
Marks & Spencer, 78
Maxim's, 81
Means test, 35
Mons, 39, 43
Monte Carlo, 80
Moore, Doris Langley, 71
Motor-bicycle, 24, 52
Motor-car manufacturers, 49, 50, 54, 55
Munich agreement, 91
Music Hall, 18, 30, 87

Naked and the Dead, The, 88
Nash, Paul, 42
National Assistance Board, 66
National Film Archive, 15
National Health, 34, 65
National Insurance, 34
Nazis, 104
Negroes, 104
'New Look', 76
Norfolk jacket, 74
Novello, Ivor, 40

Observer Review, 88
Oh, Calcutta, 88
'Old Contemptibles', 89
Orwell, George, 31, 86
'Overlord', 99
Owen, Wilfred, 41
Oxford bags, 74

Pacific Ocean, 96
Parade, 100, 107
Pall Mall, 56
Paris, 38, 76
Paris Exhibition, 15
Passchendaele, 43
Pathe Gazette, 15
Paul, Robert, 14
Payne, Jack, 56
Pepys, Samuel, 11
Philadelphia, 10
Phillips, Bertram, 15
Phonograph, 14
Photomaton, 19
Piccadilly Circus, 84
Pickford, Mary, 22
'PO Prune', 93
'Pitcher' of the 'Pink 'Un', 70
Platt, Harry, 10, 11, 19
Poincaré, President, 38
Police, 61, 63
Political parties, 30, 32, 65, 67
Pools, 57
Pop Art, 78
Pope, W. Macqueen, 28, 82
Postcards:
  collecting, 15
  colour, 17
  competition in collecting, 17
  court size, 15
  field, 38
  glamour, 71
  hymn, 17
  Korrespondenz Karte, 10
  Life model, 17, 18, 30, 80
  photographic, 15
  picture, 17
  plain official, 10
  private, 10, 15
  song, 17, 22
  view, 15
Postcard artists:
  Browne, Tom, 20
  Fitton, Frank, 18
  Fitzpatrick, Brian, 18
  Gibson, Charles Dana, 18
  Harrison, 31
  Kirchner, Raphael, 43
  Leete, Alfred, 63
  McGill, Donald, 18, 47, 104
  Spurgeon, 18
  Taylor, Arnold, 18, 56, 76
  Tempest, Douglas, 18, 22, 51, 52, 54
  Thackeray, Lance, 50
  Wilson, Oscar, 71
Postcard manufacturing firms:
  Bamforths, *passim*
  Corketts, 15
  Davidson, 20
  Ettlinger & Wrench, 17, 65, 71
  Garners, 18
  Hartman, 15
  Henderson, 18,
  Kardorama, 78
  Millar & Lang, 20, 22
  Pictorial Postcard Co., 18
  Rotary Photo Co., 71

  Stewart, 15
  Tuck, 15, 17, 18, 20, 50
  Valentine, 15, 18
Princess Ida, 58
Profumo, John, 88
Punch, 51

Queue hazard, 35

Ragtime, 24, 39
Ramsgate, 25
Rationing, 47, 89, 94
Reichstag, 76
Reith, J. C. W., 55
Reveille, 98
Rhymes of a Red-Cross Man, 40
Riley Brothers, 14
Rinkomania, 50
Robey, George, 40
Robot signs, 54, 85
Rosenberg, Isaac, 41
'Roundup', 99
RAF, 89
RFC, 19, 52
Royal Naval Exhibition, 15
Royal Navy, 46, 47
Ruhr, 75
Russia, 15, 96
  Czar of, 39
Russian boots, 75
Rutley, Ralph, 59

'Sack', 78
Salford, 36
Salvation Army, 104
Sassoon, Siegfried, 41, 44
Savoy Orpheans, 56
Schicklgruber, A., 97
Scovell, Edith, 94
'Sea-lion', 96
Service, Robert, 40
Sims, George R., 11
Skating, 50, 51
Sketches by Boz, 25
Society Pictures, 51
Somme, 40, 82
Song hits, 17, 40, 42, 43, 56, 78
Songs of a Sentimental Bloke, 39
Southend, 25
Southport, 18, 72
Strikes, 59, 66
Strip-tease, 27
Submarines, 48
Suffragettes, 63
Sunbathing, 26, 76, 85
Swanage, 20
Swift, Jonathan, 99, 100
Switz, Reginald, 14
Switzerland, 40

Tariff Reform, 30
Teddy boy, 68, 77
Teetotal League, 61
TV, 26, 27, 36, 37, 57, 87
Temperance Society, 11
Tennis, 51, 52
Ten Pin Bowling, 57
Thomas, Dylan, 94
Thomas, Queenie, 14
'Torch', 99
Transistor set, 57
Trevelyan, G. M., 60
Turkey, 71

Unemployment, 58, 59, 64
US Army, 43
USA, 18, 19, 45, 56, 96
Union Jack, 47, 104
Unionists, 30
'Unisex', 78

Vagina Rex, 100
Valentino, Rudolph, 85
Verdun, 40, 43
Victoria, Queen, 28, 60, 70
VE Day, 99
Vimy Ridge, 40
Vogue, 70, 82

Wakes, 20, 25
War:
  First World, 10, 19, 24, 38–48, 71, 95, 104
  Franco-German, 38
  Second World, 10, 26, 82, 89–99
  South African, 17
Ward, Lily, 14
Washing Machine, 33
WC, 33 37
Whiteman, Paul, 56
Wilhelm, Kaiser, 48, 94
Wimbledon, 52
Windsor Magazine, 49, 68
Wireless, 55, 56
Wolfenden Report, 27, 82, 88
Woman's Magazine, 37
Woolf, Leonard, 68
Woolton, Lord, 95
Woolworths, 95
Workhouse, 61

X-ray, 19

Yankees, 42, 96
Youth Hostels Association, 56
Ypres, 39, 43

Zeppelins, 48, 84